Fair North Riding

By the same author

Joyous Entry
Four Boon Fellows: A Yorkshire Odyssey
Moorland Tramping
Tramping in Yorkshire
Striding through Yorkshire
Broad Acres
Ground Staff
I Bought a Hotel
Poems and Songs

Rievaulx Abbey in Ryedale

Fair
North Riding

ALFRED J. BROWN

Country Life Limited
TAVISTOCK STREET COVENT GARDEN
LONDON WC2

For

DOROTHY UNA RATCLIFFE

Singer of the Dales

*Published in 1952
by Country Life Limited
Tavistock Street London WC2
Printed in Great Britain by
Tonbridge Printers Ltd
Tonbridge Kent*

Contents

Illustrations

Acknowledgements

IN the preparation of this book, I have received help from a great many kind North Riding people in all walks of life, some of whom are mentioned in the text, and to all of whom I wish to tender my grateful thanks.

In addition, I have to thank Dom Columba Cary-Elwes M.A., Prior of Ampleforth Abbey, for reading the proofs of the chapter on Ampleforth; the Rev. G. Edward Charlesworth Hon. C.F., Rector of St Peter's Church, Croft, for his kindness in showing me the rectory and church at Croft, and his recent 'Lewis Carroll' discoveries there; and a host of other kind vicars and priests in the Riding for showing me their beautiful churches.

I also owe thanks to the Rev. Monsignor C. Tindall M.A. for showing me round the Hospital of St John of God at Scorton; to Captain C. R. Child, of Catterick, for information about Catterick Camp; to R. H. B. Hamersley Esq. F.L.A.S. for facts about the Duchy of Lancaster; to G. T. Mortimer Esq. of Westerdale, and to County Councillor Henry Atkinson, of Goathland, for information about the Blackface Sheep Breeders' Association; to E. M. Conder Esq., District Officer of the Forestry Commission, for much valuable assistance on forestry; to H. G. Thornley Esq. C.B.E., D.L., Clerk of the North Riding County Council, and to S. Lee Vincent Esq., County Planning Officer, for information supplied; and to the County Librarian, North Riding, and the City Librarian, Bradford, for furnishing me with books on many occasions.

Limitations of space preclude the inclusion of a Bibliography, but I have consulted all the standard authorities and most of the modern writers who have dealt with this district, to all of whom I wish to acknowledge my indebtedness.

I should also like to thank all those unknown village people up and down the Riding who have patiently answered my questions and given me much valuable information not to be found in books.

Finally, my best thanks are due to all those country innkeepers (and their wives) who have stayed me with flagons and regaled me with true Yorkshire hospitality during my tour of the Riding. Without their help, this book would never have been written!

Foreword

THERE are various ways of presenting a picture of such a large and diverse piece of country as the North Riding of Yorkshire. The method I prefer is to begin the tour at once and let the countryside and the people speak for themselves. This is all the more desirable today when books are limited in size.

But for the benefit of those readers who like facts and figures—and a preview, as it were—I give a few facts here. The mere size of the North Riding is impressive. It covers an area of 2,128 square miles and is almost twice as big as the East Riding, but not quite so big as the West (with 2,790 square miles), nor anything like so densely populated—which is one of its charms. The North Riding, apart from Middlesbrough, has no large industrial towns and is chiefly rural in character. It has a population of rather more than half a million, as against the three and a half millions of the more industrial West Riding. Half this population centres upon Middlesbrough and Tees-side.

Broadly speaking, the North Riding includes the Yorkshire portion of Teesdale; all Swaledale, Wensleydale and the beautiful country of Rye-dale; the Cleveland hills and the North Yorkshire moors; the Hambleton and Howardian hills; the vales of Mowbray, Pickering and much of the vale of York; and a considerable stretch of the Yorkshire coastline. The endpaper map shows the boundaries clearly. All these different regions are fully covered in this book. I doubt if, in the whole of England, there is a district of similar size with a greater variety of scene and interest.

I have called this book *Fair North Riding* because that is how I regard this particular part of Yorkshire. It is impossible to exaggerate its richness and diversity, or the beauty of its landscapes in spring, summer and autumn. Even in winter, after weeks of snow, when a sudden thaw occurs, the colours are astonishing: soft russets and browns, deep, translucent greens, the gold of the bracken, and the brilliant scarlet of berries in the hedgerows. The moorland farms, with their weathered stone and rust-red pantiles, fit perfectly into the scene.

Those people who still imagine Yorkshire to be bleak and dour, with grim, inhospitable moors all around, will have an agreeable surprise when they see this fair and smiling North Riding landscape. Its softness of tone seems to be reflected in the character of the people. It may be that the softer burr of the North Riding dialect accentuates the impression of a gentle and kindly people; but that is what they are. Their voices are soft and full of music; their manners are gracious and friendly; and they have none of the aggressive stridency of the industrial part of the West Riding.

A man's books are coloured by his own preferences and prejudices. This book is concerned with scenery, history and people; with moors, dales and rivers; with moorland farms, market towns, villages and inns, historic castles, abbeys and churches; with old customs and stories; and with famous literary figures and sporting squires.

Ancient churches are scattered about the North Riding as thick as the proverbial leaves in Vallambrosa, and I have included a representative selection of them, but if one stops to describe every old church in detail, the book begins to read like a catalogue—and catalogues make dull reading.

No one can wander about the North Riding today without being made aware of the silent revolution that is taking place in the social scene. Historic mansions stand empty and desolate; others are being converted into schools and hotels. In some the squatters have taken the place of the old squires. To me it is a sad thing to see these historic houses in such a state. Great estates are being sold up and the traditional England is disappearing before our eyes. This, too, will be discussed in these pages.

I have devoted a considerable amount of space to the fascinating market towns of the Riding, for they are the focal point of the countryside, and a knowledge of them is essential to a proper understanding of the North Riding scene.

For the rest, what a wonderful story there is to tell! The coming of the monks to Whitby, Rievaulx, Byland, Jervaulx—and many another great abbey; the dawn of English poetry at Whitby with the song of Caedmon; the building of Cook's ships for his famous voyages of discovery round the world; the captivity of Mary Queen of Scots at Bolton Castle; the joustings and junketings of the Nevilles at Middleham; the pomp and pageantry at Richmond; the great Wensleydale families of Scrope, Metcalfe, Norton and Graham; the Latimers of Danby, Catherine Parr of Snape. These are only a few of the incidents and *dramatis personæ* taking part in the pageant of this fair North Riding.

Nearer to our own day, there was that meeting of a few farsighted gentlemen in the commercial room of the George & Dragon at sleepy

Yarm that was to promote the first railway and change the shape of the world. There were the glorious days of the eighteenth and nineteenth centuries when all the world was astir and the North Riding enjoyed its share of the general prosperity; there were the great days when Scarborough was at the height of its pomp, and society flocked to the sea; and the days when a certain young squire Osbaldeston was winning his laurels as master of foxhounds.

And behind all this, the ordinary men and women went about their business, much as they do today: the farmers and shepherds, the fishermen and craftsmen. For them there were the country shows, the village festivals and the sporting events of the day.

York is one obvious approach to the North Riding. It stands at the southern gateway and is the hub round which all three Ridings revolve—a county in its own right. York gives the right historical background and the right perspective for such a pilgrimage. It shines like a medieval jewel in the heart of the county. Space, alas, does not admit of a detailed description of York in this book since it lies outside the Riding, and there is more than enough to see (and describe) in the far-spreading North Riding itself in the space at my disposal; but I trust that anyone who begins his tour at York will spare time to see this ancient and beautiful city of ours.

For convenience' sake, I have started my own tour at the most northerly point in the Riding—on the Tees; but as each section is complete in itself, the reader can begin where he prefers. Helmsley (in Ryedale) for example, takes one straight to the heart of some of the loveliest scenery in North Yorkshire.

As this book goes to press, an Order has been signed by the National Parks Commission, designating an area of approximately 600 square miles of the north-eastern portion of the Riding as a National Park. If and when this Order is confirmed, thousands of tourists may take the opportunity of visiting this district for the first time.

All this new park land—and the rest of the region—is described in this book; but I should be the last to claim that I have given more than a hint of the richness and beauty of this fair North Riding in these few, crowded pages.

A. J. B.

Goathland 1950
York 1952

I. THE DALES

CHAPTER ONE

Teesdale

BORDER RIVER

TEESDALE is the most romantic approach into the North Riding of York-shire, and though the wild Tees itself is a border river and Yorkshire must share its glories with neighbouring Durham and Westmorland, there are quite enough romantic scenes and places of interest along the Yorkshire banks to claim attention.

The classic approach into Teesdale is by way of Scotch Corner (which is well inside the Yorkshire boundary) along the Great North Road. It can be approached from the south through Boroughbridge and Catterick Bridge, or from the north through Newcastle and Durham. At Scotch Corner, the two roads into Scotland divide, one (A.1) continuing due north towards Edinburgh, and the other (A.66) turning westward towards Greta Bridge, Bowes, Penrith, Carlisle and Gretna Green. This latter road leads directly to the beautiful country of the Tees.

It is only ten miles from Scotch Corner to Greta Bridge, and almost immediately you are conscious of a change in the landscape. After the flat, monotonous stretches of the Great North Road, it is exciting to get a first glimpse of the moors and fells rising between Tees and Swale. There is lovely country on either hand, and many a pretty village lies hidden in the folds of the hills. One of the finest stretches of the Tees lies almost within reach. Greta Bridge itself has been called 'the most painted and photo-graphed bridge in the British Isles'. Cotman's picture of it in the British Museum and Turner's Greta landscapes are well known. Certainly it is a lovely bridge in an exquisite setting, even though one does not see it at its best today owing to the ugly (and, one hopes, temporary) iron bridge alongside which was put up during the war to take the heavy traffic. Some of the ornamental columns of the old bridge were temporarily removed also as a wartime precaution; but if one wanders down to the river itself on the left side of the bridge by the farmhouse, one can get an idea of its original beauty. But it is not so much the bridge itself, or even the lovely Greta, that we think of as we turn the corner and come upon this little hamlet, but rather of Dickens and Scott.

It is curious how famous writers and poets can leave their mark on a village as they do. The visits of Scott and Dickens to this remote corner of Yorkshire between the years 1808 and 1838 were no more than brief interludes in its long history—Dickens especially was there for only one night, though Scott paid frequent visits to Rokeby; and yet how firmly they have each set their seal upon it! Hundreds of stagecoaches from London and York to Carlisle and Scotland have rumbled over this narrow road and baited at Greta Bridge; and long before they came, the Roman legions had marched this way. All kinds of wild dramas have been enacted there: lovesick maidens and their swains on their way to Gretna Green often stayed there—Kings' Messengers—retreating armies—Scotch drovers—all these have passed over Greta Bridge in their day, but it is of Dickens and his friend 'Phiz' that we still think today as we turn the last bend of the road and come to this welcome oasis on the king's highway.

One can picture him stumbling down from the coach on that dark night of January 31 in 1838, frozen stiff with cold, and full of foreboding as to his reception and his 'mission' as he made his way into the inn. How was he to know that this was one of the finest scenes in Yorkshire, though Scott had already discovered and immortalized it? His mind was occupied with the horrors of those dreadful boy-farming schools and their tyrannical schoolmasters. The Greta babbled over its stones unseen and unappreciated; the surrounding scenery of Rokeby and Brignall Banks, which had set Scott's heart aflame, was no concern of Dickens that night. All he and hurrying 'Phiz' wanted was a room for the night, a fire and a hot supper. (Imagine expecting a hot supper at 11.30 p.m. in a lonely roadside hotel today!). The journey of 255 miles had taken him two days, and the last part of it had been accomplished in severe weather.

Next morning, Dickens sat down and wrote his spirited account of it to his wife, and the way his pen ran away with him is a measure of his agreeable surprise at his reception the night before.

It is a pity that famous writers are not more explicit about their pilgrimages. If Dickens had stated the name of the inn at which he stayed and wrote this letter, what a lot of controversy would have been saved! There were three posting inns at Greta Bridge in those days, and it is still not known at which of the three the two travellers slept. Even the names of them are confused. There was the George, the Morritt Arms and the

In the wilds of the Pennines: Grains o' th' Beck farm and bridge, with Mickle Fell beyond.

The tower and ruins of the twelfth-century Marrick Priory have been incorporated into a farm and church on the banks of the Swale.

New Inn. It is generally thought that the large coaching house and farm with a great yard and stables, standing back from the road, but with one wing of the house abutting on the bridge, was the George, and that Dickens stayed there. The house is now divided into two residences, but Mrs Watson, who occupies the main portion near the bridge and whose husband farms the land, showed me the comfortable lounge where Dickens enjoyed the late supper and wrote his letter. This house has the best position and view, and it was the principal posting house and post office for the district. The faded words 'Post Office' can still be seen over a corner window of a little room directly facing the yard. Others say that this inn was at that time called the Morritt Arms. At any rate, this seems the obvious place at which he *should* have stayed, but it is not 'standing alone in the middle of a dreary moor'. At the opposite side of the bridge and a little distance down the road is the only surviving inn, now called the Morritt Arms but formerly known variously as the George and the New Inn! This has now been enlarged and modernized, but still retains its old-world charm, and if Dickens were alive today and came to Greta Bridge, it is the only place where he *could* stay! It is directly opposite Rokeby Park, and its delightful grounds extend to the river and beyond. It has its appropriate 'Dickens Bar', the walls of which are decorated with spirited scenes from *Pickwick* and other of Dickens's work, excellently done by J. Gilroy a few years ago. In Dickens's time, this inn was the smaller of the two near the bridge, but it was also a posting house and it is by no means certain that he did not stay there.

Finally, there was a third inn—then also known as the New Inn—standing about a quarter of a mile from the bridge in the direction of Scotch Corner. This inn is now the private residence of Mr Barkes—a gentleman farmer, but no relation to the other Barkis, he assured me! It is now called Thorpe Grange. At first sight it seems improbable that Dickens could have stayed there. Mr Barkes, however, is willing to prove that he did, and modern scholarship is on his side. This would have been the first inn that Dickens's coach would reach. It is much more isolated than the other two, and would certainly have given the impression of being alone on a dreary moor at that hour of the night. It was obviously of considerable size and importance. There are several hooks for fastening the horses' reins still on the outside of the big coaching stables; and, more important perhaps, there are corner fireplaces both downstairs and in the bedrooms—the only one of the three inns that possesses them. So there it is! Although I still like to think Dickens stayed at the George, adjoining the bridge, I confess that

B

Mr Barkes has shaken my confidence. But how fascinating it is to wander from one old inn to the other speculating on the mystery. And at least it enables one to look more carefully at the scenery, which is remarkable.

And when one looks at the scenery, one thinks of Scott rather than of Dickens. For while Dickens contented himself with a quick glance round the immediate neighbourhood next morning and then hurried off to Barnard Castle and to Bowes—staying only four days in the district to gather material and hatch the plot for *Nicholas Nickleby*—Scott was a frequent visitor to Rokeby Hall, then the home of his friend John Bacon Sawrey Morritt. J. B. S. Morritt was a patron of the arts and of literature, and had a large circle of friends. He was the founder of the famous Dilettante Society, and a great collector. Rokeby Hall was at that time famous for its magnificent collection of pictures, sculpture and *objets d'art*. The celebrated 'Rokeby Venus', by Velasquez, now in the National Gallery, hung on those walls from 1808 to 1905, together with paintings by Sir Joshua Reynolds and many others. Today, alas, Rokeby is shorn of much of its former glory, but the house and beautiful park remain. Major H. E. Morritt, the present squire of Rokeby, an authority on angling and an antiquary, gave me permission to look round the grounds. They are still much as Scott must have known them, though some of the trees he loved have gone. Scott first met Morritt in 1808, and they became close friends and often exchanged visits.

Some of Scott's best-known poems were written while he was staying at Rokeby Hall, including the long romance of *Rokeby* itself, with the well-known lyric 'O Brignall Banks are wild and fair . . .'

During Scott's visits, Morritt had a special seat and writing table set up in a cave in the woods overlooking the Greta—known as Scott's Cave—to enable him to write in seclusion. This can still be seen and, unlike many such poet's stones and caves, it is genuine. It gave me no small satisfaction to touch the wizard's desk—and hope for inspiration. (There are times when I wish that I could retire to such a cave!) Scott was enchanted with the scenery of the Greta in and around Rokeby—and no wonder! It is river scenery at its best and fairest, with noble woods and glades, and romantic reaches at every turn. Turner's famous picture of the *Meeting of the Waters* immortalizes the confluence of the Greta and Tees just beyond Scott's cave and near Mortham Tower which so fired Scott's genius. Originally a Border peel, Mortham, with a fine embattled tower and much beautiful tracery, witnessed many stirring scenes in the stormy days gone by when the other Scots were crossing the Border on their forays and pillaging the Yorkshire dales. Mortham was the most southern of the Border peels. It is believed to have been built by an earlier Rokeby when Rokeby Hall, together with the church and hamlet, was burned down by the Scots after Bannockburn, in Edward the Second's reign. It is steeped in legends and ghost stories; but has now been converted into a beautiful private residence for Major Morritt's sisters, Mrs Rhodes-Moorhouse and Mrs ffrench, who showed me round. It is the kind of romantic tower that all brave youths and maidens dream about and few are lucky enough to possess. It is perfectly furnished and full of treasures.

From Mortham, the path to the Meeting of the Waters leads over the beautiful Dairy Bridge, designed by an earlier squire of Rokeby, Sir Thomas Robinson, and to the Dairy cottage nearby.

I walked back along the banks of the Greta, passing Scott's Cave again on the other side. It looked so lovely and enchanting that I could almost imagine Scott to be sitting there, brooding on another ballad. Nothing has changed since he dreamed his dreams there—only the world beyond is quite translated! The path takes one back across the great park and out at the lodge gates by Greta Bridge, where the roar of the passing traffic falls strangely on the ears after the calm peace and beauty of the woods.

Brignall Banks lie between Greta Bridge and the village of Brignall, a mile or two up the river. They can be reached direct from the garden of the Morritt Arms hotel, which, incidentally, stands on the site of an old Roman fort. The famous banks are quite unspoilt—still as wild and fair and as green as Scott portrayed them. The scenery hereabouts is indeed as romantic as one could desire. The Greta plunges through the narrow valley and is lost in the dense woodlands, but suddenly it swings out again into the sunlight and shows one a glimpse of its incomparable beauty. By the side of the stream, far below the hamlet of Brignall itself, is a ruined chapel that lends enchantment and a pathetic solemnity to the scene. It is the old chapel of Brignall. The inevitable tree-felling is taking place beyond the chapel, and perhaps before long some of Brignall's beauty will have gone, but as I saw them on that perfect summer afternoon, Brignall Banks were still fair.

BOWES

From Greta Bridge the road—once a Roman road—continues westward through the hamlet of Rokeby to the village of Bowes, five miles away. Just before reaching Rokeby, a branch road to the right runs along the side of Rokeby Park to the ruins of Egglestone Abbey, where the old Abbey bridge crosses the Tees, and the road goes on to Barnard Castle on the Durham side of the river.

One can either make this detour on the way, or go straight on to Bowes and return to the Tees—which is what I propose to do now.

Bowes is one of the outposts of Yorkshire, standing astride the highroad to Brough and Penrith: a long, grey, stone village, with an ancient church and castle, and the old Unicorn hotel—another famous coaching inn—with its fine cobbled yard waiting to welcome weary travellers. It was to Bowes that Dickens came from Greta Bridge by way of Barnard Castle, and in this case there is no doubt about where he halted. He came to the Unicorn—and who indeed could resist it?

For as long as I care to remember, the Unicorn was in the hands of the Pickersgill family, who have often put me up and regaled me in the traditional Yorkshire fashion. They almost seemed to belong to the Dickens era! Now it has been taken over by a brewery, and when I called, Mr Jemson, the manager, was alone for the inn was being redecorated. He very kindly offered me bed and breakfast if I did not mind taking my evening meal at Dotheboys Hall. I pricked my ears up at this and thought for a moment that he was pulling my leg, but he was quite serious. Dotheboys Hall has recently changed hands too, and is now once more a boarding establishment. It has been taken over by a local garage proprietor, Mr Wearmouth, who has converted it into a transport café and hotel.

DOTHEBOYS HALL, ORIGINAL PROPRIETOR WACKFORD SQUEERS, reads the legend over the door, with an invitation to motorists and transport drivers to stop and sample its charms.

I was delighted to have a chance of dining at Dotheboys Hall and lost no time in doing so. It is the last house in the village on the left as one walks up the road, a substantial rectangular stone building, with a cobbled yard at the back, and the famous pump and stone trough in the middle. It is a strange trick of Fortune's wheel that has turned the notorious Dotheboys into a modern pull-up for lorry drivers and others, but it is surely a change for the better if half the things Dickens said about it were true. I had an adequate meal—which is more than the unfortunate boys used to have—and I gazed on Bowes Castle from the dining-room. Afterwards, Mr Wearmouth showed me over the house. There are three floors, and some of the upper rooms, with their low ceilings, are very gloomy and depressing. Without a ladder we were unable to enter the attic quarters which Mr

Wearmouth considered were used as dormitories. There are still traces of names and initials scratched or burnt into the beams. The existing bedrooms with their rows of beds for the long-distance night drivers look curiously reminiscent of a boarding school.

This is the true romance of this ancient Roman and British highway today. The roar of heavy traffic is seldom absent for long. An amazing succession of lorries, coaches and cars pass from early morning into the late hours of the night to and from Scotland to London. Tired transport men on their way from Aberdeen and Glasgow come to Dotheboys around midnight to snatch a few hours' sleep before continuing their journey. What a story Dickens might have written about this had he been alive today!

As it is, I have never quite been able to swallow the story of Dotheboys Hall. Admittedly it was a composite picture made up of bits and pieces of gossip, fact and imagination derived from different sources and schools. In his four days' tour of the district (not very long for such an indictment) Dickens questioned several people about the schools in the vicinity. This corner of Yorkshire was certainly noted for its boarding schools—there were three in Bowes and others at Startforth and Barnard Castle—and some of them were dubious places, but so were similar schools in other parts of the country. It seems rather unfair that Dickens should have selected this one school, thinly disguised, on which to heap his venom. It may, of course, all be true—much of the evidence is very strong—but I am not convinced. In one of his letters at that time he made much of the fact that the first gravestone he had stumbled on in the churchyard at Bowes

'was placed above the grave of a boy eighteen long years old, who had died suddenly, the inscription said. I suppose his heart broke—the camel falls down "suddenly" when they heap the last load upon his back—died at that wretched place. I think his ghost put Smike into my mind, upon the spot.'

I saw this gravestone too. The inscription on it reads:

> Here lies the remains of
> George Arthur Taylor
> of Trowbridge, Wilts.
> who died suddenly at
> Mr. William Shaw's Academy
> of this place April 13 – 1822
> Aged 19 years
> Young reader thou must die
> But after this the Judgment.

The entry in the Burial Register reads: 'George Arthur Taylor, a Boarder at Mr. Shaw's School, from Trowbridge, Wilts. 1822, April 20, age 19.'

The boy, it will be noticed, was nineteen years of age, not eighteen, and without a good deal more evidence one can hardly imagine that a youth of nineteen would die other than from natural causes. Mortality among young people was much higher then than it is today, and every church-yard has its quota of children who died suddenly in those years. Even today, with all the care and attention that money and modern science can procure, boys still die, alas, at boarding schools, from time to time.

In the same churchyard, I also saw the grave of William Shaw (the original Squeers) and his wife and son, who, incidentally, died at the early age of twenty-four. In death, at least, the notorious schoolmaster was made to appear highly respectable. Dickens does not seem to have noticed the most famous of all the old gravestones in the churchyard at Bowes—the one at the west end of the church itself commemorating the faithful young lovers Rodger Wrightson and Martha Railton. The story is well known, but is so remarkable that perhaps it will bear repetition. The young lovers met in secret and wished to marry, but Rodger's family objected to the match on the grounds that Martha's people—though of a similar class—had no money, and 'blood was nothing without groats'. The boy's un-pleasant sister seems to have been a very hostile witness to their clandestine meetings and opposed the marriage. Suddenly, in March, 1714, Rodger fell sick of a fever and his life was in danger. Martha was allowed to see him once more, but it was too late. He died the same evening, and on her way home the broken-hearted Martha heard 'the tolling of his passing bell'[1] and cried out 'My heart is broke.' She too died within a few hours. Both were about twenty years of age and both were buried in the one grave.

So here was another case of a youth of twenty dying in unusual circum-stances at Bowes! But this is a true and very remarkable tale.

Bowes was a Roman military station called Lavatrae, and it is full of interest to the student of history. The ruins of the Norman castle stand on the edge of this old Roman site. Like all these Border castles it suffered severely from the Scots, and not much of it is left standing. Between 1314 and 1332, when Robert Bruce was devastating the North of England, Bowes was besieged again. It was finally dismantled in the seventeenth

---

[1] Still to be heard in Richmond.

century. What remains of it is now in the care of H.M. Office of Works.

Church and castle were built in about the same period, and both stand side by side overlooking the old Stainmore Forest and the fells—stretching towards Arkengarthdale. The castle is a grim pile and the church is bare and austere, but together they seem to interpret Bowes and to bear witness to its long and chequered history.

HIGH TEES

There are various ways out of Bowes.

Having proceeded thus far, the tourist may well wish to continue along the main road over Bowes moor, past the attractive Bowes Moor hotel and across the Yorkshire boundary to Berwick, Penrith, Carlisle—and Scotland. This is a fine drive, but it is outside the scope of this book.

For my part, I am tempted to follow the old road over the Stang southward into Arkengarthdale and Swaledale, for this is one of my favourite approaches to the Dales; but as I shall be dealing with that country in a later chapter, I propose now to turn back along the Greta Bridge road as far as the little village of Rokeby where the Toll road forks left to Egglestone Abbey, Barnard Castle and the high Tees. The beautiful church of Rokeby is full of interest and well worth a visit.

Egglestone Abbey, which faces the Tees just beyond the old Toll bridge, was founded by the Premonstratensian Order of White Canons in 1190, and was extended at later periods. It is interesting historically and architecturally, and figures in Scott's *Rokeby*, but it cannot compare in beauty of setting with Rievaulx, for example, and it failed to inspire me. The fault doubtless lies in myself, but unless a ruin really excites me, I think it better to say so and be done with it.

The Tees at this point is a fine, noble river running through a limestone gorge, and the high, embattled Abbey bridge affords splendid views. I was attracted by the old legend reading:

Chaise with 2 horses	9d.
Gig or dogcart	6d.
Waggons with 3 horses	10d.
Cattle per score	1/3.
Sheep „ „	8d.
Foot passengers	½d.
Motorcars	6d.

Apart from pointing the obvious moral that it always pays to travel on foot, the mere mention of bygone vehicles such as chaises and gigs, and 'waggons with 3 horses', vividly recalls the spacious days gone by.

This fine bridge was another of the benefactions of J. B. S. Morritt and dates from 1773. Sheep and cattle still occasionally pass this way, the toll-keeper told me, but not in any quantities now. Nearby, over Thorsgill Beck, is a much older packhorse bridge which must have rendered service for 'cattle by the score' down the centuries.

Once across the Abbey bridge, and we are in Durham, which is strictly outside my territory, but if one wants to see the best of the Tees one must be prepared now and again to set foot in the rival camp. The road leads straight to the pleasant town of Barnard Castle, which is notable for its vast Bowes Museum built in French Renaissance style and housing a collection of treasures; there is also a fine Catholic church nearby, and much else besides. For Dickensians, it is chiefly of interest for the old King's Head hotel in the market place where Dickens stayed for two or three days on his Yorkshire tour. 'There is good ale to be had at the King's Head,' he said, and, having tasted it, I can vouch for its goodness even today. The hotel has been modernized, but the older portion is preserved.

It was in Barnard Castle that Dickens noticed the old clock shop with the sign 'Humphrey, Clockmaker' and a remarkable long-cased clock, which gave him the inspiration for the series of tales in *Master Humphrey's Clock*. Old Thomas Humphrey, the original of the 'Master', was one of a family of clock-makers, and was very proud of his association with the master of fiction.

Through the yard of the King's Head, a footpath leads to the ruins of Barnard Castle, but interesting as this historical castle is, I must decline to delve into the story of a Durham castle here. For me, at any rate, it cannot compare either in setting or appearance with the Yorkshire Richmond which will be considered in a later chapter. When I was last there, Barnard Castle looked sadly decayed and neglected, and the nearby mill over the river seemed to be in ruins too. I found the whole scene depressing in the extreme, and the best view from the Castle was undoubtedly the fine bridge below and the road over it back into Yorkshire.

The road goes straight to Bowes again, but a fork on the Yorkshire side of the Tees runs close to the river past Lartington, Cotherstone and Romaldkirk. These are all pleasant villages, with much of interest; Romaldkirk is particularly notable for its magnificent church, Cotherstone for its famous cheese, and Lartington is graced by the Hall. But it is the wild country to the west of this road that appeals most to me. Hunderthwaite village points the way into Baldersdale and to Hunderthwaite Moor, while Cotherstone gives the name to the adjoining moor of that name. There is fine moorland tramping here over Shacklesborough hill or up Deepdale Beck and over to Stainmore. All this is essentially walking country, though there are motoring roads into Baldersdale.

High Force, five miles beyond Middleton-in-Teesdale, is generally considered to be the finest waterfall in England. The usual approach to it is along the main road from Middleton-in-Teesdale to the comfortable High Force hotel where a footpath descends through a heavily wooded gorge to the hidden falls. There is a tollgate at the top and a charge of threepence. It seems reasonable enough, I suppose, for such a sight, but it is remarkable what a lot of glamour even a levy of threepence takes off the scene for me. It seems to tame it, and the long, gloomy approach through the ravine depressed me. No, the best way to see High Force is to approach it along the road bank itself, preferably on the Yorkshire side, and see it first from above. But whichever way you approach it (and even in spite of the threepence), it is an astonishing—even terrifying—spectacle. The wild river comes tumbling down the rocky channel over the falls and suddenly takes a leap of seventy-eight feet to the abyss below. The thunder and tumult when the Tees is in spate is deafening and unbelievable. At the point where the cataract hurls itself over the abyss there are massive pillars of basaltic rock with falls on either side. The Tees is a mighty and majestic river, and throughout its long, tumultuous career it is broken by a series of falls, but High Force is the wildest leap of all and worth more than one visit.

The only way to appreciate a river such as this is to walk along its banks and follow it from its source to its end, on foot. You do not get the same feeling for it if you follow its course in a car on a road that is rarely close enough to enable you even to see it. Six or seven hard but entrancing miles beyond High Force, past Cronkley Scar, there is another famous beauty spot and waterfall, known as Caldron Snout, which appeals to me even more than High Force. The surrounding scenery is wilder and more open; there are great vistas of moor and fell—and there is no charge for admittance. At Caldron Snout you are in the heart of high Teesdale, far away from any habitation except for the lonely Birkdale farms on the shoulders of Maize Beck beyond. After a relatively smooth passage under Dufton Fell, the Tees suddenly gathers itself for another spectacular leap, but this time it comes tumbling down the rocks in a series of falls, resembling a gigantic stairway, in mid-stream. The effect is entrancing seen either from above or below: a foaming cascade of creamy-brown water racing through the gap, and falling altogether a distance of 200 feet. Alongside the falls there is a natural rocky stairway from which one can observe it in all its beauty. And all around there are grey-green fells and rocky boulders, touched by the sunlight to an unearthly beauty of their own.

Maize Beck, which marks the boundary between Westmorland and Yorkshire, joins the Tees just below Caldron Snout, and the meeting of the two streams enhances the beauty of the scene. But more even than the beauty of the fells and the mingling waters, it is the general setting and the solitude hereabouts that appeal to me. This is undoubtedly one of the high spots of the Pennines, and it is incidentally the meeting place of three counties, Yorkshire, Westmorland and Durham. But what do county boundaries matter at such a time, with the high fells around—Mickle Fell, Birkdale Fell and Meldon Top, Widdy Bank Fell, Dufton Fell—and Cross Fell just beyond? This is the kind of country that makes any fell-walker's heart beat faster. For myself, I can never resist the challenge of the Boot of Mickle Fell—Yorkshire's highest mountain (2,591 feet)—a lovely green-clad hill, and the obvious way back to Yorkshire! But perhaps the most exciting walk from Caldron Snout is to follow the path by the side of Maize Beck, past the lonely Birkdale farms, and under Murton Fell to High Cup Nick—a vast amphitheatre gouged out of Murton Fell near Dufton village.

But this is outside the Yorkshire boundary and I have no right to be wandering there at all—at least, not in this book.

While I was thinking over three ways of leaving Caldron Snout on this present pilgrimage, enjoying the solitude and reluctant to tear myself away from such a scene, a man came striding over the hills from the direction of Birkdale. What a difference one man makes to a landscape in such a lonely spot! The curlews and the peewits and the moorland sheep fit naturally into the scene, and I had scarcely noticed them, but a man seems to breathe life into it, as Adam did in his Garden of Eden. One minute I was alone with my thoughts—and a few cows, which I was surprised to find cropping the green turf just above the Falls; in the next minute my solitude was broken and the landscape was alive.

I waited until he crossed the wooden bridge above the Falls and joined me. He looked half-farmer and half-postman, for he wore an old red-piped blue tunic over his farming clothes—and that is what he proved to be. He told me that his name was Dowson and that he had a small farm at Harwood, about four miles away; but he also acted as postman for the two farms at Birkdale and went there almost every day—about one and a half hours each way—part of which he did by bicycle. I walked back with him on the track that runs past the newly opened Cowgreen mine to Langdon Beck, and enjoyed his company and talk. He told me he loved the free, open-air life of the fells and could not bear to live anywhere else.

How delightful these chance encounters are in the lonely places! This talk of sheep and cows (he told me the cows at Caldron were there on 'adjistment' and did not belong to Birkdale) and the natural way of life on the hill-farms may not be of any great consequence, but it added a particular pleasure to my afternoon, and I made a new friend whom I hope to meet again, for he promised to take me with him on his rounds on a future occasion.

And there I must leave the higher reaches of the Tees and return to Yorkshire.

CHAPTER TWO

Yarm

YARM stands on the northern purlieus of the Riding, on the banks of the Tees, with a backward glance over its shoulder towards Durham. The Tees, deceptively sluggish and tranquil here after its earlier frenzies, makes one of its freakish loops round the town and flows behind both sides of the main street, making Yarm almost an island, so that one wonders whether one is in Yorkshire or in Durham.

But Yarm is entirely in Yorkshire, and looks pure North Riding. It is a period piece, and seems to belong to another age altogether—as indeed it does. I doubt if there is another high street in England to match Yarm's; and yet, in some curious way, the confusion of styles among the houses and inns harmonizes into a most delightful pattern. The pity is that it seems so shabby and neglected.

There are rows of dignified Georgian houses side by side with earlier and later styles, but the general impression is that of the eighteenth century, though Yarm is much older than that. The unusually wide, cobbled street immediately arrests the eye, for there is an amplitude about it that one sees so rarely today. The numerous inns, of which the rambling Ketten Ox is probably the oldest, fascinate me and I am torn between their rival charms. The Ketten Ox still has a cockloft under the high roof where cockfighting used to take place, while the Black Bull has more than once provided me with an excellent meal.

But the most famous inn of all is the old George and Dragon, within whose honest-looking walls an event took place which was to make history and to revolutionize travel throughout the world.

A bronze plaque on the wall commemorates the momentous event:

> In the Commercial Room of this Hotel
> on the 12th day of February 1820
> was held the Promoters' Meeting of the
> Stockton and Darlington Railway
> The First Public Railway in the Land
> Thos. Meynell Esq. of Yarm Presided.

Incredible to think that such a world-shaking conference took place in this quiet-looking hotel in the sleepy old town of Yarm. Perhaps they chose the George and Dragon because of its name, for 'St George he was for England', and perhaps they knew well what they were about. The mighty viaduct, soaring high above the houses over which the modern railway runs, is perhaps the best monument to their memory.

The landlord of the George showed me another little snuggery with the posting boxes where the tickets used to be left in the coaching days, and several little recesses where wigs were laid aside while the serious business of the day was discussed over a glass of stingo. It all seems like yesterday there. Indeed, as one stands outside any of the inns, one almost expects the stagecoach to rattle up the cobbled street and pick up some notable citizens of Yarm; or to catch the faint gleam of a brougham drawn up outside one of the great houses while the ladies in their crinoline gowns pay their calls.

Yarm Church stands in a quiet corner near the river; it was rebuilt in 1730, but a good deal of the original Norman building remains.

The most conspicuous building in Yarm is the little Town Hall in the middle of the High Street. The present building dates from about 1730, and stands over the site of the old Market Cross. It was purposely built high above street level so that it might not be flooded when the Tees overflowed its banks. On the outer wall, there are marks to show the height of the disastrous floods in 1771 and 1881, when Yarm was almost submerged. Floods still occur, for the Tees is an unpredictable river, but they are not so overwhelming. Another plaque honours the five Pioneers of Yarm who designed the first railway, and yet another honours the Local Volunteers who served in the South African war.

Yarm has other claims to fame. Strange as it seems today, it was once the third seaport of England when the Tees was navigable to Yarm and beyond, and when Middlesbrough was still a mere name on the mudflats. It built great ships, and from the Friarage Wood nearby the oak for one of Nelson's ships was drawn.

Yarm's charter is one of the oldest in the country, and its fair one of the most famous. Hundreds of head of cattle came to Yarm from Ireland, and thousands of sheep came from Scotland regularly to be sold at Yarm Fair in the broad High Street, and to be taken by the drovers along the old drove roads to the south.

Yarm has lived through great days, and now it seems to be falling asleep, but I like it just as it is. It should be preserved as an Ancient Monument. I would not alter a brick or a stone, and I am dismayed to learn that there is a conspiracy afoot to take up the old cobblestones and replace them with concrete. All Yarm needs—and needs badly—is a little tidying up and painting.

As you cross the bridge over the Tees (past the lovely doctor's house at the corner) you will notice the county boundary mark in the middle of it: 'N.R.' on one side, and 'C.D.' on the other. And when you leave Yarm behind and make your way to bustling Stockton, it is not so much like walking out of one county into another as like walking into a different age.

CHAPTER THREE

Croft and Lewis Carroll

CROFT is one of those surprising outposts of the North Riding that is full of interest for the tourist. It straddles both banks of the Tees, three miles south of Darlington, but Croft Spa is on the Yorkshire side over the many-arched bridge that spans the river at this spot.

The ancient church of St Peter and the coaching inn—now modernized and called the Croft Spa hotel—make a delightful picture against the bridge, together with the old rectory just beyond the church. Croft Hall, Monkend Hall and other charming Queen Anne and Georgian houses enhance the quiet beauty of this remote little village.

But it is the church and the rectory that attract the literary pilgrim; for Croft will ever be remembered as the place where Lewis Carroll spent some of his most impressionable years. His father, the Rev. Charles Dodgson (afterwards Archdeacon of Richmond), came to Croft in 1843, and remained there until 1868. His son, Charles Lutwidge, was almost twelve years old when the family (of eleven children) moved to the large rectory at Croft. Shortly afterwards, Charles was sent to school at neighbouring Richmond, and later he went to Rugby and Oxford, but Croft was his real home for some twenty-five years, and he returned there again and again.

He knew every nook in the rambling old house, and every corner of the spacious garden, part of which he turned into an ingenious toy railway. Elsewhere in the enchanting garden he played his strange games and lived in a dream-world of his own. What a marvellous place it must have been for an imaginative child of his qualities! A great deal of *Alice in Wonderland* and *Through the Looking Glass* was hatched at Croft, as some of the magazines which Lewis Carroll produced reveal.

When I was last in Croft, some excitement prevailed over recent discoveries under the floorboards of what was believed to be the old nursery, in the attic quarters. The rector, the Rev. G. Edward Charlesworth, was converting the enormous rectory into three or four flats; it seemed a pity to dismantle such a famous house, but, alas, necessary in these difficult

31

times. During the alterations, various small treasures had been unearthed from this lofty room, including the lid of a tiny doll's china tea-set, believed to have been buried there by Lewis Carroll a hundred years ago. There was also a pathetic-looking child's leather shoe, a pair of child's gloves, and several mysterious scraps of writing on paper and on wood. A glass windowpane bearing the famous initials C.L.D. painfully scratched by a child's hand, had also been discovered. Further treasures may yet come to light. For the sake of the enthusiastic young vicar (and his church funds) and of the legion of Lewis Carroll's admirers, I hope so. But whether more discoveries are made or not, the old house and the garden, and the lovely church, seem to be for ever invested with something of the Alice-in-Wonderland magic, despite the surprising fact that there is no memorial tablet in the church, either to the worthy Archdeacon himself (who did a great deal for its restoration) or to his gifted son; though there are tablets and tombs enough and to spare!

The most conspicuous object in the church is the famous seventeenth-century Milbank pew—a gigantic erection, like a royal box in a theatre—which clutters up the better part of the nave. The Milbanks lived at Halnaby Hall, some two miles distant from Croft, in the direction of Middleton Tyas, and which has since been converted into a country club, but is now in danger of demolition. Lord Byron, the poet, who married Annabella Milbank, spent part of his honeymoon at the Hall and attended service at Croft Church.

Irrespective of its literary associations, this beautiful thirteenth- and fourteenth-century church of St Peter well deserves a visit. It is built of mellow red sandstone which gives it a warm and kindly look, and the interior is full of interesting tombs of the Clervaux and Chaytor families. The present rector has compiled a pamphlet telling the history of this church, which I commend to all visitors. One of his most cherished ambitions is to perpetuate the Lewis Carroll associations by making a children's corner in the church, with a commemoration window, and I cannot imagine a more delightful way of doing honour to the famous writer and his family and at the same time giving permanent expression to his love of children. There are many quaint carvings of animals in Croft Church which Lewis Carroll studied to advantage.

The grey stone village of Muker with its back to the fells, looks on one of the fairest views in Swaledale.

Richmond Castle in Swaledale: the view from the river towards the castle ramparts, showing the Norman keep and the walls built on the rock

CHAPTER FOUR

Swaledale

HIGH SWALE

IN its higher reaches, the Swale has much in common with the Tees, but Swaledale is more secluded than Teesdale. It is shut in by high moorland ridges—those to the north stretching to the Tees, and those on the south to Wensleydale. It is partly this factor that gives the Swale its particular character and appeal. Of all the great dales, Swaledale seems to come nearest to one's ideal of a pure, unsullied dale—a true shepherd's dale.

To the walker, it offers some of the most enchanting moorland tramping in the whole county, with marvellous crossings from Swale to Tees or to Ure, over the high watersheds between the three dales. The scenery of Upper Swaledale, with its grey limestone crags and great gills, is of the kind that sets the pulses dancing for those who revel in the high solitudes of the Pennines. North, by Rogan's Seat and Water Crag over Nine Standards Rigg, or south by Great Shunner Fell or Lovely Seat—you cannot go wrong in this part of the world if you are a walker.

On the other hand, the motorist can see a great deal if he follows the main roads through the dale and through the passes. He may well find it too austere for his taste, for he can never experience the raptures of the walker who may climb the steep fellsides and get into the very heart of this enchanting country; but no one can fail to be moved by this secret, lovely dale.

It can be approached from Kirkby Stephen in the west, from Hawes in the south, over Buttertubs Pass—one of the finest motor roads in the north, affording magnificent views of the dale—or from Richmond or Reeth in the east. The last is the obvious approach from the direction of the Great North Road; but personally I like to approach Swaledale from Hawes or from Kirkby Stephen and go first to Keld.

KELD

Keld is the best centre for exploring Upper Swaledale. In several books, I (and many others) have sung its praises, and I will say no more here than that it is blessed both in its setting and in its surroundings. The main village lies just off the road, as if clinging as closely as possible to its beloved river. It hides its light under a bushel, so remote and out of the world it appears, like a community of anchorites holding no communion with the world beyond.

Keld is not, I suppose, what one would regard as a 'pretty' village: it is too shut-in for that, and it lacks an old church, but it has some lovely cottages and farms and is full of atmosphere. But there is no question of the beauty of the scenery around Keld, for this is one of the most beautiful districts I know, especially the reach of river behind Kisdon. The waterfalls, too, above and below the village are famous.

And so, for that matter, is the tiny Cat Hole inn on the outskirts of the village, facing Kisdon, where I have spent so many delightful evenings after arduous days on the tops. For a great many years the inn was in the capable hands of Mrs Hutchinson, who set her seal on this corner of the dale in the best possible way, for hers was Yorkshire hospitality at its best. When I was last in Keld, Mrs Hutchinson had retired to one of those secluded cottages in the heart of the village where I hope she may enjoy many years of well-earned rest. Many of my happiest memories are associated with glorious holidays in her hospitable inn, and with delightful nights in the kitchen-bar talking to Swaledale shepherds. Now the inn is in the care of Mr L. Hamilton who is carrying on the old traditions, and who kept a remarkable diary throughout the famous blizzard of 1947 when he was living at the neighbouring inn at Tan Hill.

THWAITE

The green hill of Kisdon shelters Keld from the east and seems to cut it off from the main dale, the Swale flowing behind the hill and rejoining the main road at Muker, three miles south. Keld, Thwaite and Muker form a trinity of sturdy, stone-built Swaledale villages, a little grey and dour, perhaps, but quite enchanting to the dales' lover. If you come over Butter-tubs Pass from Hawes, Thwaite is the first of these you will see, and it will make its own impression in its wonderful setting. Angram and Keld lie above and Muker just below. To me, these villages typify Swaledale. They are rough, workaday villages, mainly occupied by farmers and shepherds; for Swaledale is pre-eminently a hill sheep-farming country, home of the famous pure-bred Swaledale sheep, and it is to the farmers and shepherds one must go for the real story of Swaledale.[1] But for the moment, let me turn to two other famous Swaledale men.

It was at Thwaite that the famous brothers Richard and Cherry Kearton were born. You can see the little stone cottage at the farther end of the village. The sons of a gamekeeper (old Cherry Kearton), they were born naturalists and acquired their intimate knowledge of wild life as boys on these moorlands. Richard was crippled by an accident in his early years, and this helped to foster his natural gifts. Both the boys attended the village school at neighbouring Muker and are remembered by two tablets on the wall. It was during a shooting party on the moors that Richard attracted the attention of Mr Cassell, the London publisher. He prevailed on their father to let the lame Richard enter his London office, where his wonderful gifts were quickly recognized. Richard Kearton won fame as a naturalist and lecturer, while Cherry Kearton, who followed his brother to London, became famous as a pioneer of wild-life photography. The two brothers collaborated in many books, and their work revolutionized the study of wild life at close quarters.

TAN HILL

Just beyond Keld on the way to Kirkby Stephen (another fine mountain road), a branch road turns northward up Silver Hill, past the hamlet of West Stonesdale, and climbs steadily for four miles to the remote citadel of Tan Hill—an old whitewashed inn standing on the lonely moors and famous as the highest inn in England (1,732 feet). No pilgrimage to the North Riding is complete that does not include Tan Hill, for apart from its pre-eminence, this exposed and weatherbeaten inn stands in the midst of some of the wildest moorlands in Yorkshire and the views from its doors are sufficient reward for the climb. Northward, one looks out over Stainmore 'forest' and Bowes Moor and Cotherstone, towards the distant country of the Tees, and everywhere one turns there are desolate moors and craggy ridges.

Tan Hill is only a simple ale-house, but more than one traveller has found shelter there in fierce gales and has blessed its existence. Old Susan Peacock set her mark upon it, and she is commemorated on the rocks beyond the house. I never pass that way without seeming to hear her caustic tongue!

The road past the inn runs north-westward to Barras and Brough (or Bowes); and south to Arkengarthdale and back to the Swale at Reeth.

[1] See Chapter Twenty-eight, 'North Yorkshire Sheep Farms'.

ARKENGARTHDALE

Arkengarthdale, watered by Arkle Beck, is an offshoot of Swaledale and has a stark beauty of its own. This is the country of the old lead-mining industry, and you can sense it as you journey through the lonely valley, where the neighbouring ridges have a hard and sombre cast. Here and there you come across gaunt, abandoned workings, and villages that seem to live in the past. So you pass Whaw and Langthwaite, and the modernized and very comfortable 'C.B.' Inn at Arkle Town, with the straggling hamlet of Booze perched high on the ridge above. Booze, despite its encouraging name, is about the most teetotal hamlet I have ever explored hopefully from end to bitter end. But as you approach Reeth, the country softens a little; green pastures appear, and there are magnificent views, with the fierce Fremington Edge and the strange bald hill of Mount Calva dominating the scene.

To return to Swaledale proper . . .

MUKER TO REETH

Muker is a typical Swaledale village, perhaps the most striking of them all, and there are superb views between Muker and Gunnerside, an old lead-mining village which has seen more prosperous days. There are several fine passes, too, between Muker, Gunnerside and Feetham, to Askrigg in Wensleydale, which will repay the detour.

Low Row and Feetham are adjacent villages in the heart of the dale, and command fine views of the soaring fells to the south. The Punch Bowl inn at Feetham is another comfortable house and makes an excellent centre for exploring this old lead-mining district, while the moors are full of fascinating tracks for walkers.

Kearton and Healaugh point the way to Reeth which is the key-town of this middle dale—ten miles from Richmond.

Reeth stands at the junction of Arkengarthdale and Swaledale and it is so full of inns that the mere sight of them, standing shoulder to shoulder round the spacious green common, is enough to cheer any man after a hard day on the fells, especially in the rather austere region of Arkengarthdale. Who could fail to like such a smiling, inn-full place as Reeth with its wide-awake, bustling air? All the buses in the dale seem to meet here, and all the motorists, too. My problem whenever I arrive in Reeth is to decide which of the numerous inns I should enter first: the Black Bull, the Buck, the King's Arms, and the rest. My advice is to try them all in turn—and then decide for yourself! For Reeth is a kind of halfway house into Swaledale, and it is the obvious place for a halt before resuming the journey up or down dale.

REETH TO RICHMOND

From Reeth to Richmond, the scenery changes and becomes more wooded and picturesque, if less wild. As you cross the fine bridge between Reeth and Grinton, you are immediately conscious of this change in the landscape.

Grinton is the old mother church of Swaledale and it is one of those venerable churches that cannot be passed by. It has the dignity of a cathedral, and its massive tower (400 years old) seems to grow out of the rugged pile. Its oak roof looks hoary with age, and there are Norman arches and capitals. The old tombstones in the spacious churchyard emphasize its antiquity; but it is the perfection of the whole fabric—and the setting—that fire the imagination.

The position of the village, immediately beyond the bridge, with its back to the hills and its hospitable Bridge inn on the threshold, make Grinton a perfect dales village. There is a staggering road out of it into Wensleydale, and a choice of roads on either bank of the Swale to Richmond. Both roads have their advantages. The main road clings to the Swale on the southern bank, while the top road climbs away from the river towards Marske, and affords the better views. Either way, the scenery is enchanting and both roads lead in the end to the jewel of Richmond.

The ruins of Marrick Priory stand on the farther bank, a few miles from Grinton. Originally a Benedictine nunnery of the twelfth century, it is now part farm and part church. The church was rebuilt in 1811, and is used for occasional services, but the old thirteenth-century tower still stands and stirs the heart in its beautiful setting by the banks of the Swale. The farm is built on to the ruins and is really an integral part of the old priory. The walls are six feet thick and there is some fine carving over the fireplace in the great living-room.

Just beyond Marrick, on the south bank and in the grounds of a private residence, are the remains of Ellerton Abbey, consisting in the main of a fine Perpendicular tower, which I climbed to be rewarded with a superb panorama of the surrounding countryside. Ellerton was originally a priory of Cistercian nuns.

Downholme village stands on the hillside above (on the Leyburn road) and has a fine little church. Walburn Hall, a notable old Elizabethan house, once in the possession of the Scropes and now a farm, is a mile or so beyond.

On the opposite bank of the Swale stands the lovely village of Marske, which can be approached over the nearby bridge. With its ancient church and Hall, and its beautiful glade, Marske affords the best approach to Richmond.

RICHMOND

Richmond in Swaledale—ancient capital of Richmondshire—stands supreme among the market towns of Yorkshire and is one of the finest examples of an old market town in England. In 1945, it was selected by the British Council as the typical English country town. This jewel of the dale is one of the show-places of the north, and no tourist who wishes to see the best things in Yorkshire should miss it. The tour of Swaledale can be made equally well—indeed, more conveniently—from Richmond itself, where all roads meet and where the Swaledale buses begin their journeys up-dale.

Historic and famous as Richmond is, it is first and foremost a friendly and hospitable town, typifying all that is best in the county of Broad Acres, and it is in this spirit that I prefer to consider it. I like to stand at the corner of Finkle Street or Frenchgate—and just look at it. It is unlike any other market town in outline and does not conform to the North Riding pattern —having, indeed, a continental air—but it is this very irregularity that gives it its peculiar charm. There never was such a rambling old cobbled square, with such steep streets leading down to the river and the lower town. There never was such a quaint church as Holy Trinity, with shops and offices built into the main fabric. And there never was quite such a stupendous keep towering over the housetops across the square.

There are numerous inns round the square—and more round the corners; in that respect, at least, Richmond conforms strictly to the York-shire pattern, and it is in the inns that one meets the people. On one visit I ran into more people than I had bargained for. It was at Whitsuntide, when the whole of Richmond is given over to a great meet of cyclists who come from all over the North and fill every inn and guest-house in the town. Wheel to wheel, they stretch for miles and make a noble spectacle, five thousand strong! Their mayors and presidents come with them, wives and all, and take possession of every spare bed in the town for the long week-end. This is an established tradition, and long may it con-tinue! There are dances and smokers and church parades, while medieval plays are performed in the grounds of the castle. On Whit Monday, having braced themselves for a final fling, the cyclists really let themselves go at the farewell suppers and sing-songs. Then, towards midnight, they go the rounds of the King's Head, the Fleece, the Turf, the Black Lion, the Bishop Blaise, the Richmond, the Town Hall hotel—and the rest—saying farewell to each other, singing still more songs and partaking of light refreshment in the way of enormous turkeys (carved by their respective mayors), and have one for the road—and then to bed—or to breakfast, as the case may be!

On my last visit (it was in February) the town was strangely quiet, and I woke up next morning to a heavy fall of snow. Richmond had never looked more lovely than it did then. I walked down to the famous terrace below the castle. It is built on the rock, and looks down on that enchanting reach of river far below that has been immortalized by Turner and other great artists. The trees were hung with a sparkling mantle of snow, and the whole scene looked like fairyland.

At any time this is a striking view, but equally fine is the view of the great castle from the bridge below—and from many another vantage point. To see the castle at close quarters, one must enter by way of castle yard, through the barbican, and into the great court. Even after many visits, the size of the great court (450 by 300 feet), and the beautiful lawn which covers it, still astonishes. But it is the massive keep (109 feet high) that captures the imagination, even though the castle did not play a great part in history. It is of two periods: the ground storey was built in the eleventh century by Alan the Red, first Norman Earl of Richmond, and the upper storeys were added in the twelfth century. The view from the top battlements on a clear day is breathtaking. All Swaledale lies at one's feet—and what more could one ask of any view?

Of the many stories and legends associated with the castle, the most persistent is the one that tells of Potter Thompson, who found a deep cave under the castle in which Arthur lay sleeping with his knights and with the sword Excalibur by his side. Amazed by his discovery, the Potter decided to take the sword away to prove his story. As he did so, the slumbering knights awoke, and a noise like the roaring of the seas filled the cavern, while a mocking voice cried:

> 'Potter Thompson . . .
> If thou hads't either drawn the Sword
> Or blown the Horn
> Thouds't been the luckiest man
> That ever yet was born.'

Medieval Richmond was a town of great importance and witnessed many notable scenes. There were some thirteen guilds in the town, of which the Guild of Mercers, Grocers and Haberdashers is the sole survivor. Much of the ancient pageantry of medieval England is still preserved, however; for example, the tradition by which the Mayor presents a bottle of wine to the farmer who first brings to the market place a 'respectable sample of the new season's grain'.

Those who wish to delve more deeply into the history of this entrancing town should read the fascinating *Story of Richmond*, written by David Brooks, the genial and indefatigable Town Clerk of Richmond, who is steeped in its lore and legends, and who has done so much for the renovation of the famous old Georgian theatre of Richmond in Friar's Wynd. Built in 1788, some of the most celebrated actors in England have graced its stage, including Kean, Kemble and Macready. The original sunken pit was discovered in 1944, and the theatre is the only one of its kind in the country, with a unique Georgian proscenium.

There is much else to see in Richmond. There is the lovely tower of Grey Friars in the heart of the town—all that is left of the Franciscan friary founded in 1258. From the old tower the curfew bell is tolled every night at eight and the 'Prentice bell every morning. Holy Trinity church in the market square now belongs to the grammar school and the Corporation. The parish church of St Mary in Frenchgate is full of treasures, and there is a fine nineteenth-century Roman Catholic church of St Joseph and Francis Xavier in Newbiggin.

For myself, it is the old streets, shops, inns, and wynds that fascinate: Frenchgate, Friar's Wynd and the little streets that radiate from the market place. In one of these—at Hill House, Pottergate—lived Frances l'Anson, the 'sweet lass of Richmond Hill', who was wooed and won by Leonard McNally, an Irish barrister. The famous song was sent to her in the form of a love-letter. Byron's wife also lived for a time at Hill House.

Lewis Carroll, who attended the old grammar school, must have loved Richmond. You have only to stand once again in the cobbled square to appreciate that, for who could resist this comely, fairylike town?

EASBY ABBEY

There is a delightful riverside walk from Richmond to the notable ruins of Easby Abbey on the left bank of the Swale, a mile beyond the town. This Premonstratensian Abbey of St Agatha was founded in 1152. Many of its

treasures have gone to adorn other churches, including Richmond parish
church, and those of Easby and Wensley.

ASKE HALL

Just north of Richmond, on the Ravensworth road, is the magnificent
mansion of Aske Hall, the seat of the Marquess of Zetland, Lord-Lieutenant
of the North Riding. It occupies a commanding position overlooking the
Richmond country, and is full of priceless portraits and treasures. This is
one of the finest houses in Yorkshire, as befits a family which has done so
much for the county and is held in such high esteem.

CHAPTER FIVE

Around Catterick

CATTERICK BRIDGE

THERE are three 'Cattericks': the attractive village of Old Catterick itself stands back from the Great North Road, a mile south of Catterick Bridge —and a long way from Catterick Camp.

Catterick Bridge, which spans the River Swale four miles from Richmond, has several claims to fame. The original bridge was built in 1422, reconstructed in Elizabeth's time, and greatly enlarged in 1820. As the present fine bridge is adjacent to the site of the Roman camp of Cataractorium, it seems certain that a bridge must have existed here since Roman times.

Perhaps the most famous incident associated with this part of the River Swale is the recorded baptism of early Christians there by St Paulinus, the first Archbishop of York. Ten thousand people, including a Saxon king, are said to have been baptized near this spot, and the lands by the river towards the village of Brompton-on-Swale are still known as 'Holy Banks'.

For most travellers, Catterick Bridge is notable chiefly for the adjoining Bridge House hotel which has a history going back to the early fifteenth century. This famous hotel is as charming without as it is hospitable within.[1]

On my way from the Bridge House to Catterick Camp, I called at Brough Hall, which stands on the site of a Roman fort, and Sir Ralph and Lady Lawson showed me round their beautiful house. During the Second World War, Brough Hall was taken over by the Royal Air Force and served as an Operations Headquarters for Catterick Aerodrome, but now the Hall has been restored to some of its former glory. Beautiful oak panelling has been replaced and ceilings renovated. One of the most striking features of the house is the exquisite Adam staircase. The Adams added two wings to the house, and made other improvements.

The Lawson family has always remained true to the Old Faith, and, in addition to the private chapel in the Hall, an imposing church was built in the grounds in the early part of last century and is open to the public.

[1] See Chapter Thirteen, 'Some North Riding Inns and Hotels'. p. 100.

CATTERICK CAMP

Probably more contemporary Englishmen have passed through Catterick Camp than any other part of Yorkshire; and its rapid rise to pre-eminence among the military camps of the country has been remarkable.

The camp occupies a site between Catterick Bridge and Richmond, and now covers an area of twenty miles in circumference. It is a self-contained town, in size and population roughly equivalent to the town of Grantham.

To call it the 'Aldershot of the North' is a misnomer, for it has long since left Aldershot behind and is now the largest and most important military camp in England.

Modern Catterick came into existence during the First World War. It began as a small camp for Australian and Colonial troops in 1914, and by 1919 it appeared to have served its purpose. From 1919 to 1923 it lay derelict. And then, in 1925, it became the headquarters of the Royal Signals Regiment, which moved in from Maresfield in Sussex. From 1923-5, the new Catterick began to grow rapidly, and during the next ten or twelve years the Sandhurst blocks began to appear. When war broke out in 1939, it was well established as an important training centre, and during the war up to 35,000 British and Colonial troops were in training there.

Today 13,000 troops are permanently installed, in addition to over 5,000 civilian employees; and Catterick is still growing. The School of Signals is where officers for the New Army are trained. Next to it are the head-quarters of Signals Training Centre where technical personnel are trained. In addition, the Royal Armoured Corps H.Q. and the H.Q. Training Brigade is stationed at Catterick. Tank and cavalry regiments are also trained there. The 65, 66 and 68 Training Regiments, Royal Armoured Corps, now undertake the training of the National Service men in their basic training period. These regiments are staffed by officers from various tank and cavalry regiments. The School of Signals and Signals Training Centre do the same for the Signals personnel. These are some of the units which are permanently stationed at Catterick, but the camp is growing all the time.

Catterick today is the home and training centre of the New Army. New streets are appearing and new names with local Yorkshire associations, but to the soldiers of the last two wars the names of the 'lines' such as Arras, Le Cateau, St Quentin, Gaza, Somme, Hooge, Tigris, Euphrates, Shaiba and Mosul will always recall their Catterick days.

HORNBY CASTLE

Musing on Catterick, I found myself walking on what is now a tank road, pursued by a mighty, mechanized army, from which I fled.

I fled in the direction of the village of Hornby, a few miles to the south, with the intention of seeing Hornby Castle, but I was quite unable to resist the tiny church of St Mary the Virgin which graces this equally tiny village. It is very old and weathered, and, to be truthful, seemed a little neglected, but it is a jewel none the less, and the tower, part of which dates back to A.D. 1070, is remarkable, as are the ornamental Norman arches and the numerous effigies of knights and ladies.

Hornby Castle, which dominates the landscape hereabouts, is largely derelict. Until recently, it was in the possession of the Duke of Leeds, and was formerly held by the St Quintins, the Conyers and the D'Arcys. It stands in a great park which has now been split up into farmlands; and although much of the frame of the castle still stands, only one habitable wing remains—and this has been entirely remodelled. Nevertheless, the shell of the castle still retains something of its former glory, and one seems to catch an echo of its historic past as one walks around the ruins of St Quintin's Tower.

Turning towards Old Catterick village from this vantage point, one gets a glimpse of the lovely valley of the Swale beyond. And once more I found myself caught up in the teeming traffic of the Great North Road, which has a habit of reappearing in unexpected places wherever one turns in this corner of the Riding.

Anxious to see two more remarkable sights, I turned away from the road again and made my way to the village of Bolton-upon-Swale at the other side of the river.

CHAPTER SIX

Bolton-upon-Swale

PATRIARCHAL HENRY JENKINS

IT was raining fiercely when I arrived at Bolton, so I had no hesitation in making straight for the old church—first because, among its many other attractions, a church makes an excellent shelter, and second because I wanted to look once again on that unique memorial tablet to the oldest man in England, if not in the world. In a dark corner in the south wall of the nave, near the altar, I found it and picked out the florid epitaph, which begins:

> 'Blush not Marble
> To render from Oblivion
> The memory of Henry Jenkins . . .'

Born in the year 1500, Henry Jenkins was engaged as a labourer and fisherman for the first 140 years of his life. Famous as a salmon-fisher, he told one judge that old as he then was, he could dub a hook with the best man in the county. He is reported to have been able to swim across the Swale when he was over a century old and to have worked as a harvester to within a few years of his death.

There seems no reason to doubt that Jenkins did live to the ripe old age of 169 or thereabouts; it may have been a year more or a year or so less—but what does an odd year matter to such a patriarch? Parish registers were not kept in 1500 when he claims to have been born. The entry recording his death merely says: '1670 Decem. 9 Henry Jenkins, a very aged and poore man of Ellerton, buried.' The vicar could scarcely commit himself further in the circumstances. Jenkins had given evidence on the vicar's behalf some years before his death and had then been sworn as aged 'one hundred and fifty-seven'. The principal events on which the estimates of his age are based are his frequent appearances at York Assizes to give evidence of matters that occurred during his boyhood and youth. In the year 1655, Henry Jenkins gave evidence at York that he remembered a right-of-way over a property as far back as the year 1540. Two other ancient men admitted that he was a very old man when they were young.

On another occasion he gave evidence that he was sent as a boy to Northallerton with a horse-load of arrows for the battle of Flodden. He claimed to have been butler to Lord Conyers and said that he remembered the Abbot of Fountains very well and that he was between thirty and forty at the time of the Dissolution of the Monasteries. He said that he was usually given 'a quarter of a yard of roast beef and a jack of strong ale' when he went to Fountains.

He lived under six kings and through some of the most eventful years in English history. When one remembers the world-wide interest that was aroused a year or so ago when the most famous contemporary figure in English literature passed away at the age of ninety-four, one can appreciate what a remarkable physique this simple day-labourer must have had. Not for him the Spartan regime of the vegetarian, the non-smoker and abstainer. He enjoyed his roast beef and Yorkshire pudding and his jack of strong ale, and he retained his keen memory and all his wits until he died.

Henry Jenkins was a great natural—the last, perhaps, of the breed, though there are plenty of young nonagenarians like him in Yorkshire today. I have watched men far in the eighties playing darts in some of these remote North Riding villages, and drinking pints of ale into the bargain, whose backs were 'broad as bullocks'. (I had an uncle of my own who lived to be ninety-seven.)

Henry Jenkins well deserves the flowery epitaph in the church of Bolton-on-Swale and the massive monument in the churchyard which was erected by some of his admirers as far back as 1743. The village of Ellerton-on-Swale where he was born and where he spent the greater part of his life—except when he was summoned to York to give evidence—is only a stone's throw away from Bolton where he is buried.

KIPLIN HALL

Kiplin Hall stands just beyond Henry Jenkins's village of Ellerton.

The Hall is of particular interest to American tourists, since it was built by the first Lord Baltimore, Secretary of State to James I, from designs by Inigo Jones. It is a typical Jacobean building of red brick with stone quoins and mullioned windows, but looked somewhat neglected and forlorn when I called there and found it temporarily deserted. It contains a notable collection of pictures, including some of the best works of Canaletto. It was from this lovely old house that Lord Baltimore set off for America in 1633 with the idea of founding a colony there, and though he did not live to accomplish his plan, his son carried on the work and became the founder of the city of Baltimore and the State of Maryland. Strange to think that in this quiet corner of Yorkshire germinated the idea of colonizing Maryland; but Yorkshire is full of such surprises and has several other close links with America.

Topcliffe-on-Swale (near Thirsk) always lures me aside, partly to admire the fine sweep of the Swale at this point from the bridge, and partly because of Richard Rolle, the Yorkshire hermit of Hampole—famous mystic and writer—who has been called the father of English prose. The saintly Richard spent some of his early years here.

The old church has been largely rebuilt, but contains a remarkable fourteenth-century brass and other interesting memorials. There are historic sites nearby on the bank of the river, but Topcliffe today, like Dishforth, Leeming, Middleton St George and Skipton-on-Swale, is largely in the hands of the Royal Air Force, and the sky hereabouts is full of the roaring of wings. This was my own battleground during part of the war and is full of memories; but I cannot truthfully commend it to the tourist in search of peace and quiet!

SCORTON

Scorton, near Bolton-upon-Swale, is famous among lovers of archery for the 'Antient Scorton Silver Arrow' which has a history dating from Elizabeth's reign. The arrow has been shot for since 1672 and is a cherished prize of bowmen. The competition takes place in various parts of the country but was held in Scorton village again during the Festival year of 1951

The village, with its exceptionally spacious green, its charming cottages and old grammar school, makes a delightful picture. Scorton is also notable for its hospital-monastery of St John of God, a rather forbidding-looking grey building from without, but a revelation within. The hospital was opened in 1880 and caters for chronic invalids of all denominations. It is one of several such hospitals belonging to this Order in England; recently an overflow hospital to Scorton was opened at Croft, near Darlington.

Scorton is a comparatively new foundation, but thousands of patients have already been nursed there by these devoted brothers, who also run the novitiate house for young men entering the Order in England.

One might expect a hospital for incurables to suggest the motto: 'Abandon hope all ye who enter here.' On the contrary, this hospital seems to radiate hope and happiness. The reason is to be found in the attitude of the nursing brothers who only enter the Order if they have a particular vocation for nursing the sick.

I was shown round Scorton hospital by the chaplain, the Rev. Monsignor Tindall, a retired headmaster, and I found his high spirits and enthusiasm infectious. He had a joke for all the bedridden patients, and it astonished me how cheerful they all were. I had called at the hospital expecting to see a good deal of suffering and unhappiness, and instead I found everyone cracking jokes and pulling each other's legs, or having their beards trimmed and their hair cut by brother barbers—or being treated in the occupational therapy rooms.

It may seem odd to include such a place in a general book about the fair North Riding, but Scorton is an integral part of the Riding and it is everywhere known and admired in the North of England. It depends entirely on public subscription, and one of the brothers—Brother Victor (who recently died at the age of eighty)—spent the greater part of his life walking about the Yorkshire dales and towns collecting donations for his beloved hospital.

I came away from Scorton with a tremendous admiration for these unselfish men who devote their whole lives to the sick and dying and yet manage to remain so cheerful.

Bolton Castle in Wensleydale: a massive, melancholy ruin standing on the shoulder of the fells.

West Tanfield on the River Ure, showing the historic church and (to its left) the Marmion tower.

CHAPTER SEVEN

Wensleydale

WENSLEYDALE PAGEANTRY

WENSLEYDALE, the fair sister to rugged Swaledale, is scenically and historically one of the most interesting of the great Yorkshire dales. Where else will one find so many historic halls, castles and mansions, so many ruined abbeys and ancient churches, such a profusion of lovely villages, and such a wealth of spectacular scenery as is to be found in this spacious dale?

Only those who have explored the dale on foot from the source of the Ure (at Ure Head) in the high Pennines, past Blades and Lunds to the lonely Moorcock inn, or over Cotter End through Cotterdale to Hawes, can appreciate the wildness of its beginning and the beauty of its setting. Elsewhere I have described this country in some detail; it is a walker's paradise.

Fortunately, Wensleydale is favoured with good roads and the motorist can explore all the main beauty spots and subsidiary dales in a leisurely tour.

HAWES

The usual approach from Swaledale is over the famous Buttertubs Pass from Thwaite to Hawes—one of the highest passes in the country. This has the advantage of revealing superb vistas of both dales and of taking one over the high Pennines past the remarkable limestone shafts known as the 'buttertubs' owing to their churn-like formation. It also brings one directly to the old market town of Hawes, mother-town of Wensleydale, which stands at the head of the main dale (seven miles east of the Moorcock).

All roads seem to converge at Hawes. You can see them trailing over the hills from Kirkby Stephen and Kendal, from Widdale, Ribble Head and Wharfedale, and from Askrigg and Bainbridge. Hawes is a typical dales town—more typical of the dales than of the North Riding itself. It is a grey, rugged market town with a cobbled main street, narrowing near the bottom, and with its houses and inns hobnobbing together. I like to come clattering down this steep street from the fells. You feel that you have really reached your goal when you come to Hawes; its houses close in on you, and its shops invite you to enter and sample their wares. I always linger at the attractive old map shop and the book shop. Picturesque and full of atmosphere at all times, Hawes is at its best on market days when the farmers and their wives take possession of it—or when the sheep sales are on.

The rugged church dominates the dale, and everywhere there are fierce roads, twisting over the hills and tempting you to follow: to neighbouring Gayle, to Appersett, or just across the river to the tiny hamlet of Hardraw with its famous Force—one of the many wonders of Wensleydale.

BAINBRIDGE AND ASKRIGG

From Hawes, the main road goes to Bainbridge, with a branch road to neighbouring Askrigg. Bainbridge has an enchanting setting above the little River Bain—which flows out of Semer Water and into the Ure nearby. This lovely, spacious village, with its delightful green and its Rose and Crown inn should not be missed. The hunting horn used to be blown here at dusk (as at Ripon) for centuries past to guide wayfarers from the hills, but is now heard no more. Bainbridge is set in the heart of the dale and is surrounded by magnificent limestone scenery, with the lion-like hill of Addlebrough keeping guard over it and the old Roman camp on Brough hill, over the way. But for me the finest thing at Bainbridge is the old Cam High road that turns off the Countersett road and goes by leaps and bounds over the hills and far away—to Dodd Fell and Ribble Head. Metalled for the first mile or so, it turns into a broad green road that takes one into the heart of the hills. The Romans used it and perhaps made it, but more probably they adapted it from an older British track. When I was over there again recently, I met a shepherd leading his flock over it, who told me it had been used as a sheep-way from time immemorial. Equally alluring are the metalled roads to Countersett, Marsett and Stalling Busk, with the mysterious, haunting lake of Semer Water between. If anyone is looking for views, let him turn off the Cam High road towards the pretty hamlet of Countersett and he will not be disappointed. The Quakers have left their marks at Countersett and all over this valley.

Askrigg is another striking dales town nestling under the fells. The roads into it from Swaledale tumble down from the high ridge above, and this is how I prefer to approach the rugged little market town; but from

Bainbridge, the road over Yorebridge enters Askrigg from the bottom of the hill and gives a better impression of its rugged charm. There are stone-built cottages, farms and inns, an old bullring and a fine church, with a Metcalfe chapel. Up the hill, on the edge of the moorland road, stands Coleshouse, the 'Yorkshire cottage' where the late Ella Pontefract wrote her dales studies with her friend Marie Hartley, who carries on the tradition.

NAPPA

Just beyond Askrigg stands Nappa Hall, the ancestral home of the great Metcalfe clan, and now a private farm-residence. The Metcalfes are one of the oldest families in the dale, and since the thirteenth century the name of these fighting squires has been interwoven with Wensleydale story and with that of the more illustrious family of Scrope of Bolton and Danby.[1]

James Metcalfe fought at Agincourt and, in return for his services, Sir Richard Scrope of Bolton gave him a portion of his Nappa estate. Succeeding Metcalfes attained high honours in the State and became large landowners. They were renowned for their valour, their feuds, their numbers and their white horses, and were the largest English clan to fight at Flodden. One of them—Sir Christopher Metcalfe—was attended by three hundred horsemen, all of his kith and kin, mounted on white horses, when he received the appointment of High Sheriff of Yorkshire. Another, Sir Thomas ('the Black Knight'), laid siege to Raydale House beyond Semer Water. Halliwell Sutcliffe has woven their story into some of his romances.

Mary Queen of Scots spent some days at Nappa during her captivity at neighbouring Bolton Castle.

BOLTON CASTLE

Nappa Hall is really the starting-point for the romantic portion of Wensleydale, to walk through which is like walking through a book of English history. Beyond Askrigg and Aysgarth—with its tempestuous falls and fine church—and a few miles north of the village of Carperby, stands Bolton Castle—surely one of the most striking ruins in Yorkshire. From either bank, but especially on the road between West Witton and Wensley, it seems to haunt the dale, a massive, melancholy ruin standing on the shoulder of the fells in lonely splendour. In certain lights, it has a quite unearthly beauty and presents an enchanting picture. Of all the castles I have

---

[1] See *Broad Acres* for a more detailed account of the Metcalfes of Nappa.

seen, Bolton is the most eloquent and satisfying, superb in its conception and its setting. Much of this formidable fortress is still in a remarkable state of preservation. Several of the rooms may be inspected, including the suite where Mary Queen of Scots was held prisoner for six months during the year 1568.

One of my happiest memories of Bolton Castle is of seeing Dorothy Una Ratcliffe's stirring play on the unhappy Queen performed in these very rooms by the Wensleydale players. How vividly it brought the sad story to life again! With her love-affairs and desperate plans to escape, Mary gave Sir Henry Scrope and Sir Francis Knollys a great deal of anxiety, but all my sympathies are with the Queen who was so soon to lose her head.

No artist has painted the castle as vividly, or as often, as our own Fred Lawson, who lives in the little village of Castle Bolton nearby and who knows every corner of it.

BISHOPDALE AND WALDENDALE

Near the castle there are other villages which should be explored. To do so, however, entails several detours as the villages are scattered on either side of the wide valley and in the subsidiary dales. South of Aysgarth, Bishopdale and Waldendale should be seen. Both have good roads, though the Waldendale road comes to an end before the dale-head; but the walk over the watershed (and incidentally over the boundary line of the Riding) to Buckden or Starbotton is not to be despised. Whatever else the tourist misses, the lovely village of West Burton in Waldendale should be seen for its own sake; and so, for that matter, should Redmire and Preston-under-Scar, Swinithwaite and West Witton. But West Burton, with its sloping green, has such a striking setting and such an air of quiet and repose, that it delights the eye at sight. South of the river and of West Witton, Penhill Beacon rises high about the surrounding fells and dominates this part of Wensleydale, as does neighbouring Addleborough beyond Bainbridge. There are the remains of a chapel of the Knights Templar on the lower slopes of Penhill—and wonderful vistas from the top. The old green road over the shoulder is one of my particular delights.

WENSLEY

The two main roads through the dale converge at the little village of Wensley, close by the river—and properly so, for Wensley not only gives its name to the whole dale, but is also a dream-village, with an exquisite church (1245) full of treasures, including the famous Flemish brass, many Scrope shields and memorials, and the fine Bolton pew.

The great park of Bolton Hall adjoins the road at this point. The magnificent Hall was built in the seventeenth century for the first Duke of Bolton, whose wife—daughter of Lord Scrope of Bolton Castle—brought him a large portion of the Scrope estates in Wensleydale.

Readers of the Ingoldsby Legends will recall the *Lay of St. Cuthbert* or *The Devil's Dinner-Party,* the scene of which is set in Bolton Hall. It tells what happened once when the Lord Scrope's guests did not arrive in time for dinner; and what fun it is!

LEYBURN

Leyburn, a breezy old market town on the ridge above the Ure, with a vast cobbled market place surrounded by shops and inns, is a focal point for the dale. Leyburn always seems to have a sense of its own importance, and to be thriving and bustling. I like to wander about that enormous square and hear the gossip of the dale. Its famous Shawl—a limestone terrace on a ridge running northward high above the river—makes a delightful stroll and affords magnificent views of the dale. Kit Norton is said to have ridden this way with Queen Mary in her attempt to escape from Bolton Castle, and to have been overtaken on the Shawl. Whether the story is true or not, it is a romantic walk well known to generations of other Leyburn lovers.

SPENNITHORNE

From Leyburn the road divides, one branch leading to Harmby, Constable Burton and Bedale, the other to Middleham and Masham. The tiny village of Spennithorne lies between, and for the sake of its church alone, quite apart from its sylvan charms, Spennithorne is worth the slight detour involved. It is one of those ancient churches—beautifully kept—that I, for one, cannot resist, with a history reaching back over a thousand years. Among its main treasures are an oak screen reported to have come from Jervaulx Abbey, a venerable altar stone, and, among many notable architectural features, curious 'faces' carved on the capitals. The families of the Chaytors and van Straubenzees have lived here for over three hundred years in the halls by the church, and the whole village exudes an atmosphere of age and repose.

MIDDLEHAM

From Spennithorne one gets a glimpse of neighbouring Middleham—
ancient capital of Wensleydale—with its battlemented bridge and ruined
castle rising in the distance like the spires and towers of Camelot. Middleham—once known as the Windsor of the north—has not the advantage of
a position as striking as that of Bolton Castle, nor is it so well preserved,
but it makes a fine romantic picture in the distance and is a real story-book
castle. In the trim village of Middleham itself, the castle is lost, and all one's
attention is on the unusual layout of the village which seems to wander up
and down and round about the two crosses and two market places. The
roads, too, seem to go off in all directions, and only the inns and cottages
seem purposeful and firmly planted.

Horsey men and stableboys in riding-breeches strut about the cobbled
streets, and beautiful thoroughbreds come in from exercise. For Middleham is one of Yorkshire's most famous racing centres—the Newmarket of
the north—and there are many important stables up and down this
straggling village. Dante, winner of the 1945 Derby, was trained here, and
you can see the stall where he lived, with his name proudly emblazoned
over the door:

DANTE
Winner of the Derby 1945
occupied this box during
his Racing Career

Dante is the best horse that Middleham has so far bred: but many other
famous thoroughbreds have been trained at quiet Middleham. Any morning, around eleven o'clock, you will see a lovely string file out of the
stables behind the castle and walk to the famous 'gallops' on the moor
above, where, they will tell you, English queens used to ride from the
castle with their ladies (and gentlemen) five hundred years ago. Today you
will not see any queens but a rather mixed company of stableboys and
men, with an occasional pretty girl to leaven the lump: but they can all
ride like champions. Many a time I have watched the late Matthew Peacock, who might well be called the modern 'Peacock of the North',
standing up there on the 'tops' watching the sleek fillies gallop like the
wind over the green turf, with a thunder of hooves that startled me out of
my daydreams. Miles and miles of soft green turf lie between Middleham
and Penhillside—more than enough to test anyone's wind and limbs.

It is a strange experience to turn back from the exhilarating 'tops' and wander down to the mighty ruins of ancient Middleham, past the green mound known as William's Hill, the site of the original motte-and-bailey fortress. But it is the massive grey pile of the later castle that attracts the eye. It looks enormous even in ruins—a vast medley of crumbling grey walls and ramparts, with a moat and gigantic Norman keep that is still a formidable sight and one of the largest in England. It is a chastening experience to wander in this derelict palace, this fortress of kings, and to speculate on its stormy history. Before the Conquest, Middleham belonged to Gilpatrick and, after the Normans came, to Alan the Red of Richmond fame. Thence by marriage it came into the possession of the Neville family and was the seat of the Nevilles in all their splendour for some two hundred years. Richard Neville, or Warwick the Kingmaker (Lytton's 'Last of the Barons'), lorded it here, and on his death it passed to his son-in-law, afterwards Richard III. On Richard's death at Bosworth Field, it came into the possession of Henry VII and ultimately to the Lindley family. Middleham has seen days of brilliant pageantry and ruthless villainy, and one has only to wander round the ruins to feel something of its tragic history.

In the fine old church of St Alkeld and St Mary beyond, may be seen many of the arms and shields of the kings and nobles who held sway in Middleham in those troubled years, and much else of interest. Charles Kingsley was titular canon here in more peaceful days.

THE SCROPES OF DANBY

The Masham road from Middleham turns towards the river—or rather towards the two rivers, since the lovely River Cover joins the Ure at this point. Cover Bridge crosses the one and Ulshaw Bridge the other. To me, this is one of the loveliest spots in Wensleydale, and, whether you are interested in castles or not, this meeting of the two rivers and the two fine bridges cannot fail to please.

The Cover Bridge inn is well known to anglers and walkers, and the road points the way into beautiful Coverdale. Much as I should like to wander down that idyllic valley, past Coverham Abbey, Melmerby, Carlton and Scrafton, towards the dale-head, I must, on this occasion, adhere to the main dale where there is still much of interest to see; but I should like to commend quiet Coverdale to any readers who have not tasted its delights. Even without the distraction of Coverdale, Ulshaw Bridge puts me in a big enough quandary, since the by-road northward leads to many fine villages, while the main road southward to East Witton is the obvious route on this tour.

It is unusual to find an isolated Catholic chapel by a bridge of this kind—and, though it is a simple building, it is notable for the beautiful Italian Stations of the Cross, done in mosaic, and for the arms of the famous Catholic family of Scrope (of Bolton), whose present home—Danby Hall —stands in the spacious park nearby, with the Scrope eagles at the entrance gate. Nobody with any feeling for history can pass this spot without a second glance, and the scenery alone merits that. For the Scropes of Bolton, Masham and Upsal are one of the greatest families in Yorkshire—and English—history. It was Lord Scrope, Chancellor of England and Keeper of the Great Seal, who built Bolton Castle in the fourteenth century; the Scropes of Danby are his lineal descendants and they have always kept the Catholic faith. Another Lord Scrope led the dalesmen to fight at Flodden Field. Indeed there is scarcely a battle in English history in which members of this family have not played a leading part. Not only warriors but two chief justices, archbishops, high treasurers, earls, bishops and barons, figure in the long line of Scropes, and if justice were done they would still carry the title of the Earldom of Wiltes,[1] which was granted to Sir William le Scrope by Richard II in 1397 and ruthlessly set aside by Bolingbroke.

I was delighted to have an opportunity of looking round Danby Hall, where I found true Yorkshire hospitality. It always astonishes me how kind and long-suffering the owners of old country houses are to importunate writers; not only do they suffer fools gladly but usually they seem delighted to show one round, busy though they may be. My experience is that the older the families are, and the more renowned, the more courteous they are to inconvenient callers like myself. And what a beautiful house Danby Hall is, with its famous heirlooms and its wonderful gallery of Scrope portraits, from those of the earliest bearers of the title to portraits of the present time; a charming picture of Lady Jane Scrope by Reginald Brundritt had only just been added to the long line when I called.

EAST WITTON AND JERVAULX

East Witton is another of Yorkshire's surprising villages, recalling West Burton in its setting. The houses—a little too much of a pattern, perhaps; they were rebuilt at the beginning of the present century—lie on either

[1] See *The Earldom of Wiltes*, by John Henry Metcalfe.

side of a long, spacious green that slopes gently up to the hills, with trees down the middle, and an air of gentle quietude all round. The forlorn-looking Blue Lion at the crossroads beyond looks as if it is not quite sure whether a lion rampant has any right to be found in such a very sober village. It was closed. The present church is of recent date and was locked when I called. Somewhat frustrated, I continued along the deserted road which passes through some delightful wooded scenery until it reaches Jervaulx Park. The high wall hides the ruins of Jervaulx Abbey, but the key can be obtained at the lodge opposite. The grounds may be entered without a key, but the key admits one to the inner sanctuary.

At Jervaulx the setting is everything: the ruins are too scattered and the fabric too broken to give one a satisfying picture of what must have been a superb Cistercian abbey in its day; and they are somewhat dwarfed by the great house nearby, built partly out of the old stones. But as one wanders round, the abbey comes alive again and makes a splendid picture. The great trees and the green parkland emphasize the solemnity of the scene.

It was at Jervaulx that the monks made the original Wensleydale cheese and bred some of the famous Wensleydale horses; and it was here that they cultivated the lands around for some four centuries until the last un-fortunate Abbot Sedbergh took part, against his will, in the ill-fated Pilgrimage of Grace and was subsequently executed.

Between Jervaulx and Masham the dale broadens and the landscape opens out beyond Kilgram Bridge; but there is some delightful hilly country to the south of the road around the tiny hamlets of Ellingstring, Fearby and Healey, beyond which the great moorland climbs over to Nidderdale in the West Riding.

MASHAM

Masham stands near the end of Wensleydale proper, for though the River Ure has still many miles to travel past West Tanfield and Ripon to Boroughbridge, Masham marks a distinct change of scene. Perhaps it is because I always seem to go to Masham on hot, sunny days that it strikes me as an unusually sleepy market town, as Yorkshire towns go. The vast market place, with its maypole and cross, looks like some sun-drenched piazza, deserted as often as not, as if everyone were taking a siesta until five o'clock. On such occasions, I wander across to the hospitable King's Head, order tea in a comfortably drowsy mood, and relax. But of course Masham is not always so sleepy, and there is much to see in this spacious old town, including a notable church with a fine steeple which can be seen for miles, a churchyard with a unique pillar, and many attractive street corners.

Masham is dominated by neighbouring Swinton with the great park and noble mansion of Lord Swinton, part of which is now used as a Conservative college; and when you are tired of Masham you may care to wander across that spacious park and feast your eyes on the lovely vistas around, or go down to the next village of West Tanfield which marks the boundary of the North Riding at this point.

WEST TANFIELD

If you approach West Tanfield from Ripon (as I prefer to do) you will get a better impression of this attractive village from the fine bridge across the river, which is very wide and swift at this point. One half of the bridge is in the West Riding and the other half in the North Riding—or, as the legend on the keystone reads, 'DIVESION of the N. & W. Riding.'

From the bridge, there is a fine silhouette of the old church, the Marmion tower or gatehouse, the Bull inn and the red-roofed chantry cottage—a typical North Riding prospect. I never go to Tanfield without entering the church and admiring the wonderful effigies of Sir John and Lady Marmion in their imposing alabaster tomb, with its wrought-iron hearse, with prickets for candles. Although the Marmion gatehouse is in ruins, it is still a romantic sight, and whether Scott's *Marmion* is historically sound or not, these effigies of knights and ladies fill one with poetic fancies.

SNAPE CASTLE

Snape, a few miles north of West Tanfield, is a big, pleasant village, notable for its castle which faces the main road. Bereft now of its earlier splendour and partly in ruins—though two wings are occupied—Snape is still a romantic-looking castle, with its battlements, towers and parapets. For a time it was the home of Catherine Parr, widow of Lord Latimer of Danby and Snape, who subsequently became the last wife of Henry VIII. One does not know what to admire more about her, the fact that she ever consented to be that lusty villain's sixth wife, or that she won his approbation and lived to bury him, as we say in Yorkshire.

So quiet and secluded is Snape today that it is astonishing to reflect that an English queen walked out of this quiet castle to grace that troubled

Court. The chapel where Catherine Parr prayed is still in use and open to the public.

I was graciously shown round some of the main apartments, which have been largely modernized; but the fine staircase remains and the castle contains some beautiful rooms. The clock tower is still much as it was in Catherine Parr's day, and I climbed it to see the view and to wander in the footsteps of that brave queen. Her ghost still seems to hover around the home that she must often have longed to see again.

BEDALE

The westward road from Northallerton crosses the little River Wiske and gives its name to a series of charming Wiske villages—Appleton Wiske, Danby Wiske, Newby Wiske and Kirkby Wiske. It is rich, fertile country, pleasantly undulating, but not what I would call exciting to the eye.

After crossing the river near Warlaby, the road winds its way to the little village of Ainderby Steeple, with its notable church, passes through Morton-upon-Swale, and crosses the Swale in its middle course where the banks are bordered by green ings, well known to Yorkshire anglers. Over the field beyond is the pretty village of Scruton and the great hall, once the home of Roger Gale, the famous antiquary. A couple of miles farther along the road is Leeming Bar, where the quiet road is intersected by the Great North Road, which cleaves the countryside like a sword, and the traffic rushes north to Catterick and south to Boroughbridge at high speed.

Once beyond Leeming Bar, the road settles down again to country ways and very soon enters the outskirts of Bedale. Bedale (a little to the north of Snape) is an elegant little market town between the rivers Swale and the Ure, and celebrated for its fine hunting country. The Bedale hunt is one of the most famous in the Riding, and in addition the Zetland, the Cleveland, the Hurworth, and the Bilsdale are within reach—not to mention Catterick, Ripon and Thirsk racecourses nearby.

The main street of Bedale immediately strikes the eye. This broad, cobbled market street has a gentle slope and a faint suggestion of a crescent about it. It is lined with graceful Georgian houses and inns in weathered red brick, while the superb church of St Gregory at the top of the hill—and the old hall opposite—complete a delightful picture.

The dignified Early English Church is spacious, full of noteworthy detail, and contains several fine effigies. The massive fourteenth-century tower was used as a means of defence and refuge against the Border raiders.

But, alas, here again at Bedale I found the hall in a derelict condition. It was occupied by the Army during the war and afterwards came into the possession of several families of 'squatters', who looked extremely uncomfortable in their temporary quarters. The famous stucco ceiling in the great drawing-room was in a sad state, and the whole house looked forlorn and forsaken.

I hate to see these great houses falling into decay, or being turned into flats. I hate to see them being stripped of their treasures to pay taxes and death duties, and I cannot for the life of me see what good it does the country—or anyone else—to let them rot like this. I would far rather see them occupied by their lawful owners and let the country dispense with some of the death duties.

But there it is. The silent revolution goes on and the old traditional England is disappearing before our eyes. The squatters take the place of the squires. Bedale Hall belongs to the family of Beresford-Peirse (who also owned the derelict Hutton Bonville Hall). The present head of the family, Sir Henry Beresford-Peirse, Bart, is head of the Forestry Commission in Scotland. Mr. E. Beresford-Peirse kindly showed me round the gardens—now market gardens—which he looks after personally, and he gave me every possible assistance. Indeed, he was much more concerned that I should see the market garden and read a particular book about Bedale (which he offered to lend me) than that I should bother about the hall. But I came away feeling sad and angry to see it in such a state.[1]

Bedale has held a market charter since the year 1251, and in 1951 it celebrated its seven-hundredth anniversary with a great Festival of Bedale. Bedale also has a cattle-market, and it is at its best on market days, when the street is gay with country produce, and the Black Swan, the King's Head, the Green Dragon, the Waggon and Horses, and the rest, are doing a roaring trade.

WELL AND WATH

Two other interesting villages in this rich corner of the Riding are Well and Wath. Well lies in a sleepy hollow just off the main road between Snape and West Tanfield. It looks incredibly old and a little dilapidated today, but the ancient church is full of historical interest, and has many links with the Nevilles and Latimers. The Hall is next the church, behind

---

[1] Since my visit, I have learned that the York Georgian Society has taken an active interest in the fate of this fine Georgian house, and that the Bedale Rural Council has now acquired it for use as Council offices, etc.

the old almshouses. The Romans, too, had a villa here, and there is a fragment of a pavement in the church.

Interesting though Well is, I confess that I found it curiously depressing. But Wath, which can be most easily approached from Ripon (or from West Tanfield), has a church which I found exciting and stimulating, largely because of its chantry chapel (1328) which is full of monuments of the Nortons and Grahams of Norton Conyers, including a brass of Richard Norton, Chief Justice of the King's Bench, and his wife (1420). In addition, there are many vivid effigies and tombs, including a lovely alabaster piece showing Lady Catherine Graham and her husband with their six children.

NORTON CONYERS

The great Tudor house of Norton Conyers, the home of the Nortons and later of the Grahams, stands in the park beyond the village. This is another of the historic houses of Yorkshire, and I was fortunate to be shown round it by Lady Graham. It is in a perfect state of preservation and beautifully kept, the polished floors and famous staircase nearly bringing me to grief! Norton Conyers was once the home of that doughty Sir Richard Norton who took part in the Rising of the North, as the old ballad describes:

> *Thee Norton with thi nine good sonnes,*
> *They doomed to dye, alas, for ruth*
> *Thy reverent lockes thee could not save*
> *Nor them their fair and blooming Youthe . . .*

Actually, only one of the sons died and Norton himself escaped to Flanders, but the Nortons suffered severely for their loyalty to the Old Faith.

The name of Norton, like those of Scrope and Metcalfe, is a great one in the pages of Yorkshire history, and Norton Conyers was one of their proud houses. Wordsworth wove the Norton story into his 'White Doe of Rylstone'.

The house came into the possession of the Graham family around the year 1600, and has remained so ever since. Originally a battlemented house of red brick, it was considerably enlarged by Sir Bellingham Graham in the seventeenth century. Charles I once stayed five nights at Norton Conyers, and James I and Charles II also slept there in the massive four-poster bed upstairs. Among many interesting relics of Stuart days, I was shown a letter from Charles II requesting a loan of £200 from Sir R.

Graham, and an IOU for the amount. It was Sir Richard Graham who rode home from Marston Moor sorely wounded—so much of the story is true; but it is also said that his horse carried him up the broad staircase to his bedroom, leaving an imprint of one hoof which is plainly visible to-day. It may well be that one of the fiery Grahams rode upstairs, but, as Lady Graham pointed out, the present staircase was only put in in William and Mary's reign, and the hoofmark looks a little too neat to be quite genuine.

The banqueting hall and staircase are magnificent—and so is the whole of this beautiful house, which contains a superb collection of family portraits by many masters.

Charlotte Brontë, who was familiar with Norton Conyers, used it in portraying the interior of Thornfield Hall in *Jane Eyre*.

★　　　★　　　★

In the triangle of country between Middleham, Bedale and West Tanfield, on the northerly bank of the Ure, there are several other notable villages and mansions which should not be overlooked.

Thornton Steward, near Danby Hall, is a tiny little village on the hillside, with a very ancient church.

Thornton Watless, a few miles to the east, is a 'wide-open' village built round a remarkable village green, with a cricket pitch and fine old church at one end, and a lovely hall and park which has been in the possession of the Dodsworth family for many generations.

In this tour, Great Crakehall—with its spacious green and hall—to Little Crakehall and the village of Patrick Brompton, with its attractive Green Tree inn and magnificent twelfth-century church (the tower has been rebuilt), should be included.

CHAPTER EIGHT

Three Market Towns

THE NORTH RIDING is singularly rich in old market towns, some of which have already been mentioned in this book. Most of them are built round a broad main street, or square, as are so many North Riding villages, and invariably they are lined with solid stone houses, usually with russet-coloured pantile roofs, a generous sprinkling of inns, and an ancient church nearby. It is this breadth and spaciousness that seems somehow to typify the spirit of the Riding.

This pattern of squares or wide main streets is not, of course, confined to the North Riding; there are similar towns in the East and West Ridings, and in many other parts of England, for that matter. It is essentially the English style and tradition of market towns. And yet it seems to me that the majority of North Riding villages and market towns have just that little extra spaciousness that makes them so unmistakable. Consider such villages as Appleton-le-Moors or Gillamoor or High Egton—to mention only three out of scores. There is a spaciousness about the main streets that immediately proclaims their 'North Ridingness'—quite apart from the style of their architecture.

It is, perhaps, in the market towns that one can best appraise the character of the Riding and meet a representative selection of the people. And where can one do this to better advantage than in one of the old inns that line the square? Choose one of the inns on market days, and go in to rub shoulders with the farmers and townsfolk and just listen to the conversation. It may not be of any great moment—certainly it will not be very private and confidential, or they would not be talking so volubly for all to hear—but it is sure to be interesting and full of horse-sense and good humour, loud with the rich and musical North Riding speech.

I propose now to consider three typical market towns on the York-Northallerton main road which every traveller must pass through on his tour of the North Riding.

NORTHALLERTON

The ancient market town of Northallerton—the capital of the Riding—stirs the pulses in a particular way. Its exceptionally long and broad main street is so generously besprinkled with inns that one warms to it at sight—as Bacchus is alleged to have done many a long year ago; for the old poem 'In Praise of Yorkshire Ale' tells how Bacchus and his court came to this very town in search of the famous Yorkshire ale, having been told that:

> *Northallerton in Yorkshire doth excell*
> *All England, nay all Europe, for strong Ale.*

After a thorough-going carousal, Bacchus was so delighted with the ale that he swore:

> *This town is famous for strong Ale and Beer,*
> *And for the sake of this good nappy Ale*
> *Of my great favour it shall never fail.*

Whether the ale is as nappy and as potent as it was in those carefree days may be open to question, but the inns remain and make a brave show to this day.

If you arrive in Northallerton on a Thursday evening (which is half-day closing) you will probably think that every other house on the main street is an inn, for they are the only premises that seem to be lit up, and doing good business. The ancient Fleece is probably the oldest inn left standing; it occupies the site of a much older building—a house of the Austin friars.

The Golden Lion is one of the most famous of the coaching inns. The present building is a dignified Georgian house, with some Tudor remains, which must have witnessed many exciting incidents when the old North Road passed by its doors. The great coaching yard and stables behind are evidence enough of its past importance; and even today, as one wanders down the main street—especially in the early morning or at dusk—one still expects to hear the clatter and rumble of the stagecoaches. However much one may regret the good old days, one must admit that the motor car and the motor coach have done much to restore these old inns to life again. It is difficult to get a bed in any of them today at short notice.

Northallerton has much else of interest besides its inns. One of its great attractions is that it seems to combine the charms of an historic old market town with those of a modern city. It is very much in the centre of things.

Thirsk on market day: a corner of the spacious market square. The toll-gatherer still collects tolls on market days.

The steep main street of the enchanting village of Coxwold climbs towards the beautiful church of St Michael where Laurence Sterne was once incumbent

A bewildering number of roads converge on it, and from it one can travel equally well to Scotland or to London—as to any part of Yorkshire.

But the atmosphere of the old market town is ever present—witness the old market cross—and it is essentially a friendly town. You will not find many town halls with a saddler, a greengrocer, a hairdresser and a butcher occupying premises down below, and with assembly rooms for hunt balls, farmers' balls, and the like, above. Paradoxically, the Urban Council offices are quite apart, while the County Council has a magnificent modern building of its own. The main street is full of contrasts. Old bank houses rub shoulders with old inns, and dignified private residences stand cheek by jowl with little shops. The old grammar school, which has produced many famous men, may still be seen. In between the shops and the inns you can wander down little passage ways into spacious wynds and yards, and find yourself back in another age. In its heyday, Northallerton was famous for its horse fairs and for its great market.

Dominating everything else is the magnificent old church of All Saints, with its massive tower. In a sense, the church makes Northallerton what it is. Its history is long and turbulent. The Normans built it. The English armies knew it well. The Scots, who were ever a thorn in the side of the English, repeatedly attacked it. Robert Bruce's army set fire to it in the year 1318 (four years after Bannockburn), and you can still see the reddened stones in the pillar near the organ. But the old church still stands!

Three miles north of Northallerton, on the Darlington road, an obelisk commemorates the famous Battle of the Standard in 1138, in which an English army routed the Scots. The site is disputed, but whether or not the battle was fought at this precise spot—and the lie of the land suggests otherwise—it was certainly fought in the vicinity; and it was one of the turning-points in English history.

But the Scots returned to the fray many times in the succeeding centuries. 'The Scots are coming!' was a cry that often rang through the high street, and the old church tower witnessed the march of victorious armies and shared the bitterness of defeat—Bannockburn, Flodden, the Pilgrimage of Grace, and the Rising of the North. . . .

Beyond the high street, there is a new Northallerton of which the fine County Hall, headquarters of the North Riding County Council, the excellent modern County Library and the modern school, are striking evidence.

The headquarters of the North Riding County Council are imposing in

E

their modernity, as befits the capital town of the Riding, and I came away impressed with the efficient way in which this great Riding is administered. In this ultra-modern building, I was delighted to be shown an old 'bridge book' of the Riding, which the learned Clerk, Mr H. G. Thornley, produced from the muniment room for my perusal. I doubt if any other part of the county can vie with the North Riding in the number and beauty of its old bridges, and I was anxious to learn more about them. I should say that Mr Thornley knows as much about the Riding as any other man living today, and he turned over the pages of that massive old book with a kind of paternal pride. Merely to look at the exquisite sketches of some of the more famous bridges took away much of the nervous apprehension that I feel in these vast modern buildings, and gave me the comfortable feeling of being back in seventeenth- or eighteenth-century Northallerton again.

And on the whole, that is the period I much prefer.

THIRSK

Thirsk, which has a population of between two and three thousand, is an old market town after my own heart. I wish it could be preserved in perpetuity just as it is before the planners spoil it. Already it is changing a little—some of the old shops and inns have had a face-lift, so to speak, and look slightly self-conscious about it—but, on the whole, Thirsk is much as it was when I saw it twenty-odd years ago, and I can still remember how my heart jumped as first I walked into that noble square. The houses and inns are mostly of the eighteenth century, with older foundations beneath.

At first sight, the square seems to be lined almost exclusively with inns, for there are sixteen of them, with the Golden Fleece in the centre of the south side, the Three Tuns at one corner (the *old* Three Tuns is round the corner), the Golden Lion at another, and plenty of others to suit everyone's fancy and pocket. Most of them are coaching inns, and the yards behind, with their commodious stabling (now, alas, 'garaging'), are even more impressive than the frontages, which are often quite small. You can really take the air in these spacious yards, and it is easy to believe that some of them used to stable fifty to sixty horses.

Traces of the old bull-ring may also be seen in the square, near the new post office (1909), which is rather an intruder and occupies the site of the old shambles. The market cross, oddly enough, is in the grounds of the hall. Many of the other old streets are also full of interest, such as Finkle Street, Long Street, Ingramgate.

Strangely enough, the present square—old as it is—is not the original square. This even larger square lies just across the way, in Old Thirsk, and is called 'The Green'. The planners have diverted some of the outward traffic across the present square, and round the Green, so one has a glimpse of Thirsk old and new; but 'new' is only a relative term in Thirsk, since it all looks of much the same vintage. The Green, however, has a curiously deserted air, like a school playground when school is closed. It is surrounded by old houses and cottages which look so quiet and peaceful after the roaring traffic of the market place that one could almost imagine that a community of nuns lived there in seclusion.

The present market square is always swarming with traffic and people. To see it at its best and busiest, one should go there on a Monday—which is market day—and see the stalls laden with wares. It used to be said that there were more eggs in Thirsk market than in the whole of Yorkshire, but that, of course, was in the good old days before the war. Even today—but I had better not go into that! At any rate, there are lots of other stalls to tempt you with their country produce. More remarkable still, there is a toll-collector going round from stall to stall, gathering 'stallage' for the squire, who still owns the market place. All the rest of the week, there is free parking in the cobbled square—and an ideal parking place it is. But on market days, motorists, too, must pay toll, and quite right too!

One cannot begin to understand Thirsk until one realizes that it is still partly feudal, which for me is one of its great charms. Having experienced the horrors of the Planned State (which so closely resembles the Servile State), I am all in favour of feudal England. In Thirsk the squire owns the market rights, the cross, the racecourse, the water-mill, and a lot of other things besides, including the dignified hall near the church. Before you can sell a chicken in the street, or a pig in a poke, you must pay toll—and nobody seems to mind. Everyone I questioned spoke highly of the young squire and of the old one who had died a year or two ago. One shopkeeper, whose business goes back to the Middle Ages, said that Thirsk today was not quite so feudal as Helmsley, but feudal all the same. And long may it so remain!

I would not go so far as to say that everyone is perfectly content with the feudal State. It is difficult to explain the feeling of the Thirsk people as a whole. Some think that Thirsk is in a rut and should be developed. Some of them cry forward, and some back; but nobody bothers to do anything about it. Thirsk should by rights have been the county town of the North Riding instead of Northallerton, for it occupies a commanding strategic position in the middle of the Riding. But the old squire—like a Tsar of all the Russias—refused to allow the railway to come nearer than a mile from the centre of the town lest it disturb his—and the townsfolk's—peace of mind, and so Thirsk has been rather by-passed. For much the same reasons, coupled with a sturdy local independence, Thirsk has never been able to absorb neighbouring Sowerby (population 2,469), though the two places are so near together as to be almost indistinguishable. Sowerby is part of the township of Thirsk, but is a separate manor and parish. Sowerby, with its ancient church, old cottages and fine pack-horse bridge at World's End, is a pretty village well worth a visit too.

Since it has so many inns and cafés, it is not surprising that motorists and lorry drivers pull up at Thirsk. No matter how busy it seems—market days excluded—one can always find plenty of room to park a car or a six-ton lorry. It is a rare pleasure, in these 'no parking here' days, to be able to pull up anywhere and anyhow without being pounced upon by a planner! Perhaps the real romance of Thirsk today is to be found in a certain café in the square which is open day and night and which is a favourite pull-up for long-distance lorry drivers and others. When I went in there at eight o'clock one morning, I found it full of customers drinking tea and coffee and munching sandwiches. Are not these long-distance lorry men the real descendants of the old stagecoach drivers? At any rate, I like to see these modern Leviathans drive into the old square and suddenly decide to call a halt. The amount of heavy traffic passing through the town is another proof of how well situated Thirsk is for so many important roads in the vicinity.

Some of the old shops round the square have been in existence for generations—printers, stationers, chemists and so on. One locally famous firm of drapers—B. Smiths—proudly displays the sign 'Established in 1578'. Mr Hall, the present proprietor, showed me the old cellars, which include a recently discovered smuggling chamber for uncustomed goods. There has always been a Bartholomew in the firm; and I enjoyed the story of one Bartholomew and his brother who ran the firm way back in the eighteenth century, and did not quite conform to the strict family traditions. One day they set off for Manchester to buy some cotton piece-goods. It was a long, tedious journey in those days, and raining when they arrived, so they decided to relax a bit and go round the inns before transacting their business. Afterwards, they got their buying boots on, as the saying goes, and surprised the sober Manchester merchants by the extent of their purchases. A week or so later, a long train of vehicles entered

Thirsk from Manchester, piled high with bales of cloth and all manner of wares. The good townsfolk of Thirsk rubbed their eyes in amazement, for as fast as the first wagons were cleared, more arrived. It required all the capacious cellars and warehouse rooms of the firm to cope with such an influx of goods, and alas, it strained the resources of Bartholomew to breaking-point.

There was a third brother, John—an honest, hardworking farmer—and the bank asked honest John and his son to take over the firm and try to discharge their liabilities. It says much for the character and abilities of John that he did so, though it took his whole lifetime: but somewhere in the 1850's the last bill was paid off and the old firm could raise its head again. It has never looked back since.

Almost every one of these old shops and inns round the square could tell a fascinating story. The Golden Fleece was one of the most famous coaching houses on the road, and its reputation was built up by two land-lords, John and William Hall—father and son—whose portraits hang in the drawing-room. I like the old coaching clock in the entrance hall, made by Palliser of Thirsk. The Three Tuns in the corner used to be the dower house and is a notable building. The Old Three Tuns may be the oldest of all. Many of the old inns have, alas, disappeared.

Thirsk has other claims to fame. Was it not the birthplace of Thomas Lord, the founder of Lord's Cricket Ground, and of another famous cricketer, George Macaulay, who was one of Yorkshire's greatest bowlers of the present century? His mother kept the Golden Fleece. There must be something about that feudal air after all!

I have saved Thirsk's greatest glory to the last—the noble fifteenth-century church of St Mary the Virgin, which stands just outside the town on the road to Northallerton. The exterior, with its delicate, traceried battlements, is particularly striking in the evening light as one approaches Thirsk from the direction of Northallerton. The ornamented oak roof of the nave is one of the finest Perpendicular roofs in the North, but when I called there again recently it was undergoing extensive repairs owing to the ravages of the death watch beetle.

I have said nothing about the Norman castle built by Robert de Mowbray in the early part of the twelfth century, of which only the site exists in the castle garth; nor of the more famous Roger de Mowbray who succeeded him and who endowed so many abbeys and churches. The de Mowbrays made Thirsk and ruled the land for several generations. It was they who were responsible for the feudal system in Thirsk which survives in an attenuated form to this day. It is their name and fame that is com-memorated in the surrounding countryside known as the Vale of Mow-bray, of which Thirsk is the centre.

EASINGWOLD

Easingwold, which stands in the plain, on the main York-Thirsk-Northallerton road, is a sleepy old market town of mellowed red brick which caters for a large agricultural community. It is the headquarters of a rural district council covering about a hundred square miles. Although it lacks the bustle of Thirsk or the vigour of Northallerton, it has a quiet charm of its own. The market square is tucked away behind the main road, its pleasant green surrounded by old cobblestones, where the ancient bull-ring may still be traced.

The dignified old church stands on a rise on the road to Crayke and is surprisingly big, for Easingwold has seen greater days. There are some lovely Georgian houses scattered about these quiet streets, and a Catholic convent and church on the main road. The little 'private' railway that runs between Easingwold and Alne (three miles) consists of one pilot engine and a coach, and has not yet been nationalized. It used to carry passengers, but now only takes goods and parcels, so the engine driver told me.

A sleepy little place, Easingwold!

II. RYEDALE

CHAPTER NINE

The Heart of the Riding

IF I were asked to name the richest and most varied piece of country in the North Riding I would say Ryedale, using that name in its wider sense. The little River Rye runs through the middle of it, but the old wapentake of Ryedale embraces much of the enchanting country to the east and north, including Bilsdale, Riccaldale, Bransdale, Kirkdale, Farndale and Rosedale. I propose to deal with all these dales and their villages in turn because Ryedale is, in a sense, the very heart of the Riding. It is a country of smiling landscapes and constant surprises; of deep and verdant wooded valleys and bold hills, with a backcloth of ever-changing moorlands; a golden-green arcady of meandering rivers, little becks and secret dales, with lovely monastic ruins, ancient churches, historic castles, mansions and picturesque villages in astonishing profusion. Such is Ryedale—a cross-section of rural England—Yorkshire in miniature. It has almost everything the tourist could desire, including such famous ruins as Rievaulx and Byland, and such villages as Hawnby, Coxwold, Hutton-le-Hole, Lastingham, Appleton-le-Moor, Gillamoor, and many others.

Helmsley is the mother town of Ryedale and makes an excellent centre. A start can also be made from Kirbymoorside or Pickering.

HELMSLEY

Helmsley is the main gateway into Ryedale. It stands at a junction of roads from York, Thirsk, Pickering, Malton and Stokesley, and is easily accessible from north or south. I like its vast market square, with the ancient market cross and its more recent monument (designed by Sir Gilbert Scott) to the memory of the second Baron of Feversham. I like especially the pleasing frontage (and interior) of the Black Swan—an old coaching inn—where Wordsworth halted on his honeymoon journey across Yorkshire. The neighbouring Crown makes an admirable foil to the Swan, and the

71

Feversham Arms just round the corner makes another, for I have been entertained at all these noble houses and can recommend them all.

Across the square are the ruins of the castle, the keep being particularly striking. As one approaches Helmsley, the keep dominates the view, and in certain lights the grey walls have an unearthly beauty.

The existing castle was built by Robert de Roos between 1186 and 1227, and was held by his descendants for many generations. It was besieged by Sir Thomas Fairfax in the Civil War. Perhaps its most romantic occupant was the pleasure-loving George Villiers, second Duke of Buckingham, who subsequently married Fairfax's daughter.[1] The Ministry of Works is restoring some of the old apartments used by Buckingham, and these are open to the public.

After Buckingham's death, the estates were acquired by Sir Charles Duncombe. A subsequent head of the family was created Earl of Feversham and Viscount Helmsley. The castle stands in the spacious grounds of Duncombe Park. The family seat of Duncombe House, built to a design attributed to Vanbrugh (though William Wakefield was the architect) was almost entirely destroyed by a disastrous fire in 1879 and then rebuilt. For some years it has been used as a girls' boarding school, the present Lord Feversham residing at Nawton Tower, near the neighbouring village of Nawton. Nobody has shown greater zeal in the preservation of the natural beauties of the countryside or been more generous in allowing the public freely to explore his estates than the present Earl of Feversham.

One can wander where one wishes so long as one behaves in a reasonable manner. If only all landowners were as broad-minded and as zealous in resisting ugly 'development' schemes, what a lot of unpleasant legislation might have been avoided!

RIEVAULX ABBEY

Rievaulx lies three miles north of Helmsley. It can be approached on foot through Duncombe Park or by the footpath starting in Helmsley village, but travellers should be warned that this is not a continuous path.

On a first visit, the main Stokesley road towards Bilsdale is the recommended approach. About two miles up this road, the second steep branch-road to the left (signposted 'Rievaulx') goes to the sequestered village and to the abbey grounds. Before descending this road, a gate on the left leads

[1] See page 88.

directly to the famous terrace, high above the ruins. This is the best way to get a first impression of this exquisitely situated ruin, and also of a typical Ryedale landscape.

It costs a shilling to go on the terrace, but it is worth it—even to a thrifty Yorkshireman. Seen on the right kind of day, the view is quite enchanting. Ryedale is the kind of country that is at its best in sunshine, and I always associate it with warm summer days. The broad terrace is half a mile long and beautifully kept, and the vivid green lawn makes walking a delight. The terrace is designed in a series of pleasing curves, flanked by a noble belt of English trees. At one end is a circular Tuscan temple, and at the other an Ionic temple adorned by Italian pictures.

Built by Thomas Duncombe in an age when such terraces were the craze on great estates,[1] it is a fine example of this art. No doubt it is artificial, and not altogether in keeping with the graver ruins below, but it is very striking. In those days there was a continuous carriage drive from the house which entered the terrace about midway, and one can imagine the flutter of excitement in the ladies' breasts when they saw the famous view for the first time; for even after many visits one comes upon it with a glorious feeling of surprise.

The obliging caretaker will tell you all about the pictures on the ceiling, and how the Italian painter, Burnice, lay on his back for seven long years painting them in such a cunning fashion that the eyes of the horses seem to follow you round the room. I love to hear him expounding these and other mysteries.

The abbey stands deep-embosomed in the valley of the Rye, surrounded by steep, wooded hills, with other valleys converging on the scene. Far beyond, the ridge of the Hambletons flings up to the sky, with the village of Cold Kirby in the foreground.

To examine the abbey at close quarters it is necessary to leave the terrace and descend to the little dream-village of Rievaulx. Rievaulx was the first large Cistercian church to be built in England. It was started in 1131 (a few years before Fountains) and practically completed by 1175. The original building is typical of the severe Cistercian style. The more ornate quire and presbytery were added in 1230, and the result is one of the most beautiful examples of English Gothic in existence. Owing to the nature of the site, the abbey is built north by south instead of, as is usual, east by west. With the aid of the excellent pamphlet prepared by the Ministry of Works, obtainable at the gate, it is easy to follow the layout of the

[1] There are other terraces in Duncombe Park.

church and the monastic buildings. The general effect is one of entrancing beauty. The presbytery is a poem in stone and even in its ruined state looks vividly alive; the chapter house and the reconstructed cloisters are equally striking.

But are we not inclined today to think rather too much of architecture and too little of the men who designed and built these old abbeys to the glory of God? What a colossal undertaking it was for those twelve monks who left Clairvaux in France under St Bernard's direction to found a Cistercian mission centre in England. They were fortunate in finding a Norman patron in Yorkshire, one Walter l'Espec, Lord of Helmsley, who gave them this site on the banks of the Rye. Romantic as is the setting today—and it is certainly one of the most beautiful in England—it must have been wild forest land in those far-off days. But this was an age when great changes were coming over the English scene under the Norman yoke, and several such bands of pioneers were then setting forth from France to spread the Christian faith throughout Britain.

The Rievaulx monks had to divert the course of the river before they could build, but by 1136 they were already sending out missionaries to Scotland. Under the third abbot (1147–66) there are said to have been 140 monks and 600 lay brothers at Rievaulx, 'so that the church swarmed with them like a hive of bees'.

I like the story of St Aelred, destined to become the greatest abbot of them all. Shortly after he had arrived as a young novice, a fire broke out in the refectory where he was sitting with the monks, who are said to have panicked. The young Aelred seized a great flagon of ale and threw it on the flames, effectively extinguishing the fire. Thereafter Aelred went from strength to strength and eventually became the third and greatest abbot in the long history of Rievaulx.

I like, too, the oft-told tale of the rivalry between the monks of Rievaulx and of the neighbouring community at (old) Byland Abbey. The first contingent of the Byland brethren arrived in Rievaulx, after many vicissitudes, in 1143—twelve years after the foundation of Rievaulx. They, too, were presented with a site on the opposite bank of the River Rye, at Old Byland, about two miles from Rievaulx. The site was excellent and the monks got to work with a will to build their church. But, alas, the two houses were too close together. 'Each monastery could hear the other's bells at all hours of the day and night—*which was not fitting and could by no means be endured.*' So the monks of Byland collected their goods and chattels and moved off to another site at Oldstead—again not very far away. After a stay of thirty years, they moved again to their final home at Wass—still only six miles away.

There is very little other recorded history of Rievaulx to mark the monks' long sojourn of 400 years—as long a period as that of the Roman occupation. Abbot succeeded abbot, and the monks cultivated their land, tended their flocks, built and beautified their abbey, spread the Gospel and passed away. Only the lovely shell of their masterpiece and a few scattered tombstones remain to testify to their existence. But I never visit the scene without feeling their presence. The air seems full of ghosts, and the quietude seems more eloquent than the clamour of today.

BYLAND ABBEY

The Cistercian abbey of Byland has not the advantage of the romantic setting of Rievaulx. It stands immediately below the southern slope of the Hambleton hills, on the edge of the plain, but it has a challenging beauty of its own. The best view of it, I think, is from the direction of Coxwold. The broken wheel-window and the solitary turret lend a pathetic solemnity to the ruins. The fine western front, with its massive trefoil-arch doorway and tall lancet window supporting the rose window, is especially notable.

In its original state, Byland must have been a majestic sight. The mixture of styles, the rounded and pointed arches, the fine Early English Gothic, the beautiful tracery, the green and gold tiled floor, and the vastness of the cloisters—145 feet square (larger than those of Fountains or Rievaulx)—give one an idea of its former grandeur.

What strikes one today as so extraordinary is the seemingly casual way in which these early monks wandered around, without funds, and yet contrived to build these enormous churches and monastic quarters. Today, if we want to build a church, let alone a cathedral of the size of Byland, it takes years of effort and activity (whist drives, raffles, sales of work, bazaars) before a modest start can be made. But Byland was built in an age of faith.

Perhaps the most dramatic incident in Byland's long history was in Plantagenet days. In the year 1322, Edward II's retreating army was encamped on Blackhow moor, near Rievaulx, after an unsuccessful expedition against the Scots. It was not the first time that the King had travelled this road, for he had fled to York in full retreat after the Battle of Bannockburn a few years earlier. This time, however, he did not suspect pursuit. Edward had retired to Byland Abbey, and was dining with the monks when the news was brought of a sudden Scottish attack under Robert Bruce. The English flank had been turned by the Scots, who were attacking from two sides. The Battle of Byland took place at Scots Corner,[1] to the north of the neighbouring village of Oldstead. Edward fled to his capital of York, leaving his jewels to the enemy, and only escaped capture thanks to a fast horse.

The monks of Byland appear to have led quiet and exemplary lives and were highly respected; they devoted their time to cultivating their lands, and transformed the wild countryside. Roger de Mowbray, their greatest benefactor after Gundreda, ended his days by adopting the habit, and he was buried at Byland near his mother, the saintly Gundreda.[2]

COXWOLD

Within easy reach of Byland Abbey and Wass there are several other interesting villages, including Coxwold, Kilburn, Oswaldkirk, Ampleforth and Gilling. Together they make a most interesting little tour.

Coxwold is one of the jewels of the North Riding. It stands on a sloping hill—always an advantage for any village—and there is something especially gracious about its broad main street. Coxwold is a clean-built, trim sort of village, full of character and quiet dignity. The old inn, The Fauconberg Arms, half-way up the street, is perfectly in keeping with the other cottages, and it is furnished with massive oak tables and chairs from Mr Robert Thompson's famous workshop in the neighbouring village of Kilburn. The immemorial trees and the cobbled pavement suggest Coxwold's ancient lineage and stirring history.

But the crowning glory of Coxwold is its exquisite church of St Michael near the top of the village. This unique fifteenth-century church in the Perpendicular style, with its octagonal tower, trefoil parapets and pinnacles, perfect symmetry, beautiful stained glass and its crested effigies of knights and ladies, would set the seal on any village. After seeing it one feels it would be sheer greediness to expect anything else; but Coxwold has other treasures. Immediately opposite the church stands the old grammar school, now a private residence, and beyond is Colville Hall (rebuilt in the

---

[1] Not to be confused with the more familiar 'Scotch Corner' near Catterick Bridge.

[2] 'In no part of England was the dissolution of the monasteries as keenly resented or so bitterly opposed as in Yorkshire, where they had held undisputed and, for the most part, beneficial sway for nearly four hundred years.' *Ryedale* ('Country Houses', by Col. C. W. E. Duncombe C.B.E.).

seventeenth century) which commemorates the name of the ancient Norman Lords of the Manor. And at the very top of this remarkable village is the picturesque little twin-gabled Shandy Hall (which I defy anyone to pass without wanting to peep inside) where Sterne spent seven years and wrote some of his masterpieces.

But what are words to describe such a heavenly place as Coxwold? See it for yourself, especially in the evening of a summer's day when the setting sun sheds a golden glory on this lovely village, and gives it an altogether magical appearance.

NEWBURGH PRIORY

Less than a mile south of Coxwold is Newburgh Priory, one of Yorkshire's famous country houses—but once upon a time a house of the Augustinian Canons. It was founded in 1145 by the same Roger de Mowbray who helped to establish Byland Abbey. The canons, in their turn, built the existing church of Coxwold, and also created the beautiful park round the priory. One of the most distinguished canons of the Order was William of Newburgh, the father of historical criticism.

After the Dissolution, the priory came into the hands of the Belasyes family, who converted it into a magnificent country mansion. Charles I gave them the title of Fauconberg. A grandson of the second Lord Fauconberg married Oliver Cromwell's daughter, Mary, and there is a strong tradition that Cromwell's remains were removed from Westminster and secretly buried at Newburgh in the vault above the front door; the vault has never been opened. From the Fauconbergs the estate passed to the Wombwells.

Sterne was a frequent visitor to Newburgh during his incumbency at Coxwold, and in Sir George Wombwell's days Newburgh attained its second summer. Royalty were frequently entertained at their hospitable house, which is full of treasures, Roman remains, Cromwellian relics, rare books and pictures.

During the war the famous old House of Canons was used as a school.

KILBURN

Kilburn, two miles north of Coxwold, nestles under the Hambletons. The village is in two parts: High Kilburn, which stands on a terrace above, overlooking the main village of Low Kilburn. Although it does not make the instant appeal of Coxwold, Kilburn has a pleasant, old-world charm of its own.

It is a higgledy-piggledy sort of village, essentially English, with an old hall, an old church and an inn, all standing close together, with the beck running down the middle of the village. In high summer, its cottage gardens are filled with roses and country flowers, and the sun lingers on the warm colour of old brick and stonework.[1]

The village stands immediately beneath the famous White Horse of Kilburn, which was cut out of the hillside by a native of Kilburn in 1857. Seen at such close quarters, it must be confessed that it looks a strange, misshapen creature, but it improves a little when seen from a distance, though I could have wished for a more spirited representation of this noble animal. The best that can be said for it is that it is one of the White Horses of England. As it has the misfortune to be cut out of clayey soil, it needs a good deal of whitewash.

A much more interesting feature of Kilburn is the workshop of Mr Robert Thompson, the famous woodcarver, who needs no whitewash of any kind, and no praise of mine to bolster him up. When I first visited Mr Thompson, some twenty years ago, his hand-made oak furniture was beginning to be famous. Since then he has won a national reputation for his work, and his 'sign of the mouse' has become known far and wide.

In an age when first-class craftsmen are a diminishing band, it is a pleasure to meet such an artist in remote Kilburn. His father was the village joiner, and Robert Thompson worked as the village wheelwright before finding his true *métier*. He began working in English oak, using the adze to bring out the grain and lustre, and quickly developed a remarkable aptitude for wood carving. From the start, he specialized in ecclesiastical carving, and his first important commission came appropriately enough from Father Paul Nevill, O.S.B., the Headmaster of Ampleforth College.

Since then he has done magnificent work for the College library and church, as well as for the associated preparatory school at Gilling Castle. Examples of his work are now to be seen all over the country, including York Minster and Westminster Abbey, while his oak tables, chairs,

---

[1] From Kilburn, those who are interested in the Byland story should visit Hood Grange, which stands one and a half miles to the north (just off the Sutton Bank road). This was the first home of the Byland community after leaving Furness, and later on became a monastic 'cell'.

Stocking-Oldstead, with its Coronation 'Observatory', occupies a romantic position above High Kilburn, and is notable as the site of the second Byland settlement where the monks remained for twenty years and built a church and cloisters. Only a crypt remains.

cupboards and other domestic furniture adorn hundreds of private houses.

Naturally, with the growth of his business, Mr Thompson was compelled to train others to help him, most of them boys from the village school, so that today his workshops are a hive of activity.

On all his work is to be found his sign manual, a little 'church' mouse, a sign of industry in quiet places. 'Mousey Thompson', as he is called, is today one of Yorkshire's best-known craftsmen.

AMPLEFORTH ABBEY AND COLLEGE

The village of Ampleforth lies midway between Byland Abbey and Oswaldkirk. It is a straggling, sturdy village rather than a showplace, with ancient roots, as the surrounding British earthworks and tumuli prove. It is also one of the North Riding villages with a traditional sword dance and folk-play. The dance has been revived by the students of Ampleforth College.

The chief glory of Ampleforth today is the modern Benedictine Abbey of St Laurence, with the college attached. The abbey and college stand on the slopes of a hill and command a magnificent view of the wooded vale and of the Howardian hills. They can be approached equally well from the villages of Oswaldkirk or Ampleforth.

There seems to be some poetic justice in the fact that a thriving community of Benedictine monks should have taken root again in this monastic corner of Ryedale, and tourists who tire of ruins and wonder what a monastic establishment really looked like in its prime will be interested in this flourishing abbey and school.

The story of its modest beginning is as romantic as any of the older accounts of the original abbeys, but to appreciate it fully one would need to go into the story of the English Reformation and the French Revolution, which are rather outside the scope of this book.

It is said that at one period the Benedictine Order owned a fifth part of England, but at the time of the death of Elizabeth only one member of the English congregation remained—a blind old imprisoned monk, eighty-six years of age, Dom Sigebert Buckley, the last surviving monk of Westminster.

When he was turned ninety he aggregated to the English Benedictine Congregation two young monks who were the nucleus of a new Westminster, thus investing them with all the traditions and privileges of the restored abbey. That was in 1607.

These two monks and their followers settled at Dieulouard, in Lorraine, and the community grew and remained there until the French Revolution forced them to seek refuge again in England. For nine years they wandered from place to place until, in 1802, the Honourable Ann Fairfax of Gilling Castle, the last descendant of her line, gave them the use of a small house called Ampleforth Lodge, which she had built for her private chaplain, Father Bolton, himself a monk of Dieulouard.

Such was the beginning of the Ampleforth Abbey of St Laurence and of the college. In 1808, the school admitted lay students for the first time since the days of Mary Tudor. In the early years the number fluctuated between twenty and eighty, but building went on almost continuously. In 1860, the church and further houses were added. In 1893, the new monastery was built. In 1899, the seventeenth prior of Ampleforth was appointed first abbot by a decree of the Pope. The new abbey church, designed by Sir Giles Gilbert Scott, was begun, and since the appointment of Father Paul Nevill as headmaster, the college has been constantly extended and now consists of eight houses and a magnificent library in addition to the monastery and the church.

In 1929 the Ampleforth community purchased the neighbouring Gilling Castle, the ancestral home of the Fairfaxes, for use as a preparatory school, and so the wheel came full circle. Today there are some 600 boys, 72 monks, and a large staff under the two roofs. The original fortified castle at Gilling (of which the basement remains) was built in the fourteenth century. The present beautiful structure belongs to the sixteenth and eighteenth centuries. The great dining-room, 'one of the most beautiful and complete specimens of Elizabethan architecture in the country', even though now stripped of its famous original panelling, is especially noteworthy. The panelling was removed before the Ampleforth monks acquired the castle. Today the ancient house and grounds are beautifully kept, and Gilling is vigorously alive again. The famous panelling, frieze and stained glass have recently come into the market again, and an appeal has been launched to raise funds to restore these treasures to their original setting in the castle.

Of necessity, the existing buildings at Ampleforth show a confusion of styles from those of the eighteenth century to the most modern, but the general effect is pleasing and impressive. This is building on the grand scale and restores one's faith in the ability of the present generation to vie with that of the past. Every equipment of a modern school is provided for, and the spacious playing-fields are a boy's dream. The panelled library is furnished throughout with massive oak pieces by Thompson of Kilburn.

Helmsley, mother town of Ryedale, nestles under the ruined keep of the ancient castle, once the home of the notorious Duke of Buckingham.

The dignified and spacious village of Gilling, in Ryedale, with its sturdy stone cottages. Nearby are Gilling Castle and Ampleforth College.

The new abbey church, designed by Sir Giles Gilbert Scott, which is not yet complete, is in the Romanesque style, and is a magnificent conception.

It is not surprising that a school with such a history and under such guidance ranks today as one of the best public schools in England.[1]

OLD BYLAND AND CAYDALE

The village of Old Byland, one of the earlier cells of the monks of Byland Abbey, stands on a spur of the Hambletons, a good six miles from the present Byland Abbey. The road to Old Byland from Rievaulx Abbey bridge runs through the woods between two ravines: a lovely piece of country. The village is set on a broad green common graced by some ancient trees. The old church of the monks has many striking features, including a Saxon sundial, and stone dragons guarding the Norman doorway.

It was during their four year's sojourn at Old Byland that the monks (in 1146) built the little church in the nearby village of Scawton which stands on a ridge above the Rye. Everything about Scawton is on the Lilliputian scale, from the church to the inn; but both these villages are a joy to see.

A byroad from Old Byland leads to the secluded valley of Caydale (or Yowlassdale), with its solitary stone house, once a flour mill and now a private residence. Caydale is a little dream-world flanked by woods, with the great mass of Easterside Hill beyond. In spring and summer it is a paradise of wild flowers. Pure Ryedale country this, which I tremble to write about lest it be spoilt!

HAWNBY

Hawnby stands on a hill, surrounded by more hills; in the distance it looks like a citadel. It is certainly one of Ryedale's most delightful villages, in a unique and wonderful setting. Green hills and green pastures seem to suggest Hawnby best. It is a green paradise. The little Hawnby hotel is everything that a country hotel needs to be, and many times have I enjoyed its warm hospitality.

Arden Hall, the seat of the Earl of Mexborough, is situated in a wooded valley of the Rye about two miles beyond the village, and its setting among the woods can be better appreciated from the moors above. An old road climbs steeply towards Kepwick, and from the first rise the hall can be

---

[1] Among their many other activities, a group of sixth form boys have compiled an admirable guide to the school and surrounding district entitled *The Ampleforth Country*, to which I am indebted in the compilation of some of these notes.

F

seen ensconced in the woods with the beautiful lake nearby. This view from the top of Arden Great Moor is one of the highlights of Ryedale.

The seventeenth-century hall is built on the site of an old Benedictine nunnery, and is said to have sheltered Mary Queen of Scots on one occasion. There are some splendid rooms and fine panelling, and a Catholic chapel above; but the thing that most appealed to me was its homeliness and the fact that it is still lived in. I have seen so many derelict halls recently that it was a refreshing change to find one still occupied by its hereditary owner.

Hawnby church—originally built in the twelfth century—stands isolated in the quiet valley on the banks of the Rye, some distance from the village. It suffered much, in common with so many churches and villages in North Yorkshire, at the hands of the Scots, and is now largely restored; nevertheless, it has a grave beauty and an air of great antiquity. The mural monuments of the Tancred family on the east wall of the chancel are of interest.

From Hawnby there is a rich choice of roads and tracks. The nearest and most obvious excursion is to neighbouring Rievaulx and Helmsley. Another is the famous 'Sneck Yat' road over the Hambletons to the village of Boltby. This is a magnificent pass, easier to negotiate from Hawnby to Boltby than the other way round. It crosses country similar to that traversed by the better-known Sutton Bank road—and crosses the Drovers' Road—but is an altogether rougher road than Sutton Bank. For those who want to get into the heart of this corner of the Hambletons, I commend Sneck Yat!

MURTON AND COLD KIRBY

Two other nearby villages—Murton and Cold Kirby—might be included in this tour for the sake of the wonderful views they afford of the surrounding hills and dales.

Cold Kirby, with its wide, windswept street on a sloping hill is a typical North Yorkshire agricultural village, remote and a little dour, with an old church (rebuilt) and a sturdy, independent air. The view of Rievaulx and the woods above is particularly notable.

One of the great charms of all these villages is their other-worldliness: they lie far off the main roads and do not seem to belong to this bustling age. Another attraction is their picturesque cottages and farms. There is a delightful softness and mellowness about all these Ryedale villages, due in part to their clean stone and rust-coloured pantile roofs, which tone so perfectly with this North Riding landscape.

CHAPTER TEN

The Dales of Ryedale

SO MUCH for some of the villages of this rich country of Ryedale (others will be mentioned later), but villages by themselves are like jewels in a shop window without the added grace of the beautiful ladies who are to wear them, and one of the great joys of this Yorkshire countryside is that it not only provides the jewels but also the ladies; the ladies being, in this case, the dales and the landscape that go with the villages.

Some of these fair sister dales have been mentioned incidentally in the course of this text, but it may help travellers to explore them if I refer to them briefly here.

BILSDALE

Bilsdale, watered by the River Seph, is the first of the dales, and stretches from the Clevelands to its junction with the Rye near Hawnby. There is a first-class motor road from Helmsley to Stokesley through Bilsdale, a good bus service, and no excuse for not exploring the whole of this great, sprawling dale. Scenery apart, it is notable for several things. First and foremost it is famous for its great sporting traditions: I should say that more good stories and more 'characters' have come out of Bilsdale than out of any other of these dales. Bilsdale is not the most picturesque of them—it is too open for that—but it is full of character. There are two famous inns, the Buck at Chop Gate, long presided over by Garbutt Johnson, and the Spout House—or Sun Inn—which has been in the hands of the sporting Ainsley family for generations. The eldest son is always christened William, and thus the landlord is always William Ainsley—often there are three generations of Williams together. The landlord is usually the huntsman of the Bilsdale pack, too, as he is at the present time, and many are the tales you can hear of Bilsdale hunting personalities in the bar of this little, friendly inn.

Another character who set her mark on Chop Gate was old Mrs Allenby, who kept the 'Top shop' and ran a guest house in that lovely village, and who was known and beloved far and wide. Bilsdale does not seem the same without her.

Walkers who are familiar with the bleak moorland ridges that divide Bilsdale from Snilesworth and from Bransdale will need no further eulogy of mine; and those who are not will find these moors well worth their mettle.[1]

RICCALDALE AND BRANSDALE

Riccaldale is the next dale, wild in its beginnings in the high moors, and gentle and tree-covered in its lower reaches—a poet's dale. Motorists should take the road from Helmsley to Carlton, and as they reach the woods a mile or so beyond the village they will see one of the loveliest views in these dales.

Bransdale, which follows, is an extensive, beautiful dale, through which flows the Hodge beck. Beginning in the wild country of Cockagne Ridge (1,410 feet) and surrounded at the dale-head by magnificent moorland scenery, it flows past Lord Feversham's shooting lodge (Bransdale Lodge) and the unique little church of St Nicholas nearby (which should be seen). The green dale then widens and makes a fine picture against the moorland ridges on either side. There is no village in Bransdale, but there are many picturesque farms perched on the hillsides and in the valley.

There is a good road into Bransdale from the direction of Kirbymoorside and Gillamoor (or Fadmoor) right to the dale-head, and a secondary road round the other side down to Carlton and Helmsley.

In its lower reaches, the dale is variously known as Sleightholmedale, Skiplamdale, and finally Kirkdale.

The wooded, idyllic valley of Sleightholmedale, with its green pastures and footpaths, rickety bridges and lonely farms, is well known to anglers, walkers—and lovers—and is a green paradise.

KIRKDALE

From here, the Hodge flows through the green reaches of Kirkdale[2] and reserves its biggest surprise for the very end of its long journey, as it comes out of Kirkdale woods near the Kirbymoorside by-road.

---

[1] Under a War Department Order, the R.A.F. use an area of about 820 acres of moorland on Helmsley moor (5½ miles N.N.W. of Helmsley—between Bilsdale and Bransdale) as an occasional practice bombing range. The range is not used at week-ends (nor every day), and access is allowed at other times. No. H.E. bombs are dropped; but it is a pity that such a spot should have been chosen for this purpose, and it is to be hoped that when the new National Park is confirmed the range will be discontinued.

[2] Kirkdale is only two miles from Kirbymoorside, and can be visited on the journey to Helmsley.

The ancient minster church of St Gregory stands isolated just outside the woods where the river flows through a mysterious gorge. The by-road of Kirbymoorside crosses the dry bed of the stream at this point, and it was in the rocks nearby that the famous Kirkdale Cave was discovered by chance in 1821. In the cave were found the remains of some three hundred hyenas, together with the bones of numerous other wild animals, including elephant, rhinoceros, hippopotamus, tiger, bear, reindeer, lion, bison, boar and wolf. This was one of the most sensational finds of this nature ever made in England. The cave is believed to have been the home of the hyenas who preyed on the other species. The cave has since been partly demolished, but can still be traced by those who have a taste for the macabre. Even today a strange aura hovers over this gorge and over the lonely little church and its green churchyard—a sense of immemorial antiquity, of mystery and foreboding, and I never pass that way without feeling it.

The ancient church is remarkable for many things, particularly for the famous Saxon stone sundial over the inner doorway, with an antique inscription telling how 'Orm the son of Gamal' bought the church when it was 'Al-tobrocan' and 'to falan' and rebuilt it from the ground in Edward the King's day, when Tosti was Earl. That would be between 1055 and 1064. The present tower (1827) and the church were rebuilt in 1881 by the University of Oxford, who own the rectorial estate and are held responsible for spoiling the church. Even so, there is much original work to be seen and many interesting old stones, including two coffin lids ascribed to Ethelwald, King of Deira (624) and Bishop Cedd, who died in 664.

Unfortunately the church is usually locked and the key is kept at Nawton Vicarage, one and a half miles away. Kirkdale church is one of the treasures of Ryedale and should not be missed.

FARNDALE

Next, and running parallel with Bransdale, comes Farndale and the lovely River Dove. There is nothing mysterious or gloomy about Farndale: it is essentially a smiling landscape and perhaps the fairest of all these dales. Rising from the same high watershed as the Hodge, the little River Dove seems to dance down the dale as to a piper's tune; past the hamlet of Church Houses (with its comfortable Feversham Arms) down to the picturesque village of Low Mill in the middle, its banks bordered by pleasant farms, green pastures and fair woods. Everything about Farndale is bright and gay, and in high summer when the fields are full of corn, and the hedgerows and gardens with flowers, it is an unforgettable sight. In springtime it is famous for its wild daffodils which grow here in astonishing profusion and attract hundreds of visitors. There are roads on either bank with bridges at Church Houses, Low Mill and Lowna, and rough crossroads to the moors above. From Monket House there is a very rough road to Rudland Rigg and Bransdale, and from Church Houses (and Lowna) there are good roads to Blakey Rigg and Ralph Cross, and for Rosedale. Coming down dale one can turn either to Gillamoor and Kirbymoorside, or to Hutton-le-Hole and Lastingham.

Farndale, with its sporting hunt and busy farming community, is certainly one of the highlights of this Ryedale countryside.

ROSEDALE

Finally there is Rosedale, a little farther to the east, watered by the Leven, which rises at Rosedale Head near Ralph Cross and carves a course through the high moors until it broadens into a green and fertile valley. A little bare and bleak in its upper reaches, where it still bears marks of the nineteenth-century iron workings, with the gaunt pile of Rosedale Chimney still dominating it, the landscape changes around the village of Rosedale Abbey, and thereafter Rosedale becomes a broad, majestic valley, its steep slopes transformed by afforestation. There are few traces of the old Benedictine nunnery by the church, but the village itself is very much the heart of the dale—a little metropolis in a world of its own, with its inns and shops and pleasant cottages. There is another bleak hamlet above. Lower down the dale there is Hartoft End with its well-known Blacksmith's Arms and with superb walking country in the surrounding moorlands—to High Muffles and the Stape country. Farther down, the main road runs to Cropton (and Cawthorn) and the Pickering road, with a convenient loop to Lastingham and Hutton. One fierce road goes direct from Hutton to Rosedale Abbey by way of Rosedale Chimney.

Newtondale—the last of these dales—is mentioned later in this narrative.

CHAPTER ELEVEN

Around Kirbymoorside

KIRBYMOORSIDE[1] stands between Sinnington and Nawton, just off the main Pickering-Helmsley road. Motorists are inclined to by-pass the old market town as they negotiate the large island at the crossroads and see only the confused jumble of garages and workshops nearby. At first glance, from this direction, Kirbymoorside is not particularly attractive; but it improves on acquaintance and is well worth the slight detour involved. If one approaches it from Gillamoor, the first impression is quite different.

The fine old church has suffered outwardly from an unhappy 'restoration' and extension in 1873-5, though the interior is still full of beauty and interest. One of the best views of the town is from the top of Viver's Hill, the green mound behind the church, where there are the slight remains of one of the two old castles (the remains of the other castle are at the top of Castlegate).

To get the feeling of this lovable old town one need only walk up its broad main street on market day—or any other day for that matter—and let the old houses, shops and inns tell their own story: for Kirbymoorside is one of the most companionable places I know.

The old Black Swan, with its inscription '1632' over the lintel, is a fine, rambling house, full of character, with great beams and oaken doors and cheerful little rooms. From the bedroom over the porch, you can watch the whole life of this busy little town go by. Then there is the hospitable King's Head above, and the White Horse below, not forgetting the George and Dragon and the rest!

But you will look in vain among them for that legendary inn where Pope, exercising a poet's licence, made the famous George Villiers, second Duke of Buckingham, die:

---

[1] Kirbymoorside—Kirby Moorside—Kirkby Moorside: which is it? The original spelling was usually 'Kirkby Moorside', meaning 'kirk-by-the-moorside'; and this form is still favoured by the Rural District Council, and in road signs, etc. The postal and railway authorities, however, have adopted the simpler 'Kirbymoorside'; but all three forms are in use.

In the worst inn's worst room, with mat half-hung,
The floor of plaster, and the walls of dung,
On once a flock-bed, but repair'd with straw,
With tape-ty'd curtains, never meant to draw,
The George & Garter dangling from that bed
Whose tawdry yellow strove with dirty red,
Great Villiers lies—alas, how chang'd from him—
That life of pleasure, and that soul of whim!

It is true, of course, that Buckingham died in Kirbymoorside in 1687, but not in such squalid surroundings. Actually, the house where he died is now called Buckingham House and stands just below the King's Head. It is a substantial, pleasant-looking, double-fronted house (with a shop at the corner), where I was kindly allowed to see the room where Buckingham is believed to have died.

I verified the entry of his death in the faded parish register, which reads:

'Gorgos Vilrias, Lord dook of Bookingham. April 17 – 1687.'

Yes, there it is, squeezed between an obscure 'Mark Roams' and 'Robert Outhwaite' in a crowded, yellow page of names in thin, spidery script, and with nothing to show that 'Gorgos Vilrias' was anyone out of the ordinary except for the curiously spelt title that follows.

Buckingham was in possession of Helmsley Castle at the time; and it was while hunting from the castle that he was taken ill in the field and was taken to Kirbymoorside to the house where he died. At the time of his death, Buckingham had dissipated his immense fortunes and died almost penniless. His life, which reads like a Hollywood film (and what a film it would make!), has given the historians and moralists a great deal of fun.

The astonishing fact about his Yorkshire connection is this. Buckingham acquired the great Helmsley estates from his father, the first Duke, who had them by marriage. During the Civil War, Buckingham was exiled and his estates were conferred upon the Parliamentary general, Fairfax, who had laid siege to Helmsley Castle. Buckingham later returned to England and married Fairfax's daughter, Mary, and thus received back his own confiscated properties as a dowry. A curious turn of Fortune's wheel![1]

But though the shade of Buckingham still hovers over this cheerful market town, his death there was no more than an incident in its long

---

[1] Those who are interested in a modern study of this romantic figure should read Esther Chapman's spirited and sympathetic *Great Villiers*, published in 1949, which gives a detailed and moving picture of his last hours.

history. The Nevilles, who owned Kirbymoorside until 1568, and the castle at the top of the town, played a much more important part, and so did the Stutevilles, who occupied the second castle near the church.

What I like best about Kirbymoorside today is its air of friendliness and sociability. Whether you call at one of the inns, at the post office, at Mrs Goodall's busy shop round the corner, or at any of the blacksmiths, this friendliness is unmistakable. You feel at once that you are welcome and that everybody wants to help you.

Horses still play an important part in the life of the district. Apart from those used on the farms, this is great hunting country. Sinnington, just beyond Kirbymoorside, is the home of the famous Sinnington pack, of which Lord Feversham is Master. Hence it is not surprising to find so many blacksmiths' shops still flourishing in Kirbymoorside. There are three Dowsons separately engaged in the old craft, and one can stand by the forge and watch one of them shoeing a hunter or a great Shire horse in the immemorial way. There is something about the pungent smell of hot iron on hooves and the white glow of the fire that never fails to fascinate—in a way which the smell of petrol pumps certainly never can.

One of the blacksmiths, Mr W. Dowson, practises a different craft, that of wrought-iron work, and examples of his beautiful work are to be found all over the country. He is a true artist and belongs to the great English tradition of wrought-iron craftsmen.

PICKERING TO KIRBYMOORSIDE

Between Pickering and Kirbymoorside there is a group of villages which make a delightful little tour on their own, though they may, of course, be taken in conjunction with a tour of Ryedale.

Middleton, the first village beyond Pickering on the Pickering-Helmsley road, has a notable Saxon church, with a remarkable tower and some wonderful Saxon wheel crosses—one known as the 'Bound Dragon and Hart and Hounds' cross, and another the finely-carved 'Warrior' cross, with warrior, spear and dragons. Both these crosses are nine hundred years old and were only brought to light in 1948 in the ringing chamber of the tower. There are other fine wheel-head crosses of Anglo-Danish type, while on the outer walls of the tower is an Anglian cross of the eighth century. There are many other fascinating features both inside and outside this beautiful church of St Andrew's.

From Middleton the road runs through Aislaby and Wrelton to

picturesque Sinnington. By-roads from Wrelton lead to Cawthorn and Cropton. Just above the hamlet of Cawthorn is the site of the famous Roman military camps—four extensive rectangular camps (overgrown with bracken) like parade-grounds, used for military exercises. From the outer perimeter there is a wonderful view of the moors beyond, and of the Roman road through Stape to the coast.

Cropton is noteworthy as the birthplace of William Scoresby (1760), the great navigator and explorer of the Arctic, and his equally famous son, William, who accompanied his father as a boy on several voyages, sub-sequently developed into a remarkable scientist, and later joined the Church. The Scoresbys share with Captain Cook, Yorkshire's proud seafaring traditions: a remarkable trinity of North Riding sailors bred from farming stock.

APPLETON-LE-MOORS AND LASTINGHAM

To see the remaining villages, it is better to begin from the Pickering road again. After Sinnington, a by-road turns northward to Appleton-le-Moors, Spaunton and Lastingham.

Appleton-le-Moors is a typical North Riding village, built along a wide, windswept street, lined with substantial stone-built cottages. It is an honest, satisfying sort of village, rather than a showplace.

The road through it gives no promise of the surprise ahead, but a couple of miles farther on, past the Spaunton crossroads, the road descends steeply to Lastingham, one of the jewels of this corner of the Riding. I like the sudden view of the finely-sited memorial cross at the top of Lidsty Hill and the wide sweep of high moorlands beyond.

Lastingham snuggles in the valley below, under a bastion of hills. The cluster of rust-red-roofed cottages and the picturesque Blacksmith's Arms always delights me. But the chief glory of Lastingham is the ancient church of St Mary with its remarkable crypt—a complete church in itself—entered from the nave. As you enter this gracious church you will find on the table a couple of lanterns with candles, which will enable you to explore the little crypt and appreciate its beauty and great age. The first known church on this site is believed to have been built in 660 by the saintly Cedd, Bishop of East Anglia, who is buried here. Bede, who visited the church, tells us all we know about it. He describes Lastingham as 'a place . . . lying among lofty and remote mountains, in which there appeared to have been more of lurking places of robbers and dens of wild beasts than habitations of men'. The Romans, we know, had to fight fiercely to subdue the ancient British tribe who dwelt here; and no sooner had the Romans gone than the Anglo-Saxons followed and then the Danes. It was the Danes who destroyed the new monastery of Lastingham, and it was not until 1078 that Abbot Stephen of Whitby brought his monks to Lastingham and built the existing crypt and much of the present church. The apsidal crypt is the only one in England which is complete with a chancel, nave and two side aisles. Many of the stones and fragments of crossheads in the crypt belong to the earlier churches, while the altar slab is believed to have belonged to the original high altar.

The church itself suffered a disastrous 'restoration' by John Jackson, R.A., in the nineteenth century, but has since been remodelled and in its existing form it is a beautiful piece of work.

The view of Lastingham itself from the churchyard is particularly pleasing: a warm, companionable village, embosomed in the moors and protected by curious hills. The scenery around is enchanting and one gets a taste of it as one continues along the road to the neighbouring village of Hutton-le-Hole.

HUTTON-LE-HOLE

One could scarcely imagine a greater contrast in two neighbouring villages than that between Lastingham and Hutton-le-Hole. Lastingham has an air of immemorial age, while Hutton-le-Hole looks spick and span and new; it is a trim, wide-open village. To me it always suggests the Cotswolds rather than the North Riding, but Hutton is as Yorkshire as any of them! And though it may not be as old as Lastingham, it is certainly not new, as some of the dates chiselled over the doors of the cottages testify. Once it was a centre for the early Quakers, and one cottage bearing the date 1695 and the initials 'J.R.' was formerly the home of John Richardson, friend of William Penn. Another house in the centre of the village bears an inscription reading: 'By Hammer and Hand All Arts do Stand.' This was the home of Emmanuel and Betty Strickland, and later became The Hammer and Hand inn, but the nearby Crown is the only existing inn.

It is a lovely village, with the little Hutton beck, crossed by pretty white bridges, flowing through the middle of it, and the broad green common on either side. Almost every stone cottage is a joy to see, for they are all so beautifully kept, so clean and tidy, and with such delightful gardens. At either end of the sprawling village is a water splash, but there is a continuous road round, and one can admire this little moorland place from both banks of the stream.

The inn, the post office and the new village hall catch the eye, and the little gift shop with its blue sign in the very middle of it all, where Mrs Hutton does hand weaving and makes all manner of charming things.

After the cottages, it is the beautiful green common (with its quoits pitch) and the beck and the moorland background that make Hutton-le-Hole so attractive and restful: a perfect holiday centre.

And as you leave the village by the Farndale road, you pass Mr and Mrs Burnley's dream house at the end of it all, with their heavenly rock garden and view.

Hutton is truly a delectable village.

GILLAMOOR

Just beyond Hutton, the Gillamoor road swings leftward and dips down to the Dove at Lowna Bridge, then climbs steeply up the farther bank to the little church of Gillamoor perched on the very tip of the ridge. It is as well to pause here a moment and look back, for this is a famous 'surprise view' of the valley of the Dove, of Farndale and Spaunton Moor, and of the enchanting valleys between. At any season this is a superb panorama, but in summer, when the heather is in prime and the corn is ripe for harvest, it is unforgettable.

On the church wall at this corner there is an apt text from Keble, which reads:

Thou Who hast given me eyes to see
And love this sight so fair,
Give me a heart to find out Thee
And read Thee everywhere.

Gillamoor, an outpost of Farndale, is another of those spacious villages, with a wide main street and some delightful houses and farms—a breezy, honest North Yorkshire village, with its Royal Oak Inn, its flourishing local life, and strong sporting traditions. It stands at the crossroads and is ideally situated for exploring Farndale, Bransdale, Rudland Rigg, and much else.

Fadmoor—another hill village—is its near neighbour, with the key-town of Kirbymoorside three miles to the south.

NOTE: For the convenience of tourists, the outlying parts of Ryedale are included in the following three chapters. For more detailed study of the geology and natural history of this fascinating district, I would refer readers to *Ryedale*, a report on the district published by the Ryedale branch of the Council for the Preservation of Rural England.

III. THE HAMBLETON HILLS

CHAPTER TWELVE

Sutton Bank

FROM Helmsley the Thirsk road (which can be joined from Rievaulx or Byland) climbs steadily to the ridge of the Hambleton Hills, and leads to one of the most spectacular views in Yorkshire—the top of Sutton Bank. This impression is enhanced by the unexpected nature of the climax to what seems to be a normal ridge road. All the way from Helmsley, however, the country has been opening out; the long line of the Hambletons is revealed on the right, with Easterside Hill and Black Hambleton in the middle distance.

A little beyond the Hambleton hotel and the racing stables, the road comes to the brink of a tremendous chasm—or so it appears—which marks the dramatic finish to this surprising range of hills, never so impressive as in this sudden plunge to the green and golden Vale of Mowbray below.

To the left is the forbidding mass of Roulston Scar (and the head-quarters of the Yorkshire Gliding Club), softened a little by the panache of Hood Hill nearby. On the right is the equally spectacular Whitestone Cliff. On a fine day, this is a scene of great beauty; at other times—and especially when approached from the plain below—the great cliff is an awesome sight, with the mark of Druidical sacrifices still hanging over it. Deep below, in a fold of the hills, is the dark jewel of eerie Lake Gormire (said to be unfathomable).

From the top, the immense vista of plain below, with the shadowy smudge of the Pennine hills far away in the west, grips the attention. Thirsk lies due west, only six miles ahead. York Minster, Ripon, Northallerton and many other distant features may be seen. Although the view from the top of the road itself is so impressive, an even better view is to be obtained from the top of the Whitestone Cliff, where a still vaster panorama from the Ouse to the Tees is revealed. Given a clear day (and good vision!) the abbeys of Fountains, Rievaulx and Byland may be seen, as well as Castle Howard, Newburgh Priory, Duncombe Park and the castles of Sheriff Hutton and Gilling and Helmsley. I am bound to add, however, that shimmering mist frequently dims the view.

But here, if anywhere, the tourist will derive a lively impression of the vastness and variety of this great county. I, for one, never look on the scene without a lift of the heart and a feeling of pride in my Yorkshire heritage.

The road leaps down in a series of hairpin bends to the plain below, past the little village of Sutton-under-Whitestone Cliff, and so on to Thirsk.

OLD DROVE ROAD

No walker worth his shoes, however, will leave Sutton Bank by this metalled road to the plain when the old drove road to Yarm and the north can be joined near the top of the hill. This old road has a long, fighting history. The Scots knew it well, and this was probably the road they followed when they pursued Edward II's army over six hundred years ago. In more peaceful days, the road was the main cattle-way to and from the Border; and many a tale could be told of the feuds and fights among the old drovers.

The broad green road goes past High Paradise farm and straight over Arden Great Moor and Black Hambleton to Osmotherley Moor, to Slape-stones and Scarth Nick, where it joins the now metalled road to Yarm. There are numerous cross-tracks to Old Byland, Hawnby, Snilesworth and Chop Gate, or westward to Kepwick, Thimbleby and Osmotherley. This is the kind of road a walker dreams about, and I commend it to all lovers of the old road.

CHAPTER THIRTEEN

Some Hambleton Villages

IN THE VALE OF MOWBRAY

ON the western flanks of the Hambleton Hills, in the Vale of Mowbray country, there is a cluster of delightful villages which make an excellent tour of themselves. Their names alone make music, 'Thirlby, Thimbleby and Thirkleby', for example. Others are Sutton-under-Whitestone Cliff, Felixkirk, Boltby, Kirby Knowle, Cowesby, Kepwick, Nether Silton, Over Silton and Osmotherley. One approach to them is from Thirsk by the main Helmsley road.

A mile beyond Thirsk, the first by-road turns northward for Felixkirk, but if one takes this road, one misses Sutton-under-Whitestone Cliff and Thirlby (not to mention Bagby and Balk and High and Low Thirkleby, all of which lie to the south of the main road). How confusing these by-roads are, and how difficult it is to keep to a strict itinerary with so many alluring villages just off the route! Thirkleby, with its Franklands memorials, should certainly be visited on some other occasion (it can be approached from Kilburn or Coxwold); but on this tour it is better to go direct to Felixkirk.

Felixkirk (sometimes spelt Feliskirk) is on the edge of the Mowbray country. It is one of the places that have an unmistakable air of antiquity around it. It is only a tiny village, but its Norman church (dedicated to St Felix), though much restored, is interesting and contains two fine effigies, one of a knight in chain mail which is quite astonishingly lifelike, and the other of a beautiful lady in a wimple. On the hill of Mount St John's, beyond the church, there used to be a Preceptory of the Knights Hospitallers of the Order of St John on the site now occupied by the dignified residence of Mount St John's, in the possession of Mr A. J. Walker, who kindly showed me round. The house commands an extensive view of the Vale of Mowbray and the Plain of York.

On this occasion I made the detour to Boltby village first and then on to Kirby Knowle. The views are thrilling all the way. Boltby clings to the very fringe of the Hambletons and lies in the deep valley of Gurtof Beck.

From the village, the steep mountain road of 'Sneck Yat' (mentioned above) soars over the hills to Hawnby.

Kirby Knowle is a lovely little village nestling under the hills, and surrounded by superb scenery. The old church has been rebuilt, but fits perfectly into the picture, and there is a charming old manor house and many delightful cottages. The great house, oddly named New Building—though it dates from the sixteenth to seventeenth centuries—occupies a commanding position on the hillside above. Upsall Castle, the home of the Turton family, and now occupied by Mr R. H. Turton (M.P. for Thirsk), lies a mile or so to the west, and a convenient road connects the two villages. The castle was destroyed by fire in 1918 and the present structure is modern. The original fourteenth-century castle belonged to the Scropes.

Cowesby village lies in a fold of the hills where the road takes a sharp turn to the left. It is an ancient place, with a history going back to the days of Gamel. There is the great hall (rebuilt by Mr Cameron), a church, surrounded by yew trees, that looks ancient but is only a hundred years or so old and replaces one of the oldest churches in the district. The Jacobean altar rails and candlesticks are preserved.

There is an old hospital for the poorer tenants of the estate, and some charming cottages; but there is no inn, and somehow a village without an inn never quite comes alive for me. Even so, Cowesby, surrounded by such beautiful scenery, is a memorable village.

The road twists and turns, and after two pleasant miles swings round to Kepwick, a long, picturesque village which appealed to me even more than its immediate neighbours. The country is more open and varied around Kepwick, and the hall at the top of the village stands in a splendid park, with masses of pine trees standing on the hillside and giving it a curiously Scottish look. But there is no inn for the thirsty traveller in Kepwick either, so I pushed on to Nether Silton, a tiny hamlet, where a man can refresh his thirst and his soul and obtain fresh inspiration. Everything about Nether Silton appealed to me all the more: the hill, the green, and the magnificent views to be had from the monolith by the modern church.

And so I continued in the gathering dusk to the twin village of Over Silton just beyond. Again, it is only a small village, but it stands high on the ridge, with one eye on the lovely vale and the other on the Hambletons, which begin to merge into the Clevelands beyond. It would be difficult to exaggerate the fine setting and the spectacular views around

Unique in many ways among the villages of Yorkshire, Hutton-le-Hole, near Lastingham, recalls the Cotswolds rather than the rugged North.

From the top of Sutton Bank there is one of the most spectacular views in Yorkshire over Lake Gormire and the great panorama of the Vale of Mowbray.

this charming village. The Manor House at the corner seems perfectly in harmony with the spirit of the place and I had the added satisfaction of finding an old friend here, farming one of the smallholdings. They say— and who am I to doubt it?—that one can still trace the old strip system of cultivation around this ancient place. Certainly it looks as old as the hills.

My one disappointment at Over Silton was to find the little church locked; and it is a curious fact that it is always the locked churches that one wants to examine most. This particular church stands in an isolated position in the fields below the village and is quite hidden from view. It was built there to escape the notice of the barbarous Scots, and it looks very old and strangely appealing in its lovely valley. There is a fine Norman doorway and much else of interest within, but the church has been largely restored. It is closed only during the winter months. Perhaps they still expect the Scots to swoop down again?

And so I made my way a little sadly to Thimbleby—a dream-place of lovely old cottages with rust-red pantile roofs, under the hills and quite surrounded by trees. Thimbleby Hall stands hidden in a great park and I was sorely tempted to see it, but darkness was falling, so I turned for the main road and made my way to Osmotherley.

OSMOTHERLEY

Osmotherley is an endearing kind of village on the fringe of the Hambletons and the Clevelands. It lies about a mile to the east of the main Thirsk-Yarm road, but is most accessible from Northallerton. The King's Head hotel at Clack Lane End points the way to the village. It is a large village, standing on the slopes of a steep hill, with its heart around the market cross and the old stone table.

The bald facts do little justice, however, to the charm of this attractive village. The very name suggests a benevolent, motherly sort of place, full of homely stone cottages and inns, and that is exactly what Osmotherley is. The ancient church with its fine tower, and the rugged scenery around, seem entirely in character with this hill village.

Osmotherley once had a market, and once it was well known for its handloom weaving, but both are things of the past. Its Feast used to be a famous affair, which lasted a week, with old Bob Douthwaite fiddling away round the cross, year after year, and all the inns doing a roaring trade. It is said that whisky stills used to be worked on the moors and that

G

smugglers did a brisk business. But the village seems to have sobered down considerably since those glorious days. The thing that struck me most forcibly was the number of children playing in the street, and that is always a pleasant and healthy sign in any village.

The Queen Catharine inn in the middle of the village and the Three Tuns over the way are pleasant-looking inns. Legend has it that Catherine Parr—who came from Snape Castle—once spent a night at one of these inns. Like Elizabeth, she turns up all over the North Riding, and if she or Elizabeth slept in half the beds claimed for them, they must have led a very nomadic existence indeed.

Osmotherley is the sort of place that invites one to linger. The main street is full of fascinating passage-ways (mostly marked PRIVATE) that always tempt me sorely. But one passage at least is a public right-of-way and leads to an enchanting footpath over the fields to Slapestones and beyond.

The steep main road up the village climbs to Sheepwash and Scarth Nick, and affords wonderful views of the surrounding countryside. Scarth Wood Moor—a beautiful stretch of country—at the top of this road is preserved under the care of the National Trust. Snilesworth Moor adjoins it at this point. A reservoir is in process of construction just below in the valley of Cod Beck. From the ford at Sheepwash, the road cuts through the gap of Scarth Nick and plunges down to Swainby and the plain, revealing the first spectacular views of the Cleveland Hills to the west.

THE SNILESWORTH COUNTRY

I can recommend the road that runs from Osmotherley to Hawnby-in-Ryedale. The distance is only nine miles, but in that short space there is a wonderful variety of scene, culminating in one of the fairest views in the county.

Shortly after leaving Osmotherley, the road strikes the moors and passes the once famous Chequers inn at Slapestones which used to boast an immemorial turf-fire. Alas, the Chequers is no longer an inn; the famous sign 'Good Ale for Nothing Tomorrow' is down, and the turf-fire is out. But the old farmstead still makes a fine picture against the moorland background and faces Black Hambleton, the highest hill in the range. Near the inn, the Sheepwash track crosses the road and continues over the shoulder of Black Hambleton. This is part of the old Drove Road that starts at the top of Sutton Bank—and walkers will know what to do about it! Indeed, as it trails over the shoulder of Black Hambleton hereabouts, it is irresistible.

The main road continues roughly along the side of this long, raking hill, with the Cleveland and Snilesworth moors on the one hand, and the Hambletons on the other. They make a superb picture in the misty distance, these raking, tabular hills, with a succession of nabs—Black Hambleton, Easterside, Nor'moor, Sunburt Nab and Locker—marching away to the far horizon.

Half-way towards Hawnby, the road passes Snilesworth Lodge, the residence of Mr Osbert Peake, M.P. for South Leeds. With its back to the brown moors, it looks on to one of the loveliest scenes in Ryedale.

Just beyond the Lodge, a dream-like valley, through which runs the stripling river Rye, opens out of the moors. With its scattered farms, green pastures and isolated cottages it makes a memorable picture. The Rye—surely the loveliest of the smaller Yorkshire rivers—dances its way down the moors through this smiling land of deep valleys, snug farm-steads, and curious-shaped hills, looking in the late autumn like a gold and green fairyland.

There is no actual village at Snilesworth—only the dale itself, the scattered farms, and a village school. The little moorland school is said to be the loneliest in Yorkshire, and perhaps in England. Lonely it certainly is—but what a setting it has, and what views!

Mrs Weldon, who lives at Lowcote, took me to see Mrs Fenton, the popular school-teacher, who had recently retired after many years' service. She lives in a tiny cottage two miles away, and walked daily to the lonely school in all weathers. There were only six children at the school, and its future is imperilled, but I hope the Planners will not close it. All the children in and around Snilesworth have attended it for generations and everybody seems to love it. One of the pupils was the gamekeeper's son—a fine strapping lad over six feet tall. Who knows but that he—or one of the other children—may not develop into another Richard Kearton? For these little village schools have a trick of turning out unusual men and women. What a debt of gratitude we owe to these lonely country school-teachers! Theirs is one of the most difficult talks of all, and yet, in many ways, it is the most rewarding. They are an essential factor in the life of the North Riding—for Snilesworth is only one of many such isolated village schools, and it is in such schools that our future farmers and their wives are trained.

From Snilesworth I went on to Hawnby again, still unable to believe that the scenery was quite real on that magical autumn day.

MOUNT GRACE PRIORY

Mount Grace Priory stands a little to the north of Osmotherley off the main Yarm road. There is a grave beauty about this ruined priory, standing in a clearing under the Cleveland Hills, with a broken, melancholy tower in the centre and a vast cloister beyond. Experts say that Mount Grace Charterhouse is the most complete survival of the Carthusian Order in this country and that three periods are distinguishable in the remains, dating from the foundation of the house about the year 1400.

It is particularly interesting by virtue of the fact that the monks' cells may still be traced. One cell has been restored to its original design of two storeys, and gives an excellent idea of how these monks lived in silent contemplation. The great cloister—around which fifteen of these solitary cells were placed—is very striking. To enter the ruins, one must first pass up the drive and past the beautiful house of Sir Hugh Bell, which was built from a portion of the priory buildings by Thomas Lascelles in 1654, whose initials can be seen over the porch.

SOME NORTH RIDING INNS AND HOTELS

While I was preparing this book, I found myself one cold winter's evening at Staddle Bridge, on the Thirsk-Yarm road near Mount Grace Priory, between Osmotherley and Ingleby Arncliffe. It was too dark to see anything except the welcome gleam of light outside the Cleveland Tontine inn, and I had no hesitation in seeking shelter for the night there.

The Cleveland Tontine inn is a remarkable place in many ways. The first inn was opened in the year 1804 to serve the needs of mail and stage-coach passengers on the improved turnpike road to Thirsk. It owes its name to a Neapolitan, one Lorenzo Tonti, who evolved a system of raising loans on life annuities, the last survivor of those who advanced the money inheriting the whole amount. A group of Cleveland gentlemen raised a 'tontine' loan of £2,500 on these lines, acquired the site, and built the original inn—a commodious place with fine stabling and excellent accommodation for travellers. It quickly became a favourite place of call among stage-coach passengers. But, by the year 1835, coaching began to decline, and with the advent of the railways around 1846, the road was deserted and the inn became a private residence.

In 1946 the house came into the market again and was acquired by a firm of brewers for reconversion into an inn, to cater for the modern motorist. This, in itself, is rather a romance: first an inn, then a private residence, and then an inn again to serve a different epoch, but the same need.

There are other outstanding examples of converted hotels in the North Riding, such as the dignified Forest and Vale at Pickering, once a beautiful Georgian residence; the imposing Grinkle Park hotel at Easington—just off the wild Whitby-Guisborough road—which was once a mansion and still possesses most delightful grounds; and there are several others. Far more numerous, however, are the old coaching inns which have survived all the crises of the past hundred years and are still catering for the needs of the modern 'stagecoaches'—the motor car and the motor coach. Most of these have been extensively renovated and modernized, and are vastly improved in every way. Some of them, such as the Old Bridge House hotel at Catterick Bridge, the Black Swan at Helmsley, the Golden Lion at Northallerton, the Golden Fleece at Thirsk, the King's Head at Richmond (with its interesting sign showing two kings' heads), the Black Lion at Bedale and the Talbot at Malton, occupy key positions on important roads and are known to hundreds of travellers. The Old Bridge House hotel at Catterick Bridge is one of the most delightful-looking hotels I know, and one of the most comfortable. Standing at one of the key points on the Great North Road—about four miles south of Scotch Corner—it has been a familiar sight to English travellers for centuries, and all kinds of famous people have passed through its doors. It is a beautiful old house and I doubt if many hotels of the same size have such an admirable collection of French prints, old maps and pictures, or such a choice collection of old leather-bound books.

There are countless other hotels and village inns off the main roads which dispense Yorkshire hospitality to the travelling public year in and year out. Many of them have been mentioned in this book, for I must confess I have a great fondness for inns; but there are other equally good hotels which the persevering tourist will discover for himself. Many of the hotels on the Yorkshire coast can hold their own with any in London.

And since inns and hotels undoubtedly occupy much of the tourist's time and make all the difference to his enjoyment, I do not think too much attention can be devoted to them. A great deal of nonsense is talked and written about the standard of English hotels today. Many people seem to go out of their way to look for faults in every hotel—and it is the easiest thing in the world to do—and write angry letters to the newspapers about them; but they rarely trouble to write letters about the good hotels, which are today in the majority. Very often, I suspect, the fault lies in themselves quite as much as in the hotels. At any rate, I never seem to experience much difficulty in finding a perfectly comfortable hotel and getting an excellent meal to suit my needs and my pocket.

A silent revolution has taken place in the standard of English hotels of recent years, and no fair-minded traveller can fail to notice it. These luxurious hotels and Trust Houses are one sign of it, and the modernized country inns are another. The great majority of residential hotels and inns in Yorkshire today are steadily improving, and it seems about time that somebody drew attention to the fact.

IV. THE PLAIN OF YORK AND THE HOWARDIAN HILLS

CHAPTER FOURTEEN

Southern North Riding

THE southern extremity of the North Riding is shaped like an inverted triangle, with York at the apex, Malton at one corner and Easingwold at the other.

This southern strip of country contains much of interest to the tourist which is often overlooked. The direct road from York to Malton (18 miles) is a first-class modern motor road for those in a hurry to reach the coast, but, like most arterial roads, it by-passes all the interesting villages and scenery.

To the east, the valley of the Derwent marks the boundary of the North and East Ridings; but all the country to the left or north of the road lies in the North Riding. This includes part of the plain of York and the old forest of Galtres, and, further to the north-east, the gently undulating country of the Howardian Hills. It is not spectacular country like that of the Hambletons and Clevelands, but it is of historic interest, while the Howardian Hills themselves, especially in summertime, reveal many notable views and many a lovely village.

In this chapter I propose to take a quick glance at some of the more interesting features in this area.

THE PLAIN

I cannot pretend to any great enthusiasm for the flat country of the plain. Hills and dales are my delight, but the road from York to Topcliffe, or York to Easingwold, which crosses the forest of Galtres, reveals some of the best farming country of the Riding and has a quiet serenity and beauty, especially if one turns off the main road and follows the bridle-ways across the fields to one of the old farms. Farming apart, this is first-class hunting country, so my York and Ainsty friends assure me. I like the great ploughed fields and green pasture-lands with their fringe of trees, remnant of the old Galtres forest, and the gracious halls and manor houses that peep out of the woods. The roads from York to Helmsley or to Hovingham are, scenically, the more attractive.

Of the villages in this corner of the Riding, Sutton-on-the-Forest, Stillington and Marton should be seen. Sutton and Stillington, with their historic churches and halls, have a particular interest to admirers of Sterne, who held the livings of the two neighbouring parishes for twenty-five years before going to spread his wings at Coxwold. It was at Sutton that *Tristram Shandy* was begun. During his long sojourn at Sutton, Sterne was a familiar figure in York and he used the Minster library a great deal. His uncle was precentor of York Minster.

A mile beyond Marton's curious, ancient church is the site of Marton Priory, slight remains of which can be traced at Marton Abbey farm, just beyond Stillington. The site of Moxby Nunnery is also to be found outside Stillington, near Moxby Priory farm.

CRAYKE

North of Stillington there is a break in the flat lands at Crayke, a remarkable village perched on two sides of a steep hill, looking over the Vale of York and the Howardian Hills. Crayke, with its ancient church of St Cuthbert, and the modernized 'castle' on top of the surprise hill, should certainly be visited. The battlemented church was built in the fifteenth century and has a rood screen and other interesting features. It occupies— or is near—the site of a much earlier foundation, possibly monastic, where the body of St Cuthbert is said to have rested.

There is little of the original motte and bailey castle to be seen; the present structure is a private residence, but looks romantic from below. It is believed that a bishop's fortified palace stood here in the Middle Ages, and several English kings stayed here.

SHERIFF HUTTON

Eastwards, across the plain, there are two other villages that lure me aside: Sheriff Hutton and Foston (both of which can easily be approached from the York-Malton road, or direct from York).

Sheriff Hutton, with its ruined castle, stands on rising ground looking over the plain. The village itself is not especially notable. It is a busy, agricultural village sprawling along the road, with a pleasant green common and two friendly inns. One of the farms is built into the ruins of the castle itself (as at Danby), but the four remaining towers of the castle make an impressive picture, mighty even in ruins. Across the fields a road leads to Sheriff Hall park and hall.

The old castle, apart from its utilitarian uses as a granary and cowhouse, is now redundant; yet Sheriff Hutton was one of Yorkshire's most famous strongholds in the fourteenth and fifteenth centuries. The original castle, built by Bertram de Bulmer, Sheriff of Yorkshire, in the twelfth century, passed into the hands of the Nevilles, one of whom rebuilt it in the fourteenth century. It has taken part in some of the stormiest scenes in English history. Warwick the Kingmaker held sway here and plotted his villainies. Anne, wife of bloody Richard III, and Elizabeth of York, who became the wife of Henry VII, were both here: and indeed the full story of Sheriff Hutton is the story of England in the troubled years of the Wars of the Roses. Murder and intrigue, violence and conquest, pageantry and junketing—what stories these four battered towers could tell! Some shadow of it all still seems to hang around those immense towers as one wanders around and remembers the story of the little princes.

There are, however, happier memories of Anthony Woodville, brother of a queen and afterwards Earl Rivers, who retired here (like that other Shepherd Earl at Barden Tower) and devoted himself to books. It was one of his translations from the French that was the first book printed by Caxton in England. John Skelton, the poet laureate, also lived here for some time with his patron, the Duke of Norfolk.

The existing, nearby house of Sheriff Hutton Park, the residence of Admiral and Mrs Egerton, was built in 1621 by Sir Arthur Ingram (of Temple Newsam) as a hunting lodge, and was subsequently purchased by the Thompson family of York. In 1732, the Jacobean house was refaced in the Georgian style and various internal alterations were made. Today, with its beautiful Jacobean and Georgian rooms, and some striking internal features, Sheriff Hutton Park is a delightful country house.

No shadow hangs over the neighbouring villages of Thornton-le-Clay and Foston, where the Rev. Sydney Smith laboured so mightily and so wittily for twenty years. The famous 'Rector's Head', as he called the house he built for himself, still nestles among the trees between the two villages and the little church (much restored) should be visited by all admirers of this great Englishman.

CASTLE HOWARD

From Foston a road turns up the hill towards the great park of Castle Howard. The plain is left behind and the road climbs into the lovelier country of the Howardian hills. Straight as an arrow it goes from the first monument to the Obelisk two miles beyond, across the spacious park-lands to the great lake and the Coneysthorpe road. This road is open to the public and makes a beautiful drive. The magnificent palace, which was built by Sir John Vanbrugh for the Earl of Carlisle early in the eighteenth century in the ornate Baroque style of architecture, is one of the great treasures of Yorkshire, and indeed one of the stateliest houses of England. You catch glimpses of its obelisks and mausoleums as you approach Malton on the York-Malton road, but this drive from Welburn to Coneysthorpe cuts clean across the park and enables one to get a splendid view of the great mansion itself. During the war years, it was occupied by the girls of Queen Margaret's school, and part of the grounds was used by the Army; but the estate has now returned to the possession of the Howard family.

It was inevitable that both the house and grounds suffered during the war years; the worst misfortune was the disastrous fire of 1940, when the great central dome and part of the south front were destroyed. Shorn of these glories, the palace has lost a little of its original splendour, but it is still a superb residence—an amazing conception—full of wonderful features, pilasters and carved capitals, cherubs and statues.

The whole building is on the grand scale, and the beautiful setting by the lake always reminds me of Versailles. The interior design is in keeping with the palatial building; and the rooms are full of priceless marbles and pictures, including works by Canaletto, Rubens, Reynolds, Tintoretto, Van Dyck, Holbein, and many others.

At present, the house is not open to the public, but the park is.

SLINGSBY

After the glories of Castle Howard, one might well cry, 'Enough of castles and palaces!', and look for homelier fare. But there is one more un-usual ruined castle just beyond Coneysthorpe which can conveniently be seen on the same tour. Indeed, the road across the park leads directly to the 'street' village of Slingsby, on the Malton road. This castle is one of the few that does not seem ever to have been occupied. It was begun by

Sir Charles Cavendish, who fought for the Royalists at Marston Moor, and was never completed.

Towards Malton the road passes through more of the pretty 'street'[1] villages—Barton-le-Street and Appleton-le-Street (both with remarkable churches), and then to Amotherby, Swinton and Malton, with fine views of this gentle Ryedale country and the Howardian hills. This makes a delightful drive or walk.

HOVINGHAM HALL

Beyond Slingsby, on the same road, is the substantial 'street' village of Hovingham, with the famous hall belonging to the family of Sir William Worsley, Bart.

Hovingham Hall is another of Yorkshire's famous houses. Built by Thomas Worsley in 1760 in the Italianate style, it has many unusual features, not least the famous Riding School which serves as the main approach to the house, through a tunnelled entry and also serves as an admirable concert hall for the famous Hovingham festivals. The hall is full of exquisite marble, tapestries, pictures and other treasures. In the grounds there is one of the most beautiful cricket fields in Yorkshire, and most of the famous players of the past century have played on it in one of the festival matches. The Worsleys are one of Yorkshire's great cricketing families, and it gave much pleasure to everyone when the present Sir William was appointed captain of the Yorkshire eleven in the 1928-9 season.

Nunnington village, with Nunnington Hall, stands a few miles north of Hovingham, over Caulkeleys Bank. Built in 1552 by John Hickes, and altered considerably in the seventeenth century, the hall became the home of Viscount Preston, the Stuart supporter, who became Secretary for Scotland under James II. He was subsequently charged with treason and only escaped death by betraying his confederates.

The small, secluded village of Stonegrave—the name of which seems to fit it in a peculiar way—has an air of great antiquity. The ancient (restored) church contains several noteworthy features, including a remarkable Saxon wheel-head cross, and an effigy of Sir John Stonegrave (1295) among others.

Stonegrave is also the home of Dr Herbert Read, the distinguished poet and critic, who lives at the delightful old vicarage—near the farm where he was born.

---

[1] 'Street' villages. So-called because they stand on the old Roman road or 'street' which once ran from Malton through Hovingham to Aldburgh.

Harome—just beyond Nunnington in the direction of Helmsley—is another charming village with a most attractive inn (the Star) the bar of which has been entirely furnished with oak pieces made by Thompson of Kilburn.

The undulating country between Castle Howard and Oulston also has a gentle beauty and charm. I like it especially in early summer when the woods are at their richest and the fields are full of corn. That is the time to explore these and the other little hamlets and villages such as Coulton, Scackleton, Brandsby, Yearsley, Terrington, Dalby, Skewsby and Stearsly.

CHAPTER FIFTEEN

Malton

MALTON, in the eyes of many motorists rushing towards Scarborough and the coast, is just a bad bottleneck where they are held up for an hour or two on busy summer week-ends at the narrow crossroads. For others it is interesting because of its market, its racing stables, or its Roman museum —for Malton was once a very important Roman station.

To me it always suggests the Wolds, partly because it is one of the gate-ways to the Wolds, and partly because I have started so many Wolds walking-tours in the past at this cheerful old town.

There are two Maltons (as there are two Thirsks)—Old Malton and New Malton—with Norton immediately across the river, where the East Riding begins.

If you approach Malton by car from York, you have the advantage of travelling along one of the best modern roads in the country, rather monotonously flat for the first few miles, but alternately climbing and fall-ing as you pass Spital Beck and Cranbeck Bridge. Once over Whitwell Hill, the country opens out, and there are fine vistas of the Howardian Hills on the left and of the Wolds to the right, with the Derwent (and Kirkham Abbey) deep below. Glimpses of Castle Howard and its great park may be seen just before the approach to Malton. A sharp turn to the left at the Talbot hotel leads directly to the market square and to the great bus station. You can't escape the buses in Malton. Today they are part and parcel of the town, just as the stage-coaches were a century or so ago. And personally I like to see them lurching in and out of the great square, with their exciting names—Whitby, Scarborough, Ripon, York, Ryedale, Helmsley, and so on. They are, after all, the lineal descendants of the stage-coaches and they bring life and animation to the old town. For Malton is very much a key town for this great rural district, and serves all three Ridings. In the holiday season it is a sight to see the long-distance and country buses manœuvring for position in the square. It is a vast square— really two squares in one—with St Michael's rugged church (Norman) in the middle (rather obscured by the bus station), and, just round the corner, the Town Hall, where a tablet on the wall records the fact that Edmund Burke, the famous orator, represented Malton in Parliament from 1780 to 1794.

One side of the square is lined with inns, creeper-covered, and another side with shops, but the main shopping streets are round the corner.

Malton is not a particularly picturesque town. It has an honest, hard-working farmer's look about it, as befits such an important agricultural centre, and it is usually full of farmers and racing men, for the Malton stables are famous and flourishing. But it is essentially the farmers' metropolis and plays an important part in rural affairs.

Two old Malton breweries are still making the famous Malton ales which are well known to all good North Riding men; there is also one other famous inn—the Crosskeys, in Wheelgate—which has a Norman crypt and a legend associated with the old priory.

The fine Roman museum is full of interesting relics of the Roman station in Malton, the site of which is marked by a cross in Orchard Field.

Soon, I expect, the Planners will do something about that awkward bottleneck in the middle of the town where four crossroads meet, but I shall be sorry if they do, because the bottleneck is part and parcel of the Malton scene—and it slows down the traffic, which is a very good thing!

Old Malton lies on the Malton-Pickering road, just beyond the town, and has some delightful old cottages with thatched roofs, and two old-fashioned inns. But its great glory is the church of St Mary, with its massive tower, which is part of the twelfth-century Gilbertine priory. It stands in the meadows above the Derwent by the roadside, with the old Abbey House nearby. Dickens knew this church well. His friend, Charles Smithson, of Eastthorpe Hall,[1] near Malton, is buried in the churchyard.

Malton cricket field—which has trained some famous players and is one of the most attractive I know—is just beyond the church on the Pickering road.

---

[1] Now the seat of Lord Grimthorpe.

CHAPTER SIXTEEN

Pickering

PICKERING—eight flat miles beyond Malton—is no ordinary town. It is unique in many ways among the market towns of Yorkshire[1] and is one of the most ancient settlements of all. Even so, I would hazard a guess that half the motorists who pass through it never see the real Pickering. The Malton-Whitby and Scarborough-Helmsley roads by-pass it, and a slight detour is needed to penetrate into the high street. Unlike the majority of North Riding towns, Pickering is full of narrow streets and odd corners, and it is cut in two by the railway and the beck. Even the celebrated church of Sts Peter and Paul at the top of the town stands on a kind of island, and only the pertinacious traveller finds his way into it past the tombstones, though its lovely tower and spire are a familiar landmark for miles around. As for the castle, that indeed takes a bit of finding!

It is precisely this higgledy-piggledy arrangement that gives Pickering its distinctive character and charm. You never quite know what to expect round the next corner: it may be a dignified Georgian house, a tiny cottage, an antique shop, a cul-de-sac—or the castle!

The main street, which is built on a gentle slope, with steps to the pavement, is really the heart of the town, and its old shops, clubs and inns are full of character. There is a Black Swan, a White Swan, a George, and many other inns at odd corners, including the latest, the dignified Forest and Vale at the crossroads.

A narrow passage-way, with a garage on one side ('last garage for 18 miles') and the police station on the other, links the town with the famous moorland road to Whitby, though there is an alternative road past the church.

For the tourist, the chief attractions are the church and the castle. The rugged, battlemented exterior of the church and the superb spire are perfectly in keeping with this ancient town. Within, the chief glory is the mural paintings or frescoes which were accidentally discovered under a coat of whitewash in 1851, and date from the fifteenth century. They are

[1] See *Evolution of an English Town;* Gordon Home.

of immense size, beautifully drawn, and depict scenes from the lives of the saints. Unfortunately, the colours are fading fast, and extensive restoration is urgently needed if these priceless treasures are to be saved.

Another feature of interest is the American memorial tablet commemorating two surveyors, Robert King and his son, of Pickering, who helped and succeeded L'Enfant in planning the city of Washington. There are also two brasses commemorating the American Alliance, flanked by the English and American flags. In addition, there are effigies of knights and ladies, a Hepplewhite pulpit, a Georgian candelabrum, and, perhaps most interesting of all, the gracious fabric of the church itself, partly Norman and partly of the fifteenth century.

The ruins of the large Norman castle occupy a commanding position on a hilltop above Pickering beck. Several English kings have passed through its gateway, including John, Henry II, the three Edwards; and Richard II, who was held prisoner here, and who marched out of it to Pontefract to meet his death. Rosamund's Tower is said to have been occupied by the Fair Rosamund, mistress of Henry II. The castle was besieged and severely damaged by the Roundheads in the Civil Wars. It belongs to the Duchy of Lancaster.

Pickering has produced many famous men, including Francis Nicholson, the painter, and Dr John L. Kirk, a country doctor and famous collector of eighteenth-century pieces, which are now in the Kirk Museum at York. Mr F. Austin Hyde, the well-known Yorkshire dialect authority and poet, who was headmaster of Lady Lumley's Grammar School in Pickering for years, knows more about its history than anyone. John Castillo, the poet of Cleveland, is buried in the Methodist churchyard.

Pickering today is a pleasant little market town, with its antique shops (of which there are many), and its wonderful nursery gardens with their magnificent display of lupins and roses which make such a delightful picture on the outskirts of the town.

The Vale itself is not exciting country for the tourist, for it is too flat and monotonous; but it is full of pleasant little villages and fine farmlands. It is also a paradise for geologists, who will find the Vale of Pickering, with its marks of the Ice Age and the great Lake, a fascinating study.

In the grounds of Hovingham Hall, the ancestral home of the Worsley family. The lawn provides one of the finest cricket pitches in the county.

A quiet stretch of Pickering Beck. Part of Pickering's mighty castle is seen in the background, and some old–world cottages typical of the vale.

V. THE GOATHLAND COUNTRY
AND THE NORTH-EAST MOORS

CHAPTER SEVENTEEN

From Pickering to Whitby

THE MOORLAND ROAD

ONE of the most spectacular parts of the North Riding is the extensive stretch of moorland and dale lying between the Whitby-Scarborough coast road and the Vale of Pickering.

Most tourists are familiar with the famous moorland road, twenty-one miles long, from Pickering to Whitby, with the great moor of Fylingdales on the one hand and Goathland moors on the other. In late August, when the heather is at its prime, the views of these far-flung moorlands are unforgettable, but they are impressive at all seasons of the year, provided there is good visibility. I have done this journey hundreds of times and doubt if I have ever seen quite the same views. Moorlands are peculiarly susceptible to atmosphere, to changes of light, cloud shadows, veils of mist and early morning frost and sunshine, as well as to the changing seasons of the year.

From the tiny Fox and Rabbit inn, five miles beyond Pickering, past the twin villages of Lockton and Levisham, the road climbs steadily to the 900-feet level above Saltersgate, a point where even the most hardened motorist is compelled to pause for a moment on the edge of the crater of the celebrated Hole of Horcum to admire the spectacular scene. For a short distance the road skims the edge of this deep and extraordinary ravine, relic of the Ice Age, and one looks into a green oasis in the midst of the wild moorlands. Two little farms nestle in the lovely valley below, and a few twisted pine trees on the lip of the ravine bear witness to the fierce winds that blow there. Beyond the ravine, the road plunges down the 'Devil's Elbow' to the Saltersgate inn and beyond. The views of the beautiful valley of Newtondale, a little to the west, are as striking as the ravine above. Ellerbeck bridge, a few miles farther along the Whitby road, is another viewpoint on this road which reveals moorland scenery at its very best.

After passing Ellerbeck bridge, the road climbs steeply past Widow Howe and then drops to the ravine of Brocka Beck before climbing again to Silhowe. Just beyond Silhowe, the highest point is reached and there is another change of scene. The green and wooded valley of Littlebeck,[1] with its hill farms and cottages, is revealed far below to the right, while in front, a long stretch of coastline north and south of Whitby can be seen, fringed by pasturelands. It is this juxtaposition of rugged coast, blue sea and green farmlands, coupled with the sparkling air, that combines to make this surprise view so enchanting. The long, straggling village of Sleights—old and new—lies hidden below at the foot of the famous hill of Blue Bank, with the River Esk winding through the valley towards Ruswarp and its estuary at Whitby. The village of Aislaby lies on the hillside above.

It is in this lovely corner of the North Riding that important deposits of potash have recently been revealed. Shafts have been sunk at Eskdaleside, Sleights, Aislaby and Sneaton, and vast deposits of the precious mineral have been located. It is too soon to say what effect these discoveries will have on their immediate neighbourhood, but it is to be hoped that they will bring back prosperity to Whitby without spoiling the countryside.

LILLA CROSS

Newtondale, through which the Pickering-Whitby railway runs, is one of the most romantic stretches of railway in the country, and is full of surprises; but for the moment I propose to deal with the country to the east of this Pickering-Whitby moorland road. The vast State forest of Allerston, which dominates the landscape between Thornton Dale and the Fox and Rabbit inn is dealt with in a separate chapter.[2]

Most of Fylingdales moor, which extends from the forest to the coast road and runs alongside the road for several miles, is in the hands of the War Department, as the numerous ugly notices bear witness. From a tourist's point of view, this is lamentable, for this great moor is rich in old tracks and historic remains, and stretches almost to the sea.[3]

At the eleventh milestone from Whitby, marked also by a tall North Riding boundary post, an old fish-track cuts across the moor towards the famous Lilla Cross and continues in the direction of Robin Hood's Bay.

[1] See page 127.   [2] See page 131.   [3] See pages 176–7

Weatherbeaten Lilla Cross,[1] the oldest stone cross in the Riding, stands on the high ridge at Lilla Howe, near the source of the River Derwent. Lilla Howe and the nearby Louvain Howe can be seen from the road, and on the same fascinating ridge various other Howes and Crosses may be traced, e.g. High Woof Howe, Ann's Cross, York Cross and Foster Howes. All this is magnificent country, and commands fine sea views at certain vantage points, but it is foolish to attempt to explore it while the Army are in possession.

SALTERSGATE TO HACKNESS

An old road turns into the moors from the top of Saltersgate bank, opposite the Hole of Horcum. This is a very rough road, unsuitable for cars, that dips down to the valley behind Whinny Nab and Malo Cross to Newgate Foot farm. It then turns round the base of the curious pudding-shaped hill of Blakey Topping—another relic of the Ice Age—passes the ruins of Blakey Ho farm and winds its way past a few isolated farms to Red House. It then crosses Black Beck, winds past Jerry Noddle and eventually emerges from the valley at the hamlet of Langdale End, where one joins the main road for Hackness and Scarborough.

No bald description can do justice to the wild beauty of this hidden valley. Towards the Langdale End side of the valley, the upper slopes and ridges have been planted by the Forestry Commission—all this land comes within the area of Allerston Forest—but from Blakey Topping to Red House and beyond there are magnificent views, romantically sited farms, and many tempting detours into the moors and little dales.

Another approach into this intricate and fascinating country is by way of Staindale.

IN STAINDALE

Staindale is one of those little dales, lying just off the Pickering-Whitby road, which are only one remove from paradise. It can be reached by foot-path over the fields from Lockton, but the surest way to find it for a first visit is to follow the first by-road to the right, just past Lockton Lane end. It is indicated by a Y.H.A. sign.

The road climbs gently up the hill, past a few scattered farms—Mount Pleasant, High House, Whitethorne, High and Low Pastures—then dwindles to a cart-track and turns down to the isolated Low Staindale farm, which is now the Youth Hostel.

[1] See Chapter Twenty-seven, 'Stone Crosses of the North Yorkshire Moors'.

Just beyond the hostel, a footpath by the beckside leads to the lovely secluded valley of Dovedale Griff. There are several other Dovedales—this one is known locally as the Doodle—and within its limits it can challenge comparison with any of them. It is only a small valley, an off-shoot of Staindale proper, but it is surrounded by the most striking scenery, and it is uninhabited. The great moorland riggs enclose it, and it is dominated by the gaunt High Bridestones. Possibly it is the giant Bride-stones above that gives this valley its peculiar quality of strangeness, but if ever there was a hidden valley haunted by the ghosts of the Druids, this surely is it! I had this lovely valley all to myself one showery day in January and felt this atmosphere most vividly. It is the kind of secret valley where one would expect to find fauns or hobmen, for it seems to lie under the spell of an enchantment. And how quiet and peaceful it is there in the green silence, wandering along the bank of the little stream, with beautiful clumps of trees on either hand! There is a blue mistiness among the bare branches at that time of year, and a sense of spring not very far away.

As I climbed up the rigg to the level of the Bridestones, there were magnificent views all round, and the colours—even in January—were breathtaking. The bracken along the side of the griff was still russet-brown, and one of the most perfect rainbows I have ever seen spanned the head of the valley.

Up there on the heights, there is a wide vista of moorlands to the north, while to the south and east you look on to the outer fringe of Staindale forest, part of the great Allerston Forest. All the beautiful country of Langdale, Broxa, Hackness and Whisperdales lies beyond. The lonely hostel fits perfectly into the picture—just round the corner, in a little world of its own.

On my way there, I met the postman from Lockton, Mr Patrick. We went into the parlour together and had a pleasant chat with Mrs Topham, the warden, who made me tea and gave me all the gossip of the dale. What a difference to their lonely lives the postman makes! Wherever one wanders in these remote valleys of the North Riding, one meets the rural postman at some time or another, and they can tell you more about the countryside than any books. They know intimately every farm and family for miles around, and I am always delighted to meet one on his rounds.

From Low Staindale, a rough road by the side of the main stream leads to High Staindale, with its two houses, and this is getting near the heart of these vast forest lands. You can take the road up to Jingleby or climb up to the great fire tower.

On this occasion, I took the track behind the house and joined a ride which climbs over the treetops to the wastelands above. Keeping to the high plateau, it passes Blakey Topping and Newgate Foot, and swings round to join the Pickering road again at the Hole of Horcum. It is useless to attempt to describe the views from the ridge: they must be seen; and even though I came back through drenching rain, I enjoyed every yard of the way.

But what a strange, eerie atmosphere invests these vast new forests, and how eloquent is the silence that broods over them. To feel it most strongly, one should go there alone and wander along the rides that lead sometimes to the treetops and sometimes down to a dark maze of trees, or else climb to one of the great new fire-rides high above.

As one comes unexpectedly across one of these major rides that split the forest, it is as though a giant has passed that way, hacking his way through the rows of spruce and pine, wielding a two-handed sword and leaving a great clearing in his wake.

But the giant in this case is the modern bulldozer and plough, which is capable of tearing up heatherclad moorlands that have resisted Nature's effort to grow trees for a million years. Walking through the maze of trees, one does not know which to admire most, the modern machines that have broken up the savage moorlands and enabled the forest to be made, or the devoted band of forestry workers who have planted millions of trees over the past twenty-five years.

As this is one of the most striking recent developments in the North Riding. I shall be dealing more fully with the new State forests in a later chapter.[1]

[1] See pages 131–4.

CHAPTER EIGHTEEN

Goathland

MOORLAND SPA

GOATHLAND lies to the west of the Pickering-Whitby road—nine miles from Whitby. Walkers have no difficulty in finding it, but many motorists miss it altogether, so I will begin by indicating the two ways into the village from the Pickering road. The first forks left to Goathland (three miles) just after passing Ellerbeck bridge, which is exactly ten miles from Whitby. The second road forks about three miles farther along the Whitby road, near Silhowe. The other approaches to Goathland are from the direction of Egton Bridge and Beck Hole.

It is, I suppose, possible to exaggerate the beauty of this countryside, and as I happened to be living in Goathland whilst engaged on part of this book, I may well do so. Let me begin, then, by admitting that Goathland is not quite what it was: a little, unspoilt North Riding village set in the heart of the moors, with a green common running through the middle of it.

The railway (and the buses), coupled with its growing reputation as a health resort, inevitably led to its development as a small moorland spa; and while most of the new houses and hotels fit naturally into the picture, a certain amount of untidy building has taken place of recent years which mars the perfection of the scene. But even allowing for this, Goathland is a remarkable village, and is surrounded by some of the loveliest country in Yorkshire. Moreover, it has this great advantage from the tourist's point of view, that it contains more hotels and boarding houses than any other place of its size that I know. As long ago as the twelfth century, Henry I granted a place in Goathland for a hospital 'and a carucate of land for Ormerod the priest', and Goathland seems to have been catering for visitors (of one kind or another) ever since!

It is perhaps the sparkling air and immunity from excessive rain that make it so attractive to middle-aged people seeking a place of retirement. Tourists apart, farming is the main occupation, and there are small farmsteads along the common and on the moorland slopes around. These scattered farms are generally so picturesque—some of them look like stage-sets, with their weathered pantile roofs, beautiful stone frontages and moorland background—that the traveller might imagine they were not working farms, of the earth, earthy, so to say. See them snowbound in winter, or buffeted by a howling north-easter, and you will get quite a different impression. Most of them are small—with about fifty acres or so of mixed land—but many of them have considerable rights of stray on the moors for their sheep. And what these Goathland farmers do not know about moorland sheep is not of much consequence. To see them at their best, one should attend the famous Goathland Sheep Sales in October, which are among the oldest of their kind in the Riding. First comes the sale of 'yowes' (ewes) and then the 'tupps' (rams). To these two sales farmers come from far and wide to buy or sell stock, and it is an education to mix with them and listen to their comments. After the sale, you will see them, with their wonderful dogs, driving their flocks over the moorland roads and passes, and I doubt if there is a more delightful country sight than this anywhere. Or watch them at the sheepdog trials in August, and learn more of their craft. Even the names of these farms have a music of their own: Hunt House, Hazel Head, Julian Park, Partridge Hill, Hawthorn Hill, Friar's Croft, Abbot's House, Manor House—and so on.

Goathland is one of those places that exercise a powerful influence on many sorts of people, and once they fall under its spell they find it very difficult to leave. Not only is it surrounded by fine, colourful—rather than sombre—moorlands, but it has the added attraction of beautiful wooded valleys, watered by romantic streams and broken by waterfalls. The air has a crystalline purity that seems to bring out the colours to an exceptional degree, as artists long ago discovered; and the colours of the moors when the heather is at its prime, and of the bracken when turning to gold, or of the woods and scarlet berries in late autumn, are indescribable.

People who think that village life is dull might do worse than try a stay at Goathland. What with the various church activities, the Women's Institute, the Hunt and the Hunt balls, the other dances and whist drives, the Cricket Club, the Flower Show, the Sheep Sale, the Fair, the lectures, the Naturalists' Society, the Arts Council, the 'Dramatic', the Literary and Debating Society, the Plough Stots, the farming activities, not to speak of the weddings and funerals—and the 'visitors'—there is never a dull moment!

The beautiful church of St Mary, which is the first building to attract the eye as one enters the village from the Pickering road, is a comparatively new church, built in 1896. It replaces an older church which again had several predecessors. The original 'hermitage' goes back to the reign of Henry I, who gave a grant to Osmund the priest and his small fraternity to establish a cell in Goathland, and this is believed to have stood near the site of the present Abbot's House farm. Subsequently the Goathland community were attached to Whitby Abbey, and were frequently visited by the Abbots of Whitby. One of the most prized possessions of the existing church is a beautiful fifteenth-century silver chalice. It also contains some specimens of the work of Robert Thompson, the Kilburn wood-carver.

This curious blend of ancient and modern is constantly cropping up in Goathland. By what seems today a strange anomaly, this very Yorkshire stronghold belongs to the Duchy of Lancaster under an old charter.[1] Goathland forms part of the ancient Forest of Pickering, and the moorlands and farmlands are largely Crown property. Until 1924, the annual Court Leet and Court Baron were held in the village.

SWORD DANCERS AND WITCHCRAFT

Goathland is one of the few remaining villages in the North Riding with its own sword dancers and plough stots. These sword dances—of the long-sword variety—are of Scandinavian origin and are believed to have been introduced into Yorkshire by the Norsemen over a thousand years ago. The Goathland plough stots can be traced back only for about a century, but according to the late F. W. Dowson, a native of Goathland, and an authority on the folklore of the district, they are much older. The word 'stot' signified a bullock, and was applied to the young men of the village who dragged the plough round the district on Plough Monday, making merry and soliciting alms after they had made their own offerings at the church, and finishing the day with a glorious celebration at the local inn. In the old days there was great rivalry between the local teams. Subsequently the sword dancers and the plough stots joined forces, and it is in this guise that they can be seen in Goathland today performing the ancient ritual, not only on Plough Monday but on various other festive occasions through the year. All the senior team are Goathland men, most of them employed on the farms, and the boys, who comprise the second team, are of the same breed. It is astonishing to see some of them come straight from their ploughing, change into their gay costumes and dance their way round the village to the spirited music of the fiddler. There are five set

[1] See pages 125-6.

figures and a 'no man's jig', and they perform them all again and again. They money they collect goes to the hospitals.

In some districts, notably at Ampleforth, this blending of sword dances, plough stots and pageant resulted in a folk play. Such a play used to be performed at the Goathland inns in the middle of the last century, but it has been lost. The Ampleforth play is still performed.

GOATHLAND HUNT

Goathland has another link with the past in its famous Hunt, which is one of the oldest packs in the country. There was hunting of boar and deer in the royal forest of Pickering in the dim past, but the present Goathland Hunt has been in existence since 1750. Tom Ventriss was the most famous whip the Hunt has ever had. He died in 1922 at the age of 101, England's oldest huntsman, who outshines John Peel in local story. The Goathland country covers an enormous area and is tough going for hounds and followers. It runs over wild moor, and up and down steep ridges and into almost inaccessible ravines, making it a severe test of horsemanship. On special meets, notably on Boxing Day, all the village turns out and follows hounds on foot. Originally the hounds were trencher-fed, but today they are kept in fine kennels at Eskdaleside. Mr John F. Pyman is the present popular M.F.H.

INCLINE RAILWAY

Railway-minded people also have plenty to occupy their attention at Goathland. The present section of railway between Pickering and Goathland—through Newtondale and on to Grosmont—is undoubtedly one of the finest in the country. It includes the $8\frac{1}{2}$-mile stretch between Levisham and Goathland—one of the longest in this region without an intermediate station.[1] But the railway that excites most interest is the old 'Incline' between Beck Hole and Goathland—part of the original Whitby-Pickering railway—which was the third railway to be built in the country: George Stephenson helped in the survey work. Originally the coaches were drawn by horses all the way, but the gradient between the neighbouring village of Beck Hole and Goathland is so steep that the coaches had to be hauled up by rope on a revolving drum, balanced by a huge water tank weighing four tons, which descended as the coaches were being pulled up.

[1] The longest is the ten-mile stretch from Bowes to Barras.

Charles Dickens—who is constantly cropping up in Yorkshire history—was one of the passengers to use this 'quaint old railway along part of which passengers are hauled by a rope'—presumably this was on one of his visits to Mulgrave Castle. Later a wire rope was substituted and other improvements effected, but a serious accident occurred in 1864, when the rope snapped and the carriages ran backwards. In consequence, the present stretch of line was laid from Grosmont to Goathland. It entailed some tremendous engineering feats, including the construction of several high bridges. Today, one of the pleasantest valley walks in Goathland is down the abandoned Incline Railway to Grosmont, where beautiful grassland covers the old permanent way.

THE MOORS

It is, perhaps, the rich choice of walks around Goathland that, more than anything else, explains its popularity. There are local walks to the neighbouring hamlet of Beck Hole, by way of Water Ark and Thomassin Foss, or through Darnholm to Ellerbeck, and over to Tom Keld's Hole. There are the famous waterfalls of Mallyan Spout, Nelly Ayre Foss, Keld Scar Foss, and many others.

The real walking country is to be found on the high moors that encircle the village. In whichever direction one turns, there are moors crowned by ancient howes, or barrows. It is up on the tops that one really discovers the old Goathland of the ancient country of Blackamore. These moors must have been thinly peopled for thousands of years. The astonishing frequency of the howes bears witness to this. The moors have seen the Ice Age pass and they have witnessed the dawn of the new world. Palæolithic man may or may not have come so far north, but who knows? The surface of these vast moors has hardly been scratched, and time may yet reveal many discoveries. Pygmy flints and stone axes have certainly been found in north-east Yorkshire, though the majority of these howes would appear to belong to the Bronze Age. One has only to walk over these desolate wastelands to feel the strange influence of a bygone people.

One can walk over the preserved stretch of Roman road by way of Hunt House and Wheeldale lodge, and follow the footsteps of the Roman legions to Stape and on to the derelict camps at Cawthorn, or on to the villages of Newton-in-Rawcliffe and Levisham. Or one can go over Two Howes and the remarkable Simon Howe to Saltersgate and the Vale of Pickering.

Still finer are the moors to the north-west—over the high watershed by way of Three Howes, Pike Hill Moss, Glaisdale Rigg, Ralph Cross and Westerdale—into Bilsdale; or along any of the intervening riggs into Fryup Dale, Danby Dale and Rosedale.

For motorists, there are roundabout routes over the rigg roads, notably from Castleton into Rosedale or Farndale.

Indeed, wherever you turn in this region, you will see moorland scenery on the grand scale.

QUOITS AT BECK HOLE

All roads and footpaths in Goathland seem to lead to the neighbouring hamlet of Beck Hole, which lies barely a mile away in the beautiful valley of the Murk Esk.

Beck Hole is quite unspoilt, a moorland gem consisting of a handful of picturesque cottages and farms, and a tiny inn which flourishes an unusual sign—a fine oil painting of the beck itself by Algernon Newton, R.A. Once there were two inns, the present Birch Hall and the Lord Nelson, but Lord Nelson was adjudged to be redundant and lost his licence, where-upon Mr Newton very sensibly converted it into a delightful cottage in which he painted many of his famous pictures.

Beck Hole is the kind of hamlet that age does not wither nor custom stale. It is hard to believe that there ever was a little iron-smelting plant there, or a railway station; but old George Harrison, who is the un-crowned king of Beck Hole, will tell you all about both in his inimitable way if you have the good fortune to meet him there tending his garden or his honey.

Today, all is peace and quiet again and two wars have left Beck Hole quite unmoved. I doubt if an atomic bomb would be noticed there either. They are much more interested in quoits!

Here, of a summer's evening, you will find the men of Beck Hole play-ing this ancient game on the village green, with iron rings weighing five and a quarter pounds each. It is an old blacksmiths' and farmers' game, and is said to have originated with farmers throwing horseshoes about while waiting for their horses to be shod. There are blacksmiths and farmers in the Beck Hole team, too, as there are in rival teams in other North Riding villages, and they look as broad in the beam and as strong as the horses they handle.

Some of them seem nearly as old as the game itself, which has been played here for about ninety years; but they have lost nothing of their skill and enthusiasm. 'Gaiters', 'Flat 'uns', 'Q's', 'Frenchmen', 'Ringers' and 'Pot-ringers' all come alike to them, and it is astonishing how adept they are at this difficult art, which looks, at first sight, so easy—until one tries a hand! And how keen they are! 'Fetch t'collipers!' they shout, if there is any doubt about a particular throw, and the referee marches solemnly on to the pitch and measures the rival rings to a hairsbreadth. Nobody disputes his ruling. One can't argue when iron rings are flying around.

Starting a match in the early summer evening, they go on hurling the rings about until dusk—and after—and you can literally watch the sparks flying as the heavy quoits crash on top of the 'hob', or iron pin, in the ground. And woe betide you if you get in the way of one in the gathering darkness. The pitch is eleven yards from hob to hob and they play eleven a side, twenty-one up each man; so it goes on for hours.

When the Beck Hole giants won the championship of the league recently against all comers there was a mighty celebration when they arrived home in their coach. To join them in the little friendly inn after a match, and watch them drink ale and play darts just as well as they play quoits, is a memorable experience. Usually they finish with a sing-song and nearly lift the roof off. Mrs Schofield, the popular landlady, knows how to deal with them all.

Long may they flourish, these mighty smiths and farmers of Beck Hole, who play quoits and darts like champions!

AROUND BECK HOLE

The scenery around Beck Hole is in keeping with this dream-like village. The two becks meet near the village and form the Murk Esk, which flows through the deep, wooded valley to join the Esk proper at Grosmont. Some of the woods, alas, are being stripped of their trees, but even this cannot destroy the beauty of this fertile countryside. Picturesque little farms are perched on the slopes, each with its strip of cornfields and green pasture-lands, and the high moors above dominate the scene. The grass seems greener, the corn more golden and the sky bluer here than else-where, and there are delightful footpaths on either side.

You can walk to the green uplands of the neighbouring hamlet of Green End, or down the valley to Grosmont. The old village of Grosmont is spoilt by the brickworks and its tall chimneys, but the approach to it, whether one walks down the Murk Esk or along the twisting bridle-path from Green End, or down the incredible road from the high moors, is unforgettable.

One of the remarkable features of these moors above Goathland and Beck Hole is the number of green tracks that cross the moors in all directions. They are of such a vivid green that they stand out among the bracken and the heather in an exceptional way, as if a bright green strip of carpet had been lain over the dark heather. Most of these green tracks are either old 'trods' from place to place, or pack-horse tracks—and they are kept close-cropped and clean by the sheep. Occasional patches of 'intake' which have been won from the moor by an earlier generation of farmers, and walled round, have the same striking colour and can be seen for miles.

From Grosmont, one can take the spectacular motor road along Eskdaleside to Sleights and thence to Ruswarp and Whitby. But for a first visit to Goathland, the main road past the church and thence to New Wath, Julian Park and Randymere, with its great pine woods and reservoir, reveals this scenery at its best.

This is the true Goathland country, with almost every kind of scenery that anybody could desire: vast moorlands, upland farms, forest lands, steep valleys, wonderful vistas of moor and dale, and occasional glimpses of the sea. And at the end of it all is the lovely village of Egton Bridge, nestling in the valley below, and all the wild country of Eskdale beyond.

THE DUCHY OF LANCASTER

Tourists often express surprise on hearing that a considerable part of the Goathland moors and many of the surrounding farms belong to the Duchy of Lancaster—that is, to the Sovereign.

The fascinating history of the Duchy is too long to tell here in detail, but a brief note on how the Duchy of Lancaster came to acquire the estates in Yorkshire may be of interest.

The Duchy of Lancaster is an inheritance which, since 1399, has always been enjoyed by the reigning sovereign. Henry III gave to his son Edmund the possessions of the rebellious Simon de Montfort and the Earl of Ferrers in 1266. Edmund was subsequently created Earl of Lancaster in 1267 and given the castle and county of Lancaster, as well as, among others, the Pickering-Goathland properties.

Thereafter, the estates increased by various other heritages and through marriage. Henry, the fourth earl, was made Duke of Lancaster in 1351, and on his death the inheritance passed to his son-in-law, John of Gaunt, 'time-honoured Lancaster', who acquired further estates. His son, Henry of Bolingbroke, became King of England in 1399, and since that time the estates have been enjoyed by the King as Duke of Lancaster, and now by Her Majesty the Queen, in right of the Duchy of Lancaster. They have passed through many vicissitudes and changed hands at different periods of history with the Crown itself: they were put up for sale during the Commonwealth, and used by the impoverished Stuarts to raise money. They have dwindled at times to small proportions through rash sales, but from the eighteenth century they became more firmly established, through improved methods of administration, and today they are in a healthy and flourishing condition again. The modern Duchy is essentially a landed inheritance consisting mainly of agricultural estates expertly administered by the staff. From time to time new properties are bought, and the older estates are being developed on modern lines.

Far from resenting this survival of the Duchy of Lancaster in North Yorkshire, Goathland and Pickering are proud of their ancient and royal lineage.

CHAPTER NINETEEN

The Lost Valley of Littlebeck

FOR walkers there is a direct approach to the valley of Littlebeck, near Goathland, by a rough cart-road over the moor near the top of Blue Bank, with an alternative footpath direct to Falling Foss.

For motorists, the approach is more circuitous and exciting. Half-way down Blue Bank, on the Pickering-Whitby road, an innocent-looking by-road marked 'Littlebeck' debouches from the main road and turns towards the valley. It begins as a normal country lane with fields and farms on either side, but soon it plunges down the steep valley by a series of leaps and bounds (3 in 1). When it has almost reached the bottom, it swings round and soars skyward again until it turns another corner, and then plunges down to the valley in earnest, finishing up with a water splash, a final twist and an almost perpendicular leap up the other side. The narrow valley is no more than a cleft in the landscape, with precipitous slopes on either side and the prattling beck between. Across the beck, the road thrusts sharply out of the valley, and round the first bend it forks, one branch continuing straight up the steep fellside to join the coast road, the other joining it by a more devious route.

This is the way of the road to Littlebeck and it is, indeed, the way of quite a lot of roads in this part of the world, where the valleys are un-usually steep and narrow. This approach to Littlebeck down Goathland Bank is particularly spectacular; but it is all of a piece with the scenery around.

This little valley of Littlebeck—and both the tiny hamlet and the stream itself are called Littlebeck—is one of the fairest of them all. It is so difficult of access, and so cut off from the world, that it is sometimes called the lost valley, or the valley of Shangri-la. It can be approached from the Whitby-Scarborough road, or from Sleights, via Iburndale and Ugglebarnby, and by delightful footpaths; but on either side it is flanked by precipitous, wooded slopes. There are woods on either side of the stream at the narrowest part of the valley, and a footpath that climbs high above the beck, past a great cave, cut into a rocky bastion called the Hermitage.

Originally it is believed to have been used by the hermits of Eskdaleside, the most ancient of whom was St Godric the Hermit, who died in 1172; but the cave has been reconstructed. Beyond the Hermitage, the woods gradually thin out to admit the sun and the sky, while across the stream one has a sudden surprise view of one of the loveliest waterfalls in this country of waterfalls—Falling Foss—a beautiful feathery fall, surrounded by trees and illumined by shafts of sunlight. At this point, the beck plunges into a pool and continues on a new course towards the hamlet.

This lost valley is full of stories. The hamlet itself numbers only about eight cottages and farms and a chapel; but there are several almost inaccessible farms on the moorland slopes above. Some of these have scarcely any communication with the outside world, but seem quite content as they are. During the Second World War, one old woman, who had a smallholding, was approached one day by a traveller who was going the rounds trying to buy gold sovereigns. At first she refused to believe that anybody would be fool enough to give 'three pund a-piece for a gowden sovereign'; but, after much pressure, she admitted that she might have 'a twoathri' put by. Delighted to have found a customer after his arduous journey, the traveller pulled out his wallet and asked her how many she had.

' 'Appen aboot three or four hundred,' the old dame replied. The traveller was flabbergasted. He was prepared for five or six, but not for four hundred! Hurriedly explaining that he would have to go to the bank first to collect more pound notes, but that he would return the following week, he departed a wearier and a wiser man.

In the meantime, the neighbours were surprised to see the old woman's son heroically digging up a considerable slice of the surrounding moor. ' What's Reuben up to?' they asked. The general opinion was that the old woman was reclaiming a bit of the moor—'intak' ' as they call it—for the war effort; but news of the war had scarcely reached Littlebeck at the time, and the matter was rendered all the more mysterious because Reuben didn't seem to know himself either. All he knew was that the old lady had told him to dig here, there and everywhere 'for t'treeacle can' while she supervised his efforts, and by the week-end he had disembowelled a sizable piece of moorland. At last a large treacle can, firmly sealed down, was located, and when the old lady opened it she counted out four hundred gleaming golden sovereigns and put the rest back into the can.

Next Tuesday, the man returned with a fat bundle of notes and the old lady parted with her gold. As soon as his back was turned she put the notes

Moorland inn at Saltersgate: a scene on the wild moorland road between Pickering and Whitby.

Stokesley in Cleveland: a glimpse of one of the most delightful old market towns in Cleveland.

into the treacle can, and watched Reuben bury it again in a different place.

A year or two later, when the war situation was getting desperate, another man appeared—this time to try to persuade the old woman to invest some money in War Loan for the local Victory Week. After considerable persuasion she agreed to invest 'two hundred pund', and told the man to call next week.

Once more the neighbours were surprised to see Reuben wrestling with 'intak',' but this time he found the treacle can on the third day. His mother opened it eagerly and was dismayed to find that it was no longer watertight. Either she hadn't sealed it up properly, or else it had been buried in a watery bog. At any rate, the notes were "all of a mishmash'—though the gowden sovereigns were still solid! Fortunately, when the man called again he was able to reassure her. The notes might be sodden and stuck together, but the numbers were legible and they could be counted, so he persuaded her to accompany him to the nearest bank and open a proper account with the remainder.

There are many similar stories in this secluded valley, especially among the lonely farms on the moor. But there is one farm, in particular, which is noteworthy for an altogether different kind of story. This is the farm called Red Barns, on the opposite side of the valley, on the road to Ugglebarnby. For it was in this farm that the famous 'Father Postgate'—the Venerable Nicholas Postgate, D.D., then an old man of eighty-two—was taken by an exciseman named Reeves, a common informer, while he was baptizing an infant in the Catholic faith. He was subsequently charged at York Assizes on December 8, 1678, with this 'crime'. After a travesty of a trial, he was found guilty and hanged.

Reeves, the exciseman, who had hoped to gain the twenty pounds offered to such informers, never received the reward, and in a fit of remorse drowned himself in the stream at Littlebeck in a spot known as the 'Devil's Hole', which is still said to be accursed. No fish has ever been caught at the spot since that day.

Down below, in the very heart of the valley, opposite the old inn, which is now a private residence, there is a stone workshop with a butt or two of old oak weathering outside. This is yet another of the surprises of this sleepy-looking hamlet, for it is the workshop of Mr Thomas E. Whittaker, wood-carver and craftsman. There is something particularly appropriate about finding a wood-carver in this tree-clad valley. Mr Whittaker works exclusively in English oak. He follows the great tradition of English crafts-

I

men and uses the adze with great effect. From modest beginnings, he has gradually established a high reputation for his fine ecclesiastical and household furniture. All his work is done by hand, and the bulk of it by himself, though he is training one or two apprentices to help him with the preliminary work. His finished work bears his sign-manual of a little gnome, and the stamp of his genius. Massive refectory tables and chairs, Yorkshire dressers, book-ends, sanctuary stools, wine cupboards, corner cupboards, prie-dieux, are among the many beautiful examples of his work which have been admired by hundreds of visitors. Recently he completed a remarkable crucifix for the Catholic church at Lealholm and an elaborate oak screen for Ruswarp church. It is an inspiration to enter the quiet little workshop and to see some of his work in the making. One cannot imagine a more perfect background for such craftsmanship than in this forgotten valley where Time seems to stand still, and peace and holy quiet reign supreme.

CHAPTER TWENTY

North Yorkshire State Forests

THE great State forest of Allerston lies to the east of the Pickering-Whitby road, opposite the valley of Newtondale. Looking over the intervening moorlands towards the skyline, one sees an imposing phalanx of trees investing the slopes and stretching beyond the horizon. Although the immediate impression is of dense, unbroken forest, a closer survey reveals breaks in the serried ranks, and one particularly broad 'ride' culminating in a high fire-tower which dominates the scene.

There are, of course, conflicting opinions about the intrusion of these State forests into moorland and dale-country, and about the overwhelming preponderance of conifers to hardwoods. But Yorkshire is a vast county, and many of the old forests have been denuded of trees as a result of two wars. This process continues at an alarming rate all over the countryside. Hence there is room and urgent need in Yorkshire for developments of this kind so long as they are carefully controlled.

Allerston is the largest of several State forests in the North Riding; others are Ampleforth, Rosedale, Arkengarthdale and Cleveland. Allerston district consists of eight forest beats covering 25,000 acres, stretching roughly from Thornton Dale to Harwood Dale.

The heart of this great forest consists of an intricate network of beautiful little dales, strips of moorland, and so-called marginal land, fascinating in its complexity and variety. It is broken by those curious, flat-topped tabular hills, such as Jerry Noddle and High Langdale End, which are a special feature of the North Riding. Some of the smaller dales, High Dales, Low Dales and Whisperdales, for example, are famous for their natural beauty, and one trembles to think what may be their ultimate fate; but so far, farms and grazing lands in this area have been left undisturbed and only the upper slopes and moorlands are planted. In other dales, such as Troutsdale and Staindale, great areas have been planted and the dales, as one knew them, have been transformed. Inevitably there has been some displacement of moorland farming, but only to a limited extent. Most of this afforested land was largely non-productive—lean moorlands and rough marginal land, with steep, dry valleys, and thinly populated. Now, instead of the lean acres there are thousands of trees, with smallholdings here and there, and intense activity everywhere.

No one can walk through these stripling forests today without being impressed by the enormous amount of real spadework that has been done since the First World War. The first trees were planted in Dalby Forest, near Allerston village, in 1921. Since that time 13,000 acres have been planted. The remainder is either agricultural land or is to be planted later.

It takes from fifteen to twenty-five years for these new forests to reach the thinning stage when commercial production begins. Thereafter, each plantation is thinned at intervals which vary from three to ten years. The timber from the thinnings is used for pit-props, piles, fencing-stakes, pulp-board, rustic fences, telegraph poles, and the like. Already nearly a quarter of a million cubic feet of timber are being marketed each year from these thinnings. This will increase as the woods grow older, and when the trees reach maturity in about sixty years the timber will supply a much wider range of uses.

In this forest a labour force of about 350 men is employed, including foresters, foremen, gangers and forest workers. Some of the permanent staff live in the forest with their families; new hamlets are being built and smallholdings have been established for some of the men. Others live in hostels near the forest, and the rest are brought in daily from the surrounding villages.

One trained man plants about 400 trees per day, while in the nurseries at Broxa a man will transplant 25,000 seedlings per week. The nurseries produce some twenty-five million plants annually for use in all the State forests.

On the vexed question of conifers as against hardwoods, one must remember that the moors themselves will only produce carefully selected conifers. They are mostly pines, which fit well into the moorland scene, and are indeed indigenous to moorlands. Spruce and larch also seem to suit this type of country. It is rare to come across a moorland farm without its protective wall of pines.

Hardwoods can be grown in some of the more sheltered areas on favourable types of soil, particularly in the valleys and on the lower slopes; they are occasionally planted at the edge of some of the rides, but not always with success on the moorland soils. I saw one forty-acre block of young beech in Troutsdale which promised well. Oak and beech are the only valuable species that seem to flourish. But apart from the unsuitability of a great deal of the soil, hardwoods take much longer to mature than conifers and show a relatively slow financial return. On the high moorlands all conifers are by no means successful. Many of the early plantings of Sitka spruce are still 'in check', and there are bare patches of moorland showing only a few stunted trees which have scarcely grown at all in fifteen years. The few solitary trees which have had the luck to be planted on an acre of peaty soil stand out like giants among the surrounding dwarfs. Experience tends to show that the only varieties which flourish on the high moorlands are Scots pine, Corsican pine and *Pinas Contorta*. On the low moors, pines and Japanese larch give good results; while on the slopes and in the dale bottoms, Douglas firs, Norway and Sitka spruce and larches flourish.

Great difficulty was experienced in the early years in breaking up the so-called acid 'pan' on the moors. This 'pan' is a thin, hard layer of acid deposit—only about one-eighth of an inch in thickness—lying beneath the peat and sandy topsoil.

The battle of the 'pan' is one of the romances of State forestry. All the earlier types of plough used were unable to break the pan, or to keep back the heather and mulch the soil. It was not until the massive 'R.L.R.' plough was produced in 1943, largely owing to Lord Robinson's experiments, that the scales were turned. This wonderful plough can deal successfully with the roughest moorlands; it cuts a very deep furrow—of about eighteen inches—breaks the pan, and suppresses the heather—at least for several years. As a result, the later plantations on the moors are everywhere more successful.

There are, however, other difficulties to surmount. For example, the problem of serious cases of 'die-back' in some stands is by no means solved. The heather is also a persistent fighter, while the choice of the best species for various soils is still being explored. The science of forestry in England is yet in its infancy, but it is remarkable how much has been achieved in a relatively short time.

One of the most striking features of these forests is the number of new roads that have been, and are still being, constructed by means of modern bulldozers and grading machines. The roads are of two kinds: all-weather metalled roads, and fair-weather earth roads (which are not recommended in the rainy season!).

In all directions, one sees new roads and forest 'rides'—forty to sixty feet wide—as impressive in their way as any old Roman road or modern arterial road. Of the many wonderful things I saw in my tour of the forest, the roads impressed me most. One can wander for miles along mysterious

rides from one stand to another, from one forest to another, from one
dale to another—mostly without meeting a soul. Some of the views to be
had from observation points along these roads—such as the one from
Jingleby Top—are superb.

There are, of course, patches of ugliness, particularly in the early stages
of planting and deep-ploughing. The broken moor—until such time as it
is covered with young trees—is a mournful and repellent sight, but it is
surprising how soon these bare places are covered with a crop of sprightly
young trees, and how soon the wounds are healed. Elsewhere, too, the
tendency is to cover all the available uplands with trees, including the
hillocks and nabs, which to me look better as they are! But the picture as a
whole is one of vigorous life and activity. A new spirit has come to these
barren moors and dales, and a thriving young community has settled in the
heart of these vast forests.

No doubt there are some moorland lovers to whom every coniferous
forest is an offence against Nature, but, in prevailing conditions, a scheme
whereby it is hoped to supply forty per cent of our timber needs from the
home forests (instead of less than ten per cent, as at present) deserves every
encouragement.

I was impressed, too, with the precautions taken against fire. There are
warning notices everywhere, as well as fire-breaks and rides to check any
sudden outbreak. At key points, the high observation towers are constantly manned during danger periods. 'One cigarette can wipe out the
work of thirty years,' I was told; and, again—'A fire can destroy a million
trees in a few hours.' The most dangerous period is between January and
March, after frost. The older trees are less susceptible to fire than the young
plantations, while Japanese larch (which grows remarkably well here) is
reputed to be practically invulnerable to fire and acts as a fire-break.

When the general public are really fire-conscious and forest-conscious,
access to the State forests will be more generally encouraged. But there are
public rights-of-way through many parts of this beautiful countryside, and
the foresters are a friendly body of men who are always willing to help
interested visitors.

Several Natural Forest Parks have already been established in Scotland
and Wales, and it would only be poetic justice if this fine Yorkshire forest
of Allerston were one day to become a Forest Park.[1]

It would be some compensation for the loss of Fylingdales.

[1] It is, of course, now all within the area of the new National Park, but that is not quite the same
thing.

CHAPTER TWENTY-ONE

The Pickering-Scarborough Road

THE road from Pickering to Scarborough is lined with several pleasant villages, and affords striking views of the hills to the north, and the wolds to the south.

The first village beyond Pickering is Thornton Dale, which has always been considered to be one of Yorkshire's pretty villages. Although it has suffered a little in recent years, Thornton Dale makes a delightful picture, with its charming cottages and the beck running down the long main street. One of my favourite bits is the quiet backwater behind the church where a by-road runs past some beautiful gardens, crosses the stream, and then divides either towards the ancient village of Ellerburn up-dale, or to join the Pickering-Whitby road. The famous old hall is now a country club.

Allerston and Ebberston, both attractive villages, stand back from the main road. Just before reaching Ebberston crossroads, Ebberston church and lodge make one of the prettiest pictures on this road. The little hall beyond is a Georgian gem and was once the home of the famous Squire Osbaldeston.

Snainton is a long, workaday village with a picturesque and pleasant inn, The Coachman, on the outskirts.

Brompton has much to interest the literary tourist. It was at Gallows Hill farm, on the roadside beyond the church, that Wordsworth courted his future wife, Mary Hutchinson; and it was at Brompton church that they were married on October 4, 1802. The Wordsworths frequently travelled along this road to the Lakes. Brompton Hall, once the seat of the famous Cayley family (and of recent years a residential hotel), has now become a 'special' school; it seems an odd choice of milieu.

Beyond Brompton, the road passes the Downe Arms at Wykeham crossroads. Wykeham Hall, the seat of Viscount Downe, is hidden in the park near the village.

Hutton Buscel stands back from the road on the hillside above and is worth the detour. It was here that the old Squire Osbaldeston was brought up, though his house was burned down.

At East and West Ayton (with its ruined castle) a by-road turns north through Forge Valley to the beautiful country of the upper Derwent. The Scarborough road forks at the village, which is only four miles from the coast.

CHAPTER TWENTY-TWO

The Old Squires

YORKSHIRE has produced many famous squires in times past. A few of them, like Squire Waterton and Sir Tatton Sykes, have become national figures. The majority, however, have been content to rule over their own Yorkshire domains and have shunned publicity, yet each of them, in his own way, has helped to make Yorkshire what it is today.

'T'owd Squire', as he was mostly called, was generally loved and esteemed by his tenants and staff. He was a bit of a lad in his day, and a bit of an eccentric (or a martinet) in his later years; but in the main he devoted his attention to the multifarious activities of the countryside—to farming his lands, to breeding horses (about which he knew everything there was to know), and to doing a bit of hunting, shooting and fishing.

Here and there in this book I have commented on the great changes that are taking part in the pattern of country life in the North Riding, as I see it. Many of the old houses stand empty and desolate; others have been converted into schools, hotels or country clubs, or Government offices. Whether this is a good thing or a bad for the country as a whole I do not profess to know, but personally I regret the change and lament particularly the passing of the old squires. They were an integral part of the country scene and of the traditional England which is fast disappearing before our eyes, and they did a great deal of good to the country in their several ways. Fortunately, a few still remain with us, and some of them may be seen at country shows up and down Yorkshire, looking like the last remnant of the Old Guard. And long may they remain!

But there is one we will never see again, the most famous North Riding squire of them all, if not the most famous sporting squire of England. He was generally referred to as 'The Squire', sometimes as the 'Squire of England'. His real name was George Osbaldeston of Hutton Buscel, and, later, of Ebberston Lodge, both on the Pickering-Scarborough road. Hutton Buscel hall was burnt down and never rebuilt.

The Squire would have been the last to claim any academic or political distinctions. He was a sportsman first and last, though, in obedience to his

mother's wishes, he did win an election (at enormous expense) for East
Retford, and sat for that constituency for five uneasy years. He loathed
Parliament, which he seldom visited and found a great bore. He disliked
the canvassing as much as the rest. As he told a friend: 'One dirty fellow
approached me in a most patronizing manner, holding out his filthy paw,
and said, "Tip us your manus, brother sportsman! We both hunts varmints.
You kills foxes. I kills rats!" '

Politics were not the Squire's *forte;* but he excelled at all forms of sport,
especially at horsemanship. He was born in 1787, his mother going from
Hutton Buscel to London for the event. At Eton and Oxford he was con-
tinually getting into trouble on account of his escapades. His sporting
prowess was shown at Eton, where he was cock of the school in boxing,
the best cricketer and all-round athlete, and one of the most promising
oars. Cricket was his first love. He was the fastest bowler of his age and a
first-rate bat, and later he took part in some famous England matches at
Lords against the greatest players of the day. At single cricket, too, he had
few equals. The Squire was one of the first great Yorkshire cricketers and
did much to foster the game in the county.

But he was a giant at almost every game. He was a brilliant tennis player
(he beat Barre) and a first-class shot, who once killed 100 pheasants with
100 shots, and performed many similar feats. He was a dead-shot with a
duelling pistol, and was equally handy with his daddles and fought several
fights. Later on, he acted as referee in some famous prize-fights. He was a
first-class billiards player and once played for fifty hours without sleeping,
playing billiards by night and hunting by day. Several times he took part
in similar endurance feats for a wager.

His strength and stamina were phenomenal although he was only of
medium height (five feet six inches) and weight (eleven stone). In his
forties, he won some terrific rowing matches on the Thames, always for
wagers. The Squire could never resist a wager. 'Chaffing challenges and the
love of fame (i.e. at sport) have always egged me on,' he once wrote.

One of his most famous performances was to ride 200 miles within ten
hours, with changes of horses, for a wager of one thousand guineas. He did
it with over an hour to spare. On another occasion, because a pretty girl he
was squiring at a dinner party was twitted about her inferior 'bouquet' by
a rival beauty, the Squire got on his horse, rode twenty-five miles each
way to get her a bouquet that would dazzle all rivals, and was back in time
to take her in to supper. His life is full of such fantastic feats and follies, and
his autobiography (discovered long after his death) is more exciting and

amusing than most thrillers, with its prodigious feats of strength, wagers, duels, jests, amours, prize-fights, hunting exploits, quarrels, lawsuits, racing triumphs and disasters.

His greatest triumphs were in the hunting field where, in his prime as M.F.H., he was without a peer. He was Master in turn of the Quorn and the Pytchley and other leading hunts, and hunted six days a week. His fame in every kind of sport to do with riding is now a legend. When he was sixty-eight, he rode his own horse at Goodwood and only lost by a neck. But by the end of his active racing career he had lost a fortune. The Turf proved his downfall.

Not that he minded. Late in life he married a widow who looked after him like a mother, doling him out one pound each night to gamble with— he who used to play whist for £100 a trick and £1,000 the rubber.

He died in his eighty-first year and is buried in Highgate cemetery. No one ever enjoyed life more than the old Squire. He was one of the finest and most lovable sportsmen Yorkshire has ever produced. I never pass his lovely little house of Ebberston Lodge on the Scarborough road ('a mere chateau in the Italian style of architecture', he called it) without a kindly thought for this grand old squire.

VI. THE CLEVELAND COUNTRY

CHAPTER TWENTY-THREE

On Cleveland

MANY people regard the Cleveland Hills and 'Cleveland' as synonymous, but Cleveland extends far beyond the range of hills that form only the backbone of this fascinating country which includes the flat country south of the Tees and the so-called north-east moors.

But the more one talks about exact boundaries, the less likely one is to apprehend the true nature of Cleveland. Cleveland is really a kingdom within a kingdom. Although it forms an integral part of the North Riding —and perhaps the most important part—it is a self-contained community of people with strong traditions and customs of its own. The Cleveland of today is not so much a matter of precise boundaries as of market towns, villages, people and traditions. The average Cleveland man will certainly not be able to define the boundaries—some of them have very quaint ideas on the subject, according to whether they hail from the Stokesley or Guisborough districts—but he normally knows a good deal about Cleveland none the less. The Cleveland hill sheep farmers especially know their country.[1]

Stokesley, Ayton, Carlton, Ingleby Greenhow, Westerdale, Danbydale, Fryup, Glaisdale, Baysdale, Roseberry Topping, Marton, Yarm, Freeboro, Moorsholm, Skelton, Hinderwell, Guisborough—all these, and many other such places, are in Cleveland. But though Egton Bridge, Lyth and Sandsend fall within the boundaries, they do not suggest Cleveland to me.

Histories of Cleveland have been written by such giants as Atkinson, Ord, Graves, Tweddel, and others. There is some quality about this corner of the North Riding that seems to fascinate the historian and the archæologist. Other books have been devoted to its folklore, legends, sport, and to the Cleveland worthies. For Cleveland numbers among its sons such famous names as Cædmon, Captain Cook, Roger Ascham, Sir Thomas Chatham, Cholmley Turner, John Oxlee, Sir Alfred Pease, and others.

[1] See Chapter Twenty-eight.

It is therefore impossible to do justice to the richness and variety of this corner of the North Riding in the space of one brief chapter. All I can hope to do is to give my own impressions and suggest a few ways of exploring it.

THE CLEVELAND HILLS

Broadly speaking, Cleveland can be divided into two parts: the rural Cleveland, with Stokesley as the centre—and the ironstone Cleveland around Guisborough and Middlesbrough. Of the two, the ironstone district of the north-east coast is today the more important economically, but not so important, perhaps, to the tourist. There is a great deal of romance in the story of the iron, steel, alum and chemical industries of Cleveland, and stark beauty of a kind in the great mines and blast furnaces; but it is scarcely the sort of country most tourists would choose for a holiday. Here and there, in this book, I have touched on it and I must leave it at that. The other Cleveland, the country of the Cleveland hills and dales, of market towns and villages, of hill sheep farms, and of lore and legend, is the Cleveland that appeals most strongly to me.

You get a first glimpse of it as you come over Scarth Nick from Osmotherley. Or you may go from Swainby to Carlton-in-Cleveland and Ingleby Greenhow. In this case, you travel along the fringe of the hills and really *see* the Cleveland Hills. If you continue on the road from Ingleby Greenhow to Kildale and Commondale, or climb over Rudland Rigg from Ingleby Greenhow or Gillamoor, you get into the heart of the hills and enjoy some magnificent views.

As you come over Burton Howe and approach Turkey Nab, you see the main Cleveland chain coming to an abrupt end and lunging down to the smiling green plain which stretches to the Tees. The suddenness of the descent from over 1,400 feet to the low-lying plain is most dramatic, and there are exciting views of the rugged nabs and toppings that are a feature of the Clevelands—and not quite such exciting views of the smokestacks of Tees-side in the distance! You get another fine view of the hills if you follow the pass (now a motor road) from Chop Gate in Bilsdale above Raisdale Beck to Carlton-in-Cleveland. In the suddenness with which the hills leap to the plain, there is a similarity between the Clevelands and the Hambletons, but the Clevelands are much bleaker than the Hambletons. The Hambletons are soft and full of colour, and interspersed with lovely wooded valleys. The Clevelands are rugged and dour. The rigg roads and passes that run over the Cleveland chain are hard and monotonous, and the moors themselves are tinged with melancholy which the numerous howes tend to emphasize: they are also frequently enveloped in mist, but during the brief heather season they are truly magnificent.

THE WHITBY-GUISBOROUGH ROAD

The famous Whitby-Guisborough motor road (twenty-one miles) that cuts across the northern tip of the Cleveland moors reveals something of this wildness and melancholy. Many find it monotonous and forbidding, for there is scarcely a village of any consequence by the wayside—apart from Scaling—and at its loneliest part the strange hill of Freeboro rises from the desolate moor like a presiding moor deity. One can sympathize with the nervous motorist who crossed it in a blizzard and said that the only jolly thing that he saw was the Jolly Sailor inn near Moorsholm, one of the very few inns on this bleak road. There is a totally different atmosphere about this road and the other famous moorland road from Whitby to Pickering, which is so full of variety and colour.

At Barton Howl, however, which is about seven miles from Whitby on this Guisborough road, an interesting experiment in land reclamation is taking place under the National Agricultural Advisory Service. An area of about nine acres of rough moorland has been ploughed out with a Canadian prairie-buster, and grass has been sown. So successful has this been, that cattle are already grazing there, and much valuable information is expected to be gained during this five-year experiment. At several farms in the vicinity, farmers are making their own attempts to reclaim moorland with the help of Government subsidies. Great changes, therefore, may occur on this desolate stretch of moorland during the next few years.

CLEVELAND SUPERSTITIONS

You will never understand the Cleveland country unless you recognize the strange quality of mystery and melancholy that invests the remote valleys and high moors. Baysdale, Westerdale, Kildale and Danby moors all reveal it in different ways.

It is surprising that these lonely and mysterious moors have not yet produced a Cleveland *Wuthering Heights*—though one day they may well do so. What they have done is to give us a rich harvest of dialect poetry, including two of the finest traditional dialect poems in the language, 'The Cleveland Lyke-wake Dirge' and 'A Dree Neet'. Nothing so well expresses

the haunting quality of the Cleveland moors and of the faith and superstitions of the people as these strange dirges that used to be chanted over
the corpses at funerals in the remoter dales.

The real home of witchcraft was in the North Riding, especially in
Cleveland. Cleveland fairly bristled with witches and sorcerers, familiars,
wise men and hobs, boggarts and fairies, a generation or so ago. One of the
favourite tricks of the witches was to cast a spell on the cattle so that the
cows gave no milk. It makes one's hair stand on end even today to hear old
people tell of the goings-on in these lonely dales. The witches were minions
of the devil. The wise men were a kind of wizard, part sorcerer and
magician, part conjurer, but not in league with the devil. Some of them
were nothing more than cow doctors or leeches, with a lot of cunning
'magic' and fanciful 'rites' thrown in. Such was the famous Wise Man of
Stokesley, who made a good thing out of the witches' spells.

Some did straightforward bits of detective work. The wise men worked
especially on the credulity of their clients, and, by dint of cross-examination
and their own paid helpers, often performed what seemed like miracles to
the simple countryfolk of those days.

The North Riding is (or was) full of such superstitions. Fairies and mis-
chievous little hobs—some of whom did all the work while the dairymaids
slept—were always popping up. Fairies apart, there are still plenty of old
traditions lingering here and there in these dales: bee customs (or notions)
for example. When the master of the house died, it used to be the custom
for the bees to be 'put into mourning'. Strips of black material were carried
solemnly to the beehives and placed round them. Three taps with a key
were given and each hive was solemnly informed that the master was
dead. Sometimes a tray of food was carried to the bees, and they were
always clearly informed that the master was dead and that so-and-so was
the new master—and 'we hope you will be content to accept him'. But
underlying this superstitious belief in witches and fairies, there was a deep
religious faith in Cleveland that finds expression in its folk-songs and
dialect poems.

It is to the dialect writers that one must turn to get a real insight into this
fascinating corner of Yorkshire. Such rollicking rhymes as that of 'The
Race for the Bridal Garter' and 'Bridal Bands', or 'Riding t'Stang', 'Elphi
Bandy-legs', 'The Dead Pig', the famous 'Hunt o' Yatton Brig', and such
pieces as the 'Hagmena Song' reveal this aspect of Cleveland best.

Readers who are interested in this fascinating topic should turn to
F. W. Moorman's classic collection of *Yorkshire Dialect Poems*, Richard

Blakeborough's *Wit, Character, Folklore and Customs of the North Riding of Yorkshire*, and to Canon Atkinson's *Forty Years in a Moorland Parish*. Blakeborough's dialect poems and stories will be remembered as long as Cleveland exists. His son, John Fairfax Blakeborough, who lives in Westerdale, in the heart of the Clevelands, carries on the tradition, and he has deservedly won a secure niche for himself with his writings on Cleveland life and humour, and on the Cleveland Bay.

THE CLEVELAND BAY

Among horse-loving people, Cleveland is probably best known as the home of the famous Cleveland Bay breed which has never been so popular as it is today. This beautiful type of pure-bred horse is known far beyond the confines of its native county, for Cleveland Bays have been exported to almost every country in the world; and there are Cleveland studs in America founded by the Sterrikers of Pickering.

The Cleveland Bay has a long and distinguished history on the farm, as a carriage horse and on the hunting-field. The original Cleveland Bays were bred in North Yorkshire as far back as the Middle Ages. They were a strong, active, clean-legged horse much favoured by 'chapmen', and also for agricultural and pillion work. They were recognized as the finest type of horse for general farm work, and their fame extended far and wide.

From this original type, the coach horse and the hunter were evolved by crossing Cleveland with large-boned, upstanding thoroughbreds. As hunters, too, they excel, and they are very much in evidence at point-to-points.[1]

Perhaps the best place to see these beautiful animals is at one of the North Riding horse and agricultural shows, such as the delightful little show which is held at Egton in early September.

STOKESLEY

Stokesley (pronounced 'Stowsla'), the metropolis of the west part of Cleveland and the administrative centre of the Stokesley Rural District (which embraces thirty-nine parishes), is the key town. All roads converge on this delightful old market town, which seems to me to express the spirit and character of Cleveland better than any other. Its spacious main street must

---

[1] Recently, the Cleveland Bay Horse Society, which was founded in 1884 has published an interesting pamphlet setting out the history and evolution of this famous breed: *The Cleveland Bay Horse: Its History and Importance Today*, by J. Fairfax Blakeborough, and Capt. L. Edmunds of the famous Cholderton C.B. Stud.

The ancient church at Ingleby Greenhow. The village stands on the edge of some glorious Cleveland scenery.

The Market Cross at Guisborough: a corner of the ancient capital of Cleveland.

be one of the broadest in the whole Riding, and always surprises as one crosses the bridge over the little River Leven and comes upon it round the corner unawares. It is so vast, so picturesque, so unexpected in this flat stretch of country, so obviously made for markets and fairs. Some of the old Georgian houses, too, are very pleasing, and the whole town has the appearance of having been laid out in an ampler age. One has only to see Stokesley to realize that it belongs to the legendary Cleveland of old—of witches and wise men, and of real, old-fashioned country jollifications. The church and manor house fit it to perfection, and the old inns complete the picture.

You can almost see the country lads lined up outside the church after a wedding, and racing for the bridal garter, in the lusty days when it was the custom for the men to run from the church to the bride's home; the first man there could claim the right to carry the bride over the threshold into the bridal chamber and there remove her garter.

And you can see the same men, on some other occasion, 'Riding t'Stang' and administering stern justice to some unfortunate spouse accused of mal-treating his wife.

They do not, of course, practise these ancient rites today; perhaps it would be better if they did. They were better than the divorce courts. To-day Stokesley looks a little quiet and joyless; neighbouring Stockton has taken much of its former business. But it comes into its own again on market days and on the day of Stokesley Show (held on the third Thursday in September), which is the largest agricultural show in the North of England.

There are still plenty of old characters about the streets. One old bearded man who looked a born poacher, came up to me with a couple of rabbits dangling over his arm, and held forth with great indignation, in an almost incomprehensible vernacular, because a policeman had just asked him for his identity card, and suspected him of poaching. 'Me!' he said. 'Me a poacher! And I paid 5s 6d for these b——y rabbits i'Guisborough!' He went on for quite ten minutes protesting his innocence—and looking very guilty.

GREAT AYTON

Great Ayton, the near neighbour and rival of Stokesley, though it has to-day the larger population (2,309), looks even quieter than Stokesley. It has a beautiful setting under the Cleveland Hills, with Roseberry Topping conspicuous in the background and the River Leven flowing through the

K

middle of it. Its most striking feature is the High Green, on one side of which stands the famous Friends School which has produced some fine scholars.

But it is the little schoolroom round the corner (now a museum with a commemorative tablet on the wall) that produced the most famous Cleveland man of them all—Captain Cook, the greatest navigator England has known, who sailed round the world, explored Australia and New Zealand, and made many remarkable discoveries. I had the utmost difficulty in getting inside the rather disappointing museum when I was last in Ayton, since the key is kept a long way 'round the corner' and the caretaker was out. However, it was worth waiting half an hour merely to climb the stairs and to get inside the room where the young Cook learned the three R's.

Cook, the son of a farm labourer, was born at another Cleveland village a few miles to the north—Marton, near Middlesbrough—and attended school at Ayton. The cottage in which he lived with his parents during his Ayton schooldays was dismantled and taken to Australia, where it was rebuilt. Why this vandalism was ever allowed baffles me. If ever houses should have been jealously cherished where they stood, they were surely Cook's cottages at Marton and at Ayton. But the fact that the schoolroom is also so inadequately preserved and documented suggests that neither village appreciates the great sailor at his true worth.

CHAPTER TWENTY-FOUR

Some Cleveland Villages

CARLTON-IN-CLEVELAND, AND OTHERS

AROUND Stokesley there are several striking Cleveland villages. One of my favourites is Carlton-in-Cleveland, which lies just off the main Stokesley-Thirsk road, among the foothills of the main Cleveland chain.

Carlton is one of the loveliest villages in North Yorkshire. It stands on a spur of the hills, with the bold escarpment of the high Clevelands beyond. Its setting is altogether delightful and the little village itself has a gracious charm. Its street is bordered by picturesque cottages and old houses, including a delightful Queen Anne manor house, the old Rectory, two inns and other dignified houses.

The first building to catch the eye as one approaches Carlton-in-Cleveland from Stokesley is the beautiful new church, built in the style of the fourteenth century. New churches and old villages seldom mix, but the church of St Botolph at Carlton fits perfectly into the scene. It was built towards the end of last century by the late Canon Kyle, the famous sporting parson, farmer and publican. The church is a fine memorial to his genius and good taste. His grave can be seen in the beautifully-kept churchyard.[1]

At the farther end of this enchanting village, the road forks, one arm going straight over the Clevelands to Chop Gate in Bilsdale, and affording marvellous views of the hills and the plain; the other turns towards the neighbouring village of Faceby, beneath Whorl Hill (once the lair of a dragon, according to local tradition). From Faceby the lovely valley of Scugdale can be explored.

Ancient Whorlton, on Whorl Hill, a curious conical mound, has the ruins of a historic castle and of a gloomy church buried in an avenue of yews. Whorlton, indeed, is entirely composed of ruins, which I found depressing, but the scenery is delightful. Swainby, a long, straggling village, just below the hill, is a lively little place, without any particular

[1] And see pages 172-4.

claims to beauty, but it has the practical value of rejoining the main Stokesley road.

Another village that appeals strongly to me is Hutton Rudby, a few miles north of Swainby. This is one of those pretty villages that is an instant delight to the eye. It is more spacious than Carlton and is built round a wide green common on a little hill, with an avenue of trees. I like its mellow old cottages and Wheatsheaf inn at the bottom, and the old crenelated house alongside. Its beautiful old church stands detached from the village in the vale below, on the banks of the River Leven.

ON LOCKED CHURCHES

I had heard much of one particular church and was disappointed to find the door resolutely locked in the middle of the morning. No doubt there was an adequate reason for this, but nothing is more disappointing to the interested tourist than a locked church. The days when one had leisure enough to find the caretaker, sexton, vicar or whatnot, and return to the remote church again, look round and then return the key, are gone for ever, I fear, and I suggest that all country churches should be open for visitors and worshippers at all times. Several of the churches mentioned in this book were only entered after a determined search and struggle of this kind. At one church I visited—on a quiet road—I asked the housekeeper at the rectory why the church was kept locked.

'We keep it locked because it isn't safe really,' she replied. 'You never know who is coming' (looking at me darkly).

'But may I have the key?' I asked.

'What do you want it for?' she asked, still dubious.

'To see the church!' I replied, rather shortly, I fear, for the whole business of struggling in vain to open the door, finding the vicarage, waiting ages for someone to answer the bell and getting back to the church after my colloquy with the suspicious caretaker, had taken half an hour of precious time. It quite spoilt the visit to the church for me. It was not a specially striking church; I have seen many more beautiful ones open to the public. There did not seem anything likely to tempt miscreants except, perhaps, the offertory boxes, but that is a risk that all churches must run, and surely it is better to keep the churches open and used—and risk it— rather than to keep them locked—and empty. It is an odd commentary on modern times if we dare not keep the churches open lest a robber enters.

At other churches, the door handles are so tricky or stiff that one comes away with a feeling of frustration, thinking they too are locked; and it doesn't help a lot when one is told afterwards that the church was not really locked at all, only 'very difficult' to enter unless you know the secret of turning of the handle or the trick of lifting the sneck. Many of the locks do not appear to have been oiled since the sixteenth century.

I am a strong man and I am prepared to wrestle with any lock or door handle until it yields or bursts—but imagine a timid, frail woman wanting to enter the church to say her prayers! It's enough to shake anybody's faith!

THREE INGLEBYS AND AN ANCIENT CHURCH

Ingleby Arncliffe and Ingleby Cross, on the main Stokesley road near Swainby, have the advantage of fine surrounding scenery, and both have interesting features.

Ingleby Greenhow, which lies between Stokesley, Kirby and Kildale, on the edge of some of the finest scenery in the Clevelands, is the pick of the bunch. Until recently, the fine Elizabethan manor house and the whole estate was in the hands of the family of Lord de L'Isle and Dudley, one of whose ancestors was the famous Sir Philip Sidney. Recently, alas, the estate came on the market. The ancient Norman church stands isolated from the village, surrounded by great trees, and although partly rebuilt in 1741, it is full of curious carvings, strange dragons, basilisks, pigs, whales, and the like. Traces of the original seventh-century Anglican church and parts of a Danish foundation remain. Tusks of boars were found under the floor of the nave. The two bells are among the oldest three in Yorkshire and were cast about 600 years ago. It is strange how some old churches retain their ancient atmosphere more than others. This church of St Andrew always moves me profoundly, despite its various renovations.

The Dudley Arms in the little village above the church has often ministered to my needs after a day on the hills. Anyone wishing to explore some of the highest and loneliest moors in the North Riding should take the road from Ingleby Greenhow up Turkey Nab, over Ingleby Moor and Burton Howe to Bloworth, and over to Bransdale—or to Gillamoor and Farndale.

CHAPTER TWENTY-FIVE

Roseberry Topping and Guisborough

GUISBOROUGH, the ancient capital of Cleveland, lies between Great Ayton and Saltburn, in the ironstone region. If one approaches Guisborough from the Whitby road, the various mineshafts and slag-heaps in the vicinity reveal the iron mines, but from Great Ayton the main road runs alongside the north-eastern ramparts of the Clevelands and affords a fine close-up view of Roseberry Topping, Easby Hill and Cook's Monument.

Admirers of Cook should climb 'monument hill' and see the obelisk on top, which bears an inscription reading:

In Memory of Captain Cook
The celebrated circumnavigator
A man in nautical knowledge inferior to none.
In Zeal, Prudence and Energy superior to most.
Regardless of Danger, he opened an Intercourse
with the Friendly Isles and other parts of the
Southern Hemisphere
Born at Marton in 1728
Massacred at Owhyee 1779

They might perhaps have added that Cook also 'opened an intercourse' with Australia and New Zealand.

There are wonderful views of the Clevelands from the monument (1,064 feet) and even better views from the summit of the neighbouring sugarloaf hill of Roseberry Topping (1,057 feet) which really is the monarch of the chain, even though it is by no means the highest point. Its isolated position on the fringe of the Cleveland hills, and its peculiar pie shape, like a miniature Mont Blanc, make it conspicuous all over north-east Yorkshire. A footpath through the fields takes one up the grassy slopes to the massive rocks on top. The easy ascent does not prepare one for the precipitous slab of sheer rock to the foot of the peak far below on the farther side. From the summit, Roseberry Topping has the majesty of a real mountain and there is something peculiarly of Cleveland about it, for not only does

Roseberry Topping figure in many of the old legends, rhymes and plays, but it does seem to express the very spirit of this mysterious country. I like the description of it by Margery Moorpout, a character in John Reed's play, *The Register Office*: 'It's t'biggest hill i' all Yorkshire. It's aboon a mahle an' a hauf heegh, an' as cawd as ice at t'top i' t' yattest day i' summer, that it is!'

From the summit, one can see the ships on the North Sea, the smoke belt of Tees-side, and all the far-spreading country of the Cleveland Hills.

After these high delights, Guisborough comes somewhat as an anti-climax. The approach to it from this direction is flat and uninteresting, and the new suburbs and long main street, smirched a little by the industrial air, lack the charm of Stokesley and Yarm today. The surrounding iron mines and blast furnaces have left their mark on it. How marvellous this part of Cleveland must have been before the iron mines were opened! But there are some delightful old houses, and the cobbled verges and trees make a pretty picture. Then, as one comes to the farther end of Westgate, where the road climbs slightly towards the church and the priory, ancient Guisborough comes into its own. This particular corner of the town, with its old market cross, its inns and its sturdy church on the hill above, always excites me. It is pure Cleveland. The rebuilt church of St Nicholas is spacious and full of interest, and it has one exceptionally famous monument, the finely carved Bruce cenotaph of blue marble which used to rest in the priory. This noble tomb was built to commemorate Robert Bruce, claimant to the Scottish throne, who was buried in the priory in 1294.

Of the great Augustinian priory, founded by Robert de Brus in 1119 and one of the greatest conventual houses in England, only the east end of the choir of the church, the gatehouse and a vaulted fragment remain. But is there such another East window anywhere? It is one of the most solemn and beautiful things I have ever seen: a prayer in stone.

The remains of the priory stand in the grounds of Guisborough Hall, the property of Lord Guisborough. In the beautiful gardens adjacent to the ruins, there is a remarkable grove of lime trees, possibly used as a burial ground for the monks. Nearby is a huge horse-chestnut tree, said to be the largest (that is, having the biggest spread) in England: it is over 600 years old.

Guisborough was once famous for its alum mines, originally discovered by Sir Thomas Challoner, ambassador to the Spanish Court, who was said to have stolen the secret for its manufacture from the Pope. In the nineteenth century, it enjoyed new prosperity from its iron mines and later with its steel foundries, but the iron and steel trade have now moved to Tees-side and to the coast.

Pease is a name that figures largely in Cleveland history, and the late Sir Alfred Edward Pease, Bart., of Pinchinthorpe, Guisborough, was one of the greatest modern authorities on Cleveland customs. His Introduction to his *Dictionary of the Dialect of the North Riding of Yorkshire* contains some fascinating memories, while the dictionary itself is indispensable to any student of the North Riding.

Between Guisborough and Redcar there are several places of interest to the tourist, including Kirkleatham, Upleatham, and Skelton Castle.

CHAPTER TWENTY-SIX

Kirkleatham and Upleatham

KIRKLEATHAM

KIRKLEATHAM, two miles south of Redcar, is a remarkable village, and up to a couple of years ago was a famous show-place with its great hall, King's House, church, mausoleum, Lord Mayor's hospital and magnificent museum. Now, alas, Kirkleatham has been stripped of many of its glories, and when I saw it recently there was an air of sadness and decay over it. The change came about in 1948, on the death of the last owner of the hall, when the estate was sold and many of the treasures dispersed. Today the whole village seems rather like a museum and memorial to a vanished age. The massive, battlemented hall, the ancestral home of the Turner family (and later of the Newcomens and Vansittarts) was unoccupied when I called, and looked strangely desolate; but when I peeped into the spacious stables I was delighted to find that they were full of thoroughbreds, having recently been rented by Mr Calvert, of Redcar. An obliging groom showed me some of *his* treasures; they were, indeed, the only really living things I saw in Kirkleatham and they seemed perplexed to find themselves in such unfamiliar quarters.

Empty houses, especially ancestral homes with great traditions like Kirkleatham, are strangely depressing to the spirit when they stand mournful and forsaken in their parks, surrounded by immemorial trees. How much better they looked when they were to be seen in all their glory, full of happy people and the sound of music and laughter never far away!

Opposite the hall is the church, rebuilt in 1762 in the classical style by Cholmley Turner and containing many memorial tablets. The most interesting feature of all is the massive Renaissance mausoleum which dwarfs the church. It is entered through a dark doorway near the chancel, and I found the dim religious light of the late autumn afternoon, and the marble tombs, stone coffins, effigies and statues all round me rather overpowering. It reminded me vividly of the death-chamber scene in *Romeo and Juliet*. The octagonal mausoleum is an astonishing piece of work. It was built by the redoubtable Cholmley Turner in 1740 (and rebuilt from the same stones in 1839) as a memorial to his son, Marwood William Turner, but other earlier and later members of the Turner-Newcomen families are also buried or commemorated there, including the great Sir William Turner who became Lord Mayor of London in 1669. It was he who subsequently built and endowed the hospital in the village. This is another remarkable building and, in some ways, the most interesting of all. It was built by Sir William as a home for aged men and women and also as a school for young boys and girls, and everything about the building emphasizes this dual purpose and its occupation by the two sexes. I like the statues of the two children on the roof and of the old man and woman at the gates. The chapel, which forms the centrepiece, was rebuilt by Cholmley Turner in 1742. It has a marble floor, a magnificent gilt candelabrum, twin galleries for the boys and girls, and two splendid gilded chairs presented to Sir William by Charles II. Its most striking feature, however, is the lovely Italian stained glass window through which the light streams with quite astonishing brilliance. The central design in vivid colours depicts the Adoration of the Kings; the Madonna and Child are especially beautiful. Side panels show Sir William Turner in his mayoral robes and his brother John in legal attire. I found the whole window and chapel enchanting.

It seems a great pity that the treasures of the museum have now been scattered, but even so there is still much to see and admire in this remarkable village of Kirkleatham.

UPLEATHAM

Upleatham, a few miles to the south, has none of the glories of the sister-village, though it has a long, exciting history and was once the home of the famous Robert de Brus. Today it has the distinction of possessing one of the tiniest churches in England. This is really a remnant of the original twelfth-century church which was once the largest church in the district. The church stands isolated at the entrance to the village, and, with its tiny tower and foreshortened nave, makes a quaint and pathetic picture in its little God's Acre.

It is now used as a museum (and mortuary chapel) and contains a few stone coffin lids, but its main interest today is its smallness and history.

The nineteenth-century church in the village contains an exquisite twelfth-century font taken from the older church—a rare specimen of finely carved stone work.

SKELTON CASTLE

Skelton-in-Cleveland, near Brotton, the administrative centre of an urban district and a typical Cleveland ironstone town, has two churches—a plain eighteenth-century church near the castle, not now used, and a splendid nineteenth-century church which seems to dominate the whole country-side. This is noteworthy for its fine tower and spirited modern west window in vivid colours.

But it is the castle that is the chief attraction in Skelton today. Rebuilt in the eighteenth century, it is surrounded by beautiful parklands, all the more remarkable because Skelton is near the heart of the ironstone country. Originally the home of the Bruces and the Fauconbergs, it has been in the possession of the Stevenson-Wharton family for many generations—and Wharton is a name that means much in Cleveland story. One of the best-known members of the family was the eccentric Mrs Margaret Wharton, who earned the soubriquet of 'Peg Pennyworth' owing to her habit of 'purchasing penn'orths of whatever comestible she fancied'. She was both generous and parsimonious at the same time, and in this she was not perhaps alone!

Perhaps some of her eccentricity was inherited by her relative, the famous John Hall Stevenson, author of *Crazy Tales* and *Makarony Fables*—the 'Eugenius' of Sterne's *Tristram Shandy*. Sterne and Stevenson were bosom cronies and Sterne was a frequent visitor to Skelton Castle. Many were the uproarious evenings these two eccentrics enjoyed together, and many the rhymes they dashed off between their cups. Fletcher tells a tale of Stevenson's aversion—which amounted almost to a mania—to the east wind. 'He would never leave his bed so long as the weathercock showed that the breath of heaven came from that objectionable quarter.' This was very trying for his guests, so one day Sterne bribed a boy to climb to the weathercock and fix it firmly to the west! Stevenson got up immediately —and stayed up for several days on end!

A fine portrait of John Hall Stevenson occupies the place of honour in the dining-room of the castle today among a galaxy of other Hall Steven-sons and Whartons. The present castle was built just after John Hall Stevenson's death in 1785, and it is an imposing pile.

Many of the Wharton family have played an important part in York-shire history and sport. The present squire of Skelton is the popular master of the Cleveland Hunt, one of the most sporting packs in the country.

CHAPTER TWENTY-SEVEN

Eskdale

THE ESK

THE ESK is the guardian river of Cleveland and it is touched by all the rugged beauty of that wild countryside. Rising in the heart of Westerdale, it flows through the majestic valley of Eskdale to its ultimate haven at Whitby. There are stupendous roads on either bank throughout most of its course, and often the river is buried deep in the valley while the rigg roads soar high above.

To get a complete picture of Eskdale, I would suggest a tour from Whitby to Ruswarp and Sleights and thence along Eskdaleside to Grosmont, and along the private (toll) road to Egton Bridge—a beautiful village much favoured by anglers for its salmon fishing, and by holiday-makers for its enchanting surroundings. From Egton Bridge the road continues to the village of Glaisdale by way of the famous Limber Hill, at the foot of which is to be seen the romantic Beggars Bridge—a beautiful old packhorse bridge, overshadowed, alas, by two hideous iron bridges. (For walkers, the well-known footpath through Arncliffe woods is, of course, the obvious approach to Glaisdale.) Then over the shoulder of the hill to scattered Lealholm—a delightful Cleveland village—and on through Houlsike—past another famous packbridge, called Duck Bridge—to Danby, Castleton, Westerdale, and to Commondale, returning by the Guisborough-Whitby road.

Even this route—like most prescribed routes—misses many of the highlights of Eskdale, which can only be explored on foot.

Apart from the picturesque stone cottages and farms, some of the buildings reveal specimens of curious 'carved heads' which are to be found occasionally in Cleveland and Ryedale. Some of the Cleveland heads are attributed to John Castillo, the Cleveland poet, who was also a mason, and examples can be seen at Glaisdale, Lealholm, Fryup—and elsewhere. They are not, apparently, of any great age, but they are an interesting link with an old tradition.

Glaisdale village does not give one any idea of the valley of Glaisdale itself which debouches southward from Eskdale proper far into the moors beyond. There is a motor road into Glaisdale, but it comes to an end near Glaisdale Head which, again, can only be reached on foot, like the rigg road beyond, which continues over the watershed to Rosedale.[1] This watershed is full of exciting possibilities for walkers, as the one-inch map will show.

I would advise the motorist to take the alternative fork between Glaisdale village and Lealholm through Fryup, which will give him a taste of both Great and Little Fryup dales, as well as of the delectable hamlet itself. This is pure North Riding. Do not ask me why it is called Fryup, or why near Fryup Hall you will pass Fairy Cross Plain, because, disregarding all Scandinavian origins and myths, I can only tell you that when the early Yorkshire settlers came to these parts they became famous for their expert manipulation of the frying-pan, especially in the matter of ham and eggs, which was their staple diet. Wherever the stockpot was low, they said 'we will have a fry-up today', and their great and little fry-ups became so famous that the hamlet and the dales adopted the obvious name, by which they have been known ever since. As for the fairies, these dales are full of fairies, and here at Fairy Cross Plain they hold their revels as all true believers in fairies can testify.

Past Fryup, the road swings round the foot of Danby Rigg to Danby Castle, once the seat of the proud Latimers and Nevilles, and now half ruined castle and half farm. The fine farmhouse is built on to the ruins, and cattle tread where once the lords and ladies walked. Even in ruins, Danby has a proud and noble look, as befits its ancient lineage.[2] Catherine Parr, the last wife of the much-married Henry VIII (and herself four times a bride), married the third Lord Latimer for her second husband, and shortly after his demise she was at Court (1543) where she 'received the attentions of both Sir Thomas Seymour and of the King'. There are records of her dress bills being paid out of the Exchequer on the King's orders.

The marriage was solemnized in the upper oratory at Hampton Court in July, 1543. Henry VIII died in 1547 and Catherine, who was now thirty-four years old, married Sir Thomas Seymour as her fourth and last spouse four months later, but died two years afterwards in childbirth.

---

[1] There is a rough road, possible for determined motorists, from Egton Bridge, past High Hamer farm into Rosedale.

[2] The best account of Danby Castle is to be found in the late Canon Atkinson's book, *Forty Years in a Moorland Parish;* though Thomas Horsfall's *The Manor of Well and Snape* presents a fascinating picture of the Latimer family.

The arms of the Nevilles may still be seen on the medieval Duck bridge near Danby Castle. The panelled room of the castle is still preserved and contains a fine oak chest.

DANBY-IN-CLEVELAND

The delightful village of Danby-in-Cleveland—or Dale End, as it is also called—stands at the crossroads, a couple of miles beyond the castle, with pretty Ainthorpe nearby. The roads hereabouts are confusing, and one can easily take a wrong turning; but there is no mistaking Danby itself. It has about it an air of finality as if one has reached journey's end, even though the twisting road continues to Castleton and Westerdale and the wild moors beyond. All the roads seem to converge near the cosy little Duke of Wellington inn, and it is here, or at the neighbouring Fox and Hounds at Ainthorpe, that I like to call a halt and take a leisurely look at this fascinating piece of country.

Danby Dale (like Glaisdale) cuts deep into the moors to the south, and unless one penetrates into the dale one never gets near the true Danby country. The church stands two miles up-dale from the village (through Ainthorpe). The famous rectory is midway between the village and the church, while Danby Beacon, with its commanding radar station, which can be seen for miles around, stands on the high moors north-east of the village. But it is the church, with its sturdy fifteenth-century tower, which dominates Danby Dale, and it is the spirit of the late Canon Atkinson, who was vicar in this lonely parish for fifty-three years, which pervades it. His grave is in the lovely churchyard, which John Castillo, the poet of Cleveland, described as the most romantic and poetical of any in Cleveland.

Nobody has better understood the character of this remote Cleveland countryside and its people than the old Canon, who ministered so lovingly to his flock and wrote so finely about the history and folklore of this dale. His *Forty Years in a Moorland Parish* is the classic book on Cleveland, and this, and all his other scholarly books, was published by his good friend and neighbour, Macmillan, whose house stands farther up the dale.

CASTLETON AND THE MOORS

Castleton, two miles beyond Danby, is a large, grim-looking, stone village, notable rather for its situation than for its beauty. It is full of inns (always a strong recommendation to me) and it stands at the crossroads with its back to the hills, surrounded by magnificent scenery. To the north, a fierce road climbs up to Commondale or the Guisborough road. Another road soars to Kildale. But the roads that appeal most strongly to me are those to Westerdale and Baysdale, and one over Castleton Rigg.

Westerdale and the wild country of Baysdale beck, with Baysdale Abbey farm on the site of an old Cistercian monastery, are really in the heart of the Cleveland Hills, and for walkers this country is sheer delight, with rough moorland crossings to Kildale and Bransdale.

CASTLETON RIGG

The road that I would recommend to motorists is the one that turns southward at the top of Castleton village and runs over Castleton Rigg to Ralph Cross and the dales country, gradually climbing to 1,400 feet near Ralph Cross.

This is one of the key roads to this spectacular part of Cleveland. It cuts clean across the high moors and commands a wonderful panorama of dale and moor, with such landmarks as Roseberry Topping and Monument Hill, and the distant sea-coast, plainly visible in clear weather.

Seen from this height, Danby Dale really comes to life, and one can appreciate not only the strange isolation of the old church, but also the scattered farms that cling to the steep shoulder of the dale almost to the watershed. This surely is one of the most idyllic dales of all: the kind of place a man dreams of retiring to after a lifetime in the cities. But a hundred years ago, when Canon Atkinson came here as a young man, it must have been much wilder and more inaccessible.

Ralph Cross (1,409 feet), a fine, tall stone cross of great age, marks the summit of the high pass and the junction of several roads: one which leads into the green valley of Rosedale, which widens into view at this point, another over Blakey Rigg to Hutton-le-Hole and Gillamoor, and the third an alternative fork through Farndale.

Any of these roads can be recommended. The Rosedale road has the merit of showing one the whole of Rosedale from the watershed to the village of Rosedale Abbey, and then on to Hartoft End, Cropton and the Pickering road (with offshoots to Rosedale 'Chimney' and over to Hutton-le-Hole and Lastingham).

The Blakey Rigg road keeps to the high moors for the longest distance, and connects with Gillamoor or Hutton-le-Hole.

The Farndale road enters Farndale at the village of Church Houses and then runs through this lovely valley towards Gillamoor, Hutton-le-Hole and Kirbymoorside.

For myself, I prefer the road that sticks to the high moors for as long as possible. I remember once motoring with a lady and gentleman over the Ralph Cross road on a rather dull summer's day. They had spent much of their life in foreign countries, in the Diplomatic Service, and when I came to the fork I turned towards Farndale, feeling sure that my companions would prefer the softer pastoral scenery of the dale; but I was mistaken. The lady was Yorkshire-born, and she was on her mettle immediately. 'Why are we leaving the moors?' she asked through the bleak wind. I explained the reason for my choice. 'Oh, please, let us stick to the ridge as long as we can. I love moors best, no matter what sort of a day it is!'

My heart warmed to her, because I felt just the same. If you love moors, a high moorland road always appeals more than a road through the dale, no matter how beautiful the dale may be; and Farndale *is* a lovely dale. To some, moors are sullen and repellent except when the sun shines and the heather is in bloom. To others, the more bleak and inclement the day, the more they love the wild 'tops'. One of the great attractions of this North Riding country is that one can indulge either taste so easily in the same district.

On a clear day there is no difficulty about finding one's way over these moors so long as one keeps to the main roads or defined tracks. The difficulties begin when one diverges from the roads and follows some seductive track in doubtful weather. If mist suddenly descends, or a storm breaks, the moors that had seemed so familiar and friendly assume quite a different aspect. They become menacing and dangerous. Landmarks disappear from the horizon and a writhing mist rubs everything out. Here in the Clevelands, mists sometimes descend with astonishing swiftness, as I know to my cost. It is at such times that one blesses such prominent old monuments as Ralph Cross.

Just beyond Ralph Cross, on the Blakey Rigg road, there is a white-washed wayside inn called the Lion, which stands out like a beacon in a storm. More than once I have stumbled inside it, drenched to the skin and half crazy with moor-mist, and at such times I would not have exchanged its simple comforts for all the luxuries of the Ritz.

Generally, however, in the summer months at least, one can rely on clear skies and good visibility, and then the only problem is to choose which of these several enchanting roads to follow.

Ralph Cross, or 'Old Ralph', on Castleton Rigg, Westerdale, is one of the most famous of the old stone crosses of the North Riding. Wayfarers put coins in the cavity on the top of the cross for poor pilgrims.

Walking sheep on a moorland road. Hill-sheep farming forms the backbone of the agricultural life of the North Riding.

STONE CROSSES OF THE NORTH YORKSHIRE MOORS

These ancient stone crosses are a notable feature of the north-east York-shire moors, as are the numerous howes or barrows. The crosses often stand on or near a howe. Generally they are sited on high ground, on an old track, or near a junction of several ways, and one of their functions was to guide wayfarers over the moors, as well as to bless their comings and goings and to foster the Christian faith after the Dark Ages.

'The erection of crosses became general in this country soon after the introduction of Christianity amongst the Anglo-Saxons. They were with-out doubt in the first place erected as a terror to evil spirits and as a reminder of our holy religion . . .'[1]

An old treatise on the Ten Commandments printed in 1496 says:

'For this reason ben crosses by ye waye that when folke passynge see the crosses they sholde thynk on Hym that deyed on the Crosse, and worshyppe Hym above all things . . .'

They were used by Celtic missionaries to tell the story of the Gospel to the pagan tribes and they were thus the first churches. 'Near them the mendicants stationed themselves asking for alms, hence the saying: 'He begs like a cripple at a cross.'[1]

From the rude earlier crosses, more ornate crosses on steps originated, and from them the market crosses. Crosses were also erected to com-memorate great victories, and to mark resting places on the way to burial. Other uses were:

'Where four cross roads met; at the entrance to a village; and where during the perambulation of boundaries, the processionists rested and regaled themselves.

'They also marked the site of a murder or sudden death.

'They were used to denote the division of parishes and at the *turning* of public roads to serve as guides.'[1]

Many of these ancient crosses were ruthlessly destroyed after the Reforma-tion, but the North Riding, which kept the Faith, still cherishes quite a number of them.

The oldest and most famous is Lilla Cross, which stands near Lilla Howe on the highest part of Fylingdales moor (between the Saltersgate-Whitby and Whitby-Scarborough roads). Since the Army took possession

[1] T. H. Woodward, in *The Crosses on the North York Moors* (Horne & Son).

L

of these moors, the safety of this fine old cross has been imperilled, and it is proposed to move it to a place of safety. It seems a pity that this should be necessary, for this ancient cross has stood on this high ridge like a guardian angel for possibly a thousand years (one estimate places it as far back as the seventh century).

An old road from Whitby via Hawsker, and another from Whitby via Sneaton to Pickering, joined near Lilla Cross, and other old tracks to Robin Hood's Bay and Hackness and Saltersgate converge nearby.

The remains of several other crosses may still be found on these old ways, e.g. Postgate Cross, John Cross, York Cross, Ann's Cross, etc.

Malo Cross stands at the end of Whinny Nab, near Blakey Topping, whilst Mauley Cross stands just off the Roman road to Stape. Percy Cross is on Kildale Moor, and others are Swarth Howe Cross, Stump Cross, Bolton Cross, Job Cross. One of the most familiar crosses is the old Abbey Cross of Whitby Abbey, standing in the Abbey Plain.

RALPH CROSS

Ralph Cross, on Castleton Rigg, always attracts attention owing to its exceptional height (nine feet) and to the old custom of putting a coin in the cavity on the top for the next poor pilgrim. This is a very ancient tradition in this part of Yorkshire and one which I never like to neglect.

The tradition goes back to the days when needy pilgrims tramped over this wild countryside, long before the existing metalled roads were made, and to the time when tuppence was tuppence and would buy a hungry man a meal! If you are passing that way and reach up to the top of the shaft to place your coin, you will generally find a few coppers already there.

I remember once taking two somewhat sophisticated ladies over this road and stopping at the cross. Although they seemed impressed by the legend, they were inclined to scoff at its significance today. All the same, I persuaded them to leave silver coins instead of the usual pennies. Strangely enough, we had not gone more than a hundred yards beyond the cross when we passed the scruffiest-looking tramp I have ever seen! He looked like the genuine Old Man of the Mountains, with his long, shaggy beard, bushy eyebrows and wild, unkempt appearance. Although I have crossed this moorland road scores of times, I have never had the luck to meet such a pilgrim before or since. It was as if the hobs who frequent the region, and are jealous of its traditions, had conspired to produce him in this dramatic fashion. I thought I caught a twinkle in his roguish eyes when he saw my fair companions, as if he guessed that they at least would have honoured the old custom and left a few coppers for him; but I would have liked to have seen his expression when he climbed up to the cross and scooped up two shining shillings—and my two coppers! He cannot have gleaned such a harvest from 'Owd Ralph' before. It must have seemed like a miracle to him.

Actually, there are two Ralph Crosses near this point. The tall one by the roadside is Ralph Cross (East) or 'Old Ralph', and the other, about two hundred yards farther west in the heather is called Ralph Cross (West) or 'Young Ralph'.

There is a third cross about a quarter of a mile down the Rosedale Road. This is always freshly whitewashed. It has a very broad, almost square, stone for pedestal, and a rounded stone on top. It is called White Cross or, more popularly, 'Fat Betty', and looks indeed more like a snowman than a cross.

Interesting as these old stone crosses are from the point of view of history, even more striking is the way in which they seem to invest these particular moorlands with a strange, religious solemnity, not to be found elsewhere. The neighbouring howes and 'standing stones' seem to emphasize the pervading atmosphere; and if one walks over these moors at night, alone, the old Cleveland dirges take on a new significance:

> . . . When thoo frae hence away art pass'd
>   Ivvery neet an' all;
> To Whinnymoor thoo cooms at last,
>   An' Christ tak up thy saul.
>
> If ivver thoo gav' owther hosen or shoon,
>   Ivvery neet an' all;
> Clap thee doon an' put 'em on,
>   An' Christ tak up thy saul.
>
> But if hosen or shoon thoo nivver gav nean,
>   Ivvery neet an' all;
> T'whinnies'll prick thee sair to t' bean,
>   An' Christ tak up thy saul! . . .

CHAPTER TWENTY-EIGHT

North Yorkshire Sheep Farms

HILL-SHEEP FARMING forms the backbone of the agricultural life of the North Riding, particularly in Cleveland, the Dales, and on the north-east moorlands. One hears so much today about the commercial side of the woollen industry and about the fantastic prices recorded at the wool sales in Australia, that one might be forgiven for assuming that all sheep now carry a golden fleece, and that sheep farming is a sure way of making a quick fortune. This may or may not be true of some of the big Dominion sheep breeders, but it is certainly not true of the small North Riding hill farmers. It is the city dealers and brokers who make the fortunes, not the farmers. The price paid to the North Riding farmer for his fleeces is still very low—though the same wool soars in value where the dealers compete for it in the saleroom.

Most of the sheep on the North Yorkshire moors belong to the Blackface family. During the past century, the Blackface or Moor sheep have been gradually improved through intensive efforts, and three distinct varieties have evolved: the Scotch Blackface, the Rough Fell, and the Swaledale. Originally, the hardy Scotch Blackface was the most popular and vast numbers of this breed still live on the moors, but of recent years the pure-bred Swaledale has come into greater favour and seems to be gradually ousting the rough Blackface in popularity.

The Blackface Sheep Breeders' Association of North Yorkshire, originally founded in 1820 to counteract sheep-stealing, looks after the interests of the hill farmers and lays down strict rules and regulations concerning such matters as sheep marks, right of stray, 'heafed' or market values, close seasons, and so on. The Swaledale Sheep Breeders' Association plays a similar role for the pure-bred Swaledales, which are as carefully selected as attested cattle.

Anyone who is under the illusion that hill-sheep farming is simply 'dog and stick' farming, as it is sometimes called, and that any fool could make a living by it, should attend a meeting of one of these Associations and hear the dalesmen themselves talk about their sheep. Or he should visit one of the famous North Riding Shows, such as the Danby Agricultural Show, one of the best Blackface and Swaledale sheep shows in the North, or the popular Goathland sheep sales in October. These meetings are the best introduction to the local farmers and to the sheep they breed. Hill-sheep farming today is an exact science and requires years of arduous training and experience. Even the designation of the 'simple' marks by which the sheep are recognized are rather baffling to the layman. This is what the Association guide-book says of them:

> 'These marks explain themselves, with the possible exception of the pitch mark. It will be noticed that generally the ear mark comes first, the horn burn follows, then the pitch mark and the colour, red, blue or black, last. It may be as well to explain that in marking sheep horns the letters should be put on so that they can be read with the man and sheep facing one another; the far or right horn burn being read from the end of the horn towards the head and the near horn mark reads from the head towards the end of the horn. The lug mark is generally described as upper or under marked. When some sheep are said to be marked on the buttock and others on the hip, the same spot is meant. It is advisable to be particular about the exact spot and direction of both rud mark and the pitch. Allowance ought always to be made for the growth of the wool, on the lambs particularly, when pitch-marking. Care should be taken to put the top of the mark well up to the backbone.'

Typical marks are:

> 'J. Peirson, Hawthorn Hill: Near ear stoud; twice slit far; F.K. near horn; black on back.'
>
> 'R. Smailes, Manor Farm: Near ear underhalved and slit, stoud far; horn burn T.R.; pitch mark T.R.; rud along back.'
>
> 'J. W. Kirk: Near ear stoud and underbit, V upperbit far ear. J.J. both horns; rud back of head and on back.'

There are hundreds of these complicated marks in the Marks Book, and every hill farmer can recognize his own sheep and those of his neighbours for miles around, no matter how dirty and bedraggled they may appear to a stranger. But to the layman it is by no means easy to distinguish one sheep from another when crossing the high moors, apart from the fact that they will rarely let a stranger get close enough to them to examine their markings.

The sheep farmer seldom crosses the moor without his dog, and it is astonishing how adept these sheepdogs are at rounding up the scattered flock and doing precisely what their master requires with a minimum of whistling and fuss. This can be observed at most of the agricultural shows, where the sheepdog trials are always a popular attraction; but I prefer to see the dogs at work on the moors, in their natural surroundings. It is a delightful sight to watch them race up the steep fellside and send the flock stampeding across the heather to the shepherd. At one moment the sheep look immobile and ungainly in their long fleeces, but next minute they 'bound as to the tabors' sound' and go where the dog directs them.

These Blackface sheep are 'heafed' or 'hefted' (this is, bred) to the moors and spend their whole lives on the bleak 'tops', except for brief interludes at lambing time (often they lamb on the moors, too), and for shearing, dipping or in severe snowstorms, when they are brought down to the lowlands. But frequently snow falls unexpectedly in great depth, and hundreds of sheep are buried and lost. Some of them make their way down to the pastures on their own, or stray into a neighbouring farmer's lands and are returned later.

When the farm changes hands, the flock remains on the moors and passes to the new owner. They are the real assets of the hill-sheep farmer and the 'hefted' value of the flock is the most important factor in the sale.

Every farmer has his particular stint or stray on the surrounding moorlands. Sometimes it extends to some thousands of acres and entails the most arduous walking; often it is a relatively restricted stray of a few hundred acres. The astonishing thing is that the sheep know and recognize their own boundaries, though these are often very vaguely marked by a few stone stoups or a gully. Born and bred to their particular stray, 'heafed' to their own moors, they rarely stray far beyond their boundaries, though there are of course exceptions, and it is these wanderers that cause the hill farmer so much trouble. Periodically he rounds them up with the help of his dog and 'grounds' them on their own stint, and gradually the lambs learn to stick to their own territory.

'Heafted hoggets weeant mix wi' strange sheep,' one farmer told me. 'One flock hods another off but they maistlins stick to their own stray. Heaftin new stock is a varry ticklish job!'

Scores of times, when I have been crossing these moorland roads on bitter winter nights, I have come upon them lying down in the middle of the road which some of them seem to prefer to the green verge alongside, or to the heather itself. If one is walking, they do not trouble to move, and even if one is in a car, they blink at the headlights and rarely attempt to get up until the car has come to a standstill. But in the wild gales that blow with such fury over the moors you will see some of them huddling into the hollows under the rocks and high ridges, but rarely troubling to seek shelter in the valleys.

Like the curlews, the plovers and the grouse that lurk in the ling, or flash past overhead uttering their familiar cries, these sheep form an integral part of the moorland scene as they move slowly across the distant ridge, or huddle by a boulder and merge imperceptibly into the landscape. Though their attention may seem to be concentrated on their ceaseless search for the sweet morsels of green grassland and young heather shoots, they are watching every move of the lonely figure crossing their terrain, and if one approaches too close to their beat, they are away after their leader like a well-trained army in retreat; but only so far as to be out of immediate range.

Beautiful as lambs, ungainly as mature sheep, they are far more intelligent than the poets would bid us believe; and these moorland sheep are as hardy as any animal can be.

Recently I was coming over a lonely moorland road by car late at night, after a heavy fall of snow. Almost three miles from the sheltered village, the headlights picked out the ghostly figure of a farmer on a track above the road, driving a flock of Swaledale sheep from the moors. He told me that they had wandered from their usual stray on the high moors during the snow, to a valley seven miles away, where a neighbouring farmer had given them shelter, identified them by their marks and passed on the message to their owner. He had been over to collect them that evening, and also a ram from another farm. I persuaded my friend, much against his inclination, to step out of the bitter wind and get into the car and drive the last mile or so with me at crawling pace, while his wonderful dog kept the sheep together just in front of us and cajoled them on without attempting to molest them, as if it sensed their weariness. The sheep trudged on remarkably well, considering their long tramp home, but the old ram was clearly feeling the strain of the journey and lagged behind. I thought he was lame and wanted to put him in the car too, but my friend would not hear of it; he wasn't lame, he said, only tired, and the sooner he was in the sheepfold the better. To me, the sight of that old ram struggling gamely along the hard road in the freezing cold night summed up the drama of these brave hill sheep. They never give in until they die. And how many of them do die lonely deaths on the high moors! One need not go very far over the tops to come across the torn carcase of more than one of this hardy breed. I have seen them die in remote hollows with nobody to succour them, and I have seen what the foxes have done to them a day or so later.

Watching his ram stumbling over the hard road, my farmer friend could not bear to sit in the car any longer. He got out and turned his sheep into a gate that led to the outlying field of his farm. There was still a long way to go, but he preferred to go the hard way with them.

No, I doubt if many fortunes are to be made by this kind of sheep-farming; but it must bring its own reward. Most of the North Yorkshire hill farms are small—fifty or sixty acres of mixed land, but with right of stray over a few thousand acres of moorland which have to be covered on foot. You can see the farmers working from dawn to dark—and long after—by the aid of inadequate storm-lanterns, especially in the worst wintry weather and at lambing time. I have seen them carrying heavy bundles of fodder on their backs and climbing to the grazing ground on the high moors in the late winter months to get their ewes in good condition for lambing time. I doubt if the average city man could carry such a burden half a mile on the level without heart failure, but distance and steep ridges mean nothing to the tough hill farmers.

'I aim to be foddering 'em when t'seven o'clock train whistles up t'valley,' one said to me, and he did it every evening as regular as the clock. Then he would have a good hour's walk home in the dark and he would be lucky to finish work at his farm by nine p.m. after starting at dawn. I take my hat off to these North Riding sheep farmers; they are a remarkable breed of men and they shepherd a remarkable breed of sheep.

CHAPTER TWENTY-NINE

Village Life

THE contemporary life of the countryside is far more vividly portrayed in the regional country newspapers than in the national press. In the North Riding, weekly journals such as the *Whitby Gazette*, the *Malton Gazette*, the *Cleveland Standard*, the *Craven Herald*, the *Thirsk Times*, and many others, cover a wide area and have correspondents in all the chief villages, who see to it that no local event goes unnoticed.

In the moorland villages in and around Eskdale, for example, it is said that the *Whitby Gazette* (which is published on Fridays and has a circulation area of 1,500 square miles) has been read from cover to cover by Saturday morning, and woe betide the editor if he has allowed the slightest slip to enter into any of the reports. Every phase of country life is reflected in the ample pages of these newspapers, and even in these days of restricted news-print they contrive to publish broad, generous journals of many pages that seem to typify the broad acres they cover.

The average country reader turns first of all to the reports of the latest agricultural show and sheep sales, and of the latest meet—while the ladies turn first to the marriages and deaths, and then to the social events of the week. No one who wishes to enter fully into the life of the county can afford to neglect the local country newspapers; they help to keep the countryside alive and to keep remote villages in touch with their neighbours.

The monthly periodicals, too, such as the *Dalesman*, *Yorkshire Illustrated* and *Yorkshire Life*, all play their part in the life of the countryside, and also serve as a direct link between the town and country reader.

Without the country press, life in some of the scattered villages would be a very lonely affair indeed.

Here and there in this book, reference has been made to various aspects of village life; but to do justice to the multifarious activities (and characters) of any large North Riding village would call for another book of this size.

If space permitted, I should like to write something about the Old Men of the village who form, as it were, the backbone of the community and who continue to practise their arduous crafts at an age when most city

men have long since retired from the fray. Old Henry Jenkins, who was
the daddy of them all, was doubtless an exceptionally virile man, but in
almost any North Riding village you will find some ancient or other who
belongs to the same remarkable breed. Some of them are still dry-walling
at eighty and ninety; others are invariably to be found lending a hand at
harvest time and doing odd jobs about the farm that call for considerable
strength and skill, and then retiring to the village inn of an evening to play
darts or quoits (and sup ale) with the best of them! No village function is
complete without them, whether it be a cricket match, a harvest festival, a
wedding, a funeral, a flower show, a meet or a village concert. They are
part and parcel of the village life and of the North Riding scene, and without their shrewd, weatherbeaten faces, the village would not be the
same.

I should like, too, to say something about the women of the villages
who contrive in some remarkable way to look after their menfolk and
children, and keep their homes spotless throughout the year, and yet find
time to take part in a continuous round of social activities—and village
gossip!

But if the limits of space imposed on me by present paper restrictions
prevent me from dealing adequately with these facets of village life, I cannot conclude this brief interlude without paying tribute to two other
types of men who play such an important part in village affairs—the
country doctor and the country parson.

The revolutionary changes effected by the new National Health Service
in the towns have not yet made much outward difference in the life of the
country doctor, except to make him work still harder and to leave him no
time for a gossip. In that respect it is undoubtedly a misfortune, for in the
old days the doctor was not only expected to listen to the gossip of the
farm, but also to bring the latest news from the world beyond. In some
remote North Riding districts, the doctor's practice extends for fifty-odd
miles. In addition to the country town or village where he lives, he has to
serve a string of scattered hamlets and isolated farms up-dale. Quite apart
from his arduous routine round, he is liable to be called upon to render
assistance at one of these lonely outposts at any hour of the night in all
seasons of the year; and anyone familiar with this rugged hill country will
realize what that means. Some of these practices have been handed down
from father to son for several generations and the doctor knows every
family intimately for miles around. No praise could be too high for the
work they do every day under incredible difficulties, and it is a perpetual

mystery to me how they keep it up. It will be a pity if the silent revolution
that is taking place should destroy the friendly bonds that bind the country
doctor and his patients, and substitute a cold State service instead.

And finally, the parson. For the parson, too, plays a more important
role (on his miserable stipend) in the lives of his flock in remote country
parishes than he does in the cities, as anyone who has lived among such a
community for any length of time will know. He is expected to be at their
beck and call throughout the week for innumerable social activities which
play a much bigger part in rural life than they do in the towns. He has to
act as their friend and counsellor in all their personal problems and afflic-
tions, officiate at all the services and find something fresh to say twice or
thrice each Sunday, and to be able to deputize for any speaker who fails to
turn up for his lecture at the last minute. He must play his part at weddings
and funerals—and here again it must be noted that country weddings and
funerals are much more solemn and spectacular affairs, much more
intimate and at the same time more 'public' than are the everyday weddings and funerals in the cities. In a country village, everybody knows
everybody else, and everybody attends all the weddings and funerals,
either as an official guest or mourner, or else 'unofficially', which comes to
much the same thing. The vicar has to strike the right note of grief or joy
consonant with the occasion: not an easy thing to do 'regular away', as
they say in Yorkshire. In addition to all this (and much else!), if he should
happen to be in possession of one of those ancient churches which are so
frequently to be found in Yorkshire villages, he is expected to be an
authority on the history and architecture of the building, and on the
archæology of the district in general, and to be able to answer the questions
and satisfy the curiosity of a constant procession of visitors.

The North Riding has produced many remarkable clergymen (of all
denominations) and it has also been blessed (and sometimes embarrassed)
by famous literary churchmen from other parts of England, and delightful
antiquaries like Canon Atkinson of Danby-in-Cleveland, to whom reference
has been made elsewhere.

Richmond can claim several famous scholars of its own—men like
Canon Tate who became headmaster of Richmond's famous grammar
school and lived to see several of his pupils attain high honours. Eccentrics,
too, like the Rev. Wm. Towler Kingsley (a cousin of Charles Kingsley)
who held the living of South Kilvington, near Thirsk, for over fifty years,
have left their mark on the county. Kingsley was a great practical
joker and lived to the ripe age of 101. He was known as 'England's oldest

parson', and was also an accomplished wood-carver, as his church bears witness.

Two of the most famous literary parsons associated with the North Riding are, of course, Sydney Smith, co-founder and first editor of the *Edinburgh Review*, and Laurence Sterne, author of *Tristram Shandy*. Sydney Smith, the great wit and controversialist, spent twenty years of his vigorous life at Foston, a tiny village off the York-Malton road, as a tablet in the little church testifies. Sterne held the livings of Sutton-on-the-Forest, Stillington and, finally, of Coxwold where he wrote some of his most famous books and kept the whole neighbourhood on tenterhooks for a long time. Space, alas, does not permit me to do justice to any of these figures here, but I would like to pay a passing tribute to a more typical North Riding parson in the person of Canon Kyle, who held the living of Carlton-in-Cleveland from 1894 to his death in 1943. An Irishman by birth, the Rev. J. L. Kyle came to Carlton as a young man and became as popular in North Yorkshire as the Vicar of Bray, whose song he used to sing with great gusto. When he was presented to the living, Carlton had been without a church for about fifteen years. The previous incumbent—another remarkable man—had himself built a new church on the site of the old one largely by his own efforts, for he acted both as architect, stone-mason and builder, and raised the money by a vigorous campaign. The church was completed in two years and was described as 'the prettiest church in Cleveland'. It was opened in 1879, but within another two years it was destroyed by fire. Incendiarism was suspected and subsequently the vicar himself stood trial on the charge, but was acquitted for lack of evidence. Shortly afterwards, however, he was inhibited for another offence against the Church. The wretched man, having incurred the hostility of his parishioners, never lived this down, though he appears to have been innocent of the charge of setting fire to his own church. He remained in Carlton, a lonely, pitiable figure, until his death in 1894. The well-known novel *Peccavi* was written round his strange life.

When Parson Kyle came to Carlton in 1894-5, the church and beautiful village were therefore very much under a cloud. With commendable zeal, the sporting vicar set about the formidable task of raising yet more money to build another new church so soon after the last, and he engaged a first-class architect to prepare plans. This—the present dignified church—was completed and consecrated in October, 1897. It is a fine church with a tower, built of local stone in the fourteenth-century style of English Gothic. But the indefatigable vicar was not content until he had added a new peal of bells, including a 'wheat bell' subscribed for by Cleveland farmers in thanksgiving for a bumper harvest. Many other treasures followed, and then he set about the task of building the new schools.

At the same time, he not only farmed his own glebe most efficiently, but also acquired and worked another farm; he was an enthusiastic farmer and understood the spiritual and temporal needs of his farming parishioners the better for it. His sermons were full of pungent illustrations from the farm, of the earth earthy, and he often dropped into the vernacular to give point to his remarks. He was in great demand at harvest festivals, and was extremely popular over a wide district. 'He talked of cows and bulls and sheeap and pigs and sichlike things,' said one farmer to me. 'We understood him . . .' But of course he talked of other things too. A fine, robust figure of a man, as much at home on a horse or in the fields as in the pulpit, unconventional in attire and manner, he won the hearts of the sturdy North Riding people and talked their own language. In his love of the soil, his cordial relations with his flock, his outspoken sermons, strong common sense and in his pamphleteering, he had much in common with Sydney Smith, without that giant's intellectual powers. He was, however, a master of forthright English prose, as his numerous contributions to the *Economic Review* and other periodicals show. Although I have not a great deal of sympathy with the general run of 'sporting parsons' as such, the beloved Canon combined the two roles to perfection. An excellent horseman, he followed hounds whenever his duties permitted, and thought nothing of riding forty miles to preach a sermon and riding to hounds the following day, believing strongly in the old motto *mens sana in corpore sano*.

He never went to the extremes a former vicar of Carlton (Parson Brown) is said to have done. The story goes that once when Brown, a fanatical hunting man, heard the sound of the Bilsdale pack outside his church in the middle of a wedding ceremony, he left the couple at the altar and rushed out to unrobe, telling the couple to 'Come again tomorrow'—and mounted his waiting horse and was off like the wind.

Canon Kyle was always a parson first and last. He took over one of the village inns (Fox and Hounds), next door to the vicarage, at a time when feeling against a parson having anything to do with drink was much stronger than it is today. He encountered a good deal of criticism and abuse, but he acquired possession of the inn simply to reform it, as he explained in his interesting pamphlet *Why I Keep a Public House*.

It is perhaps his open-hearted kindliness and his lovable personality which explain the popularity of the late Canon Kyle more than anything else, coupled with his Irish origin and wit, for Irish stock flourishes on Yorkshire soil. He was all things to all men, yet never sacrificed his principles to curry favour. The nicest tribute I heard paid to him (and I have heard many) was delivered by the sexton who showed me his grave. 'The Canon was a gentleman, he was, and everybody loved him.' The beautiful church which he built is the best memorial to his life's work; but it is strange that among the multitude of tablets and tributes that adorn its walls, there is not one to the memory of the beloved Canon himself. And probably that is how he would have wished it to be.

These, then, are a few of the parsons who have left their mark on some of the country parishes of North Yorkshire. There are scores of others, not perhaps all quite so renowned in the worldly sense, but whose names are remembered with affection and gratitude in their own parishes. Many of them have written nothing beyond a guide-book to their ancient churches, but the tourist (and the writer) is under a debt of gratitude to them. In this chapter I have only scratched the surface of this subject; a whole book could be devoted to them—indeed many books, if one were to include all the noteworthy Catholic vicars and Nonconformist ministers.

In my perambulations around Yorkshire gathering material for this book, I have received a great deal of help from many kind vicars and priests. Often I must have been a great nuisance to them, dropping in on them at most inconvenient times to seek information. To all of them I should like to take this opportunity of offering my thanks for their unfailing kindness and assistance.

VII: TOWARDS THE COAST

CHAPTER THIRTY

In Harwood-dale

TUCKED away in the south-east corner of the North Riding is delectable Harwood-dale. Half-way between Whitby and Scarborough on the coast road, a by-way turns southward towards the moors into a little green world of its own. After the endless expanses of moorland on either side, the descent into this lush green valley provides a delightful contrast. Harwood-dale is the gateway to some beautiful country, but it is not until one has reached the old Mill Inn in the heart of the dale that one appreciates the sudden change of scene. The hedges are thick with wild roses and honeysuckle, and the scattered farms fit naturally into the scene. Clumps of oak and beech and thorn, and beautifully patterned fields, stretch far up the steep slopes of the dale, with a peaty beck in the bottom.

Beyond the inn, the road forks. The left branch turns to the scattered village a mile beyond, and the other climbs up Reasty Bank to the rigg road above. I like to pause for a moment at this spot and survey the country around, for this is one of those enchanting landscapes which reveal Yorkshire at its best and fairest.

AT BUMBLE BEE

Just above the inn, on the slopes of the dale, is a smallholding with the delightful name of Bumble Bee Hole where I stayed on this tour, and I am tempted to turn this chapter into a eulogy of Bumble Bee cottage and of the excellent farm fare provided at this Shandyean refuge by my friend Mrs Readman—not forgetting the view from my window!

There is a lot to be said for keeping a smallholding—rather than a large one—with just two fields, a couple of cows, pigs and horses, and two dozen ducks and geese and hens—especially in such an Arcadian setting as Harwood-dale. It ensures a well-stocked larder, and a life of contentment, with plenty of time to stand and stare at the scenery and take part in the social life of the dale, if my stay at Bumble Bee is any criterion. For let nobody run away with the idea that life in a little sequestered dale such as this is a dull, monotonous thing. On the contrary, with its horse fairs, sheep sales, cattle shows, and so forth, it is far more varied and exciting than life in a great city.

'Reasty Top'—a long, raking, tabular hill—dominates Harwood-dale. It derives its local name from the dialect word 'reast', meaning to jib or stall, as applied to horses straining up a severe hill such as this (for example, 'He *reasted* at it').

And anyone who ascends 'Reasty Bank' the hard way will have no difficulty in grasping its meaning. Once on top, however, you have your reward in a magnificent view of dale and moor—and sea, for the coast is only a few miles distant, with Scarborough just round the corner.

WAR DEPARTMENT

When first I discovered Harwood-dale and the heights above, many years ago, I felt that I had stumbled into an unsullied paradise of miniature dales, deep-set valleys, 'lost' villages, moorland becks, and immemorial trees. Even today, I can still remember the feeling of ecstasy which came upon me when I first followed the beautiful River Derwent from its source beneath Lilla Howe to its junction with Jugger Howe beck near the valley of Langdale. Today, alas, the scene has changed. The War Department has taken permanent possession of the surrounding moor (of Fylingdales) and parts of it now look like a blasted heath. In addition to cutting new concrete roads into, or making unsightly gun emplacements at, strategic beauty spots, the Department has established a permanent camp at Low North in one of the most beautiful corners of Harwood-dale, so that, instead of the voice of the cuckoo, the harsh crackle of rifle and machine-gun fire and the roar of anti-tank and heavy artillery is heard in this once beautiful land. It seems an odd corner to choose for these warlike demonstrations when there are so many other waste lands far away from such natural beauty spots; but of course the War Department has an answer to that.

At the same time, the Forestry Commission is busily planting the adjacent slopes with millions of young trees, and cutting still more roads across its strips of moorland.

Still, though Harwood-dale is not the Garden of Eden it once was, much of the essential beauty as seen from Bumble Bee Hole still survives

The harbour at Staithes, under the cliffs. Staithes, a dour, rugged fishing village where Captain Cook served his early apprenticeship, is famous for its seafaring traditions.

Runswick, fair sister to rugged Staithes, is a dream-village with a perfect bay and a great arc of blue sea fringed by golden sands.

in the dale itself—and in the sister dales. It is the moors that have suffered most.

I went along to the new military camp at Low North and followed the road alongside the beck towards the famous beauty-spot known as Beck Meeting, where the young Derwent is joined by Jugger Howe (now Low North) beck. Unfortunately, the peaceful meeting of the waters—still a lovely scene—was disturbed by a group of forestry workers who were hauling tree trunks near this very spot and churning the crystal stream into a muddy mess. The forestry workers, as usual, were friendly and helpful, and the foreman went out of his way to show me exactly how far I could proceed beyond that spot without too much risk of being cut to pieces by an anti-tank shell or riddled with machine-gun fire. I was happy to learn that I might still advance (with caution) as far as High Langdale End farm so long as I took advantage of the cover provided by the trees and the rigg end. Before continuing the steep ascent, I turned to look once more on the beautiful ravine through which the River Derwent runs between the steep sides of Barns Cliff Moor and Langdale Side Moor. It has always impressed me as one of the loveliest and greenest gorges in the whole of this fertile country. But the nearby sound of machine-gun fire, interspersed with the boom of the distant heavy guns, rather marred my meditations. I pressed on up the shoulder of the hill on a forestry track and made my way to the remote farm above, which occupies a commanding position overlooking the camp and the Derwent basin. Here the crackle of rifle fire and heavy guns was more alarming, and I was relieved to find some joiners and decorators at work in the building. The farm was requisitioned and un-occupied for some years, but has now been made habitable again and returned to the dispossessed tenant. He must be a brave man to risk it again. I was now within sight of my first objective—High Langdale Rigg End—at the foot of which I found a group of forestry workers tending the newly-planted Japanese larch and Sitka spruce. I talked to the Chief Forester, Mr Marsh, and obtained his permission to climb Langdale Rigg. A pretty tussle seems to be going on between the Forestry Commission and the War Department as to the exact line of demarcation between their respective lands. Although all this corner of Langdale Forest has been planted and belongs to the Forestry Commission, the Army has included it in the Fylingdales range and occasional shells fall perilously near. This Gilbertian situation could only happen in England, and I must confess that all my sympathies are with the Forestry Commission, and especially with those forestry workers who risk their lives on these border-lands. I had

M

Langdale Rigg End all to myself; it was thrilling to stride on top of the rigg again and survey the moorlands. From that high vantage point one can see the whole of Fylingdales moor, the Derwent basin, Lilla Cross, High Woof Howe, Blakey Topping, Jerry Noddle, Black Noddle, Whinny Nab, and parts of Staindale and Troutsdale. It is one of the finest viewpoints in the Riding, but it is sad to think that it is no longer safe.

The fact remains that there are public rights of way over these border-lands which the villagers of Harwood-dale still use, and so long as one keeps within the forestry area one is reasonably safe. But Fylingdales moor—itself is now highly dangerous—an odd paradox in the heart of a National Park!

From the top of 'Reasty Bank' a rough farm road descends into perhaps the most idyllic of all this network of little dales. It is called Whisperdales. When I first came upon it I thought it was too lovely to be quite true, with its poetic name, and its solitary farmstead at the head of the little, secluded, tree-clad valley.

Happily, it is not much changed, though the Forestry Commission has taken it over, and is briskly felling old trees here and there and replanting the bare places. The trouble is that the old, gnarled, misshapen oak and ash, which are useless from a commercial point of view, are so much more picturesque in this kind of dale than the straight conifers. However, Mr Chapman, the tenant of the farm, seemed to think that in another ten or twenty years, when the nabs are well covered again, the dale will look as good as ever. New tracks in Whisperdales are also being made, but so far there is no real road through it, and if one wants to explore it, the only way to do so is on foot. As I climbed out of it and looked back, Whisper-dales still seemed to me as lovely a spot as the heart of man could desire—the perfect setting for an artist; but Mr Chapman does not think much of it from a farmer's point of view.

There is a rough road out of it into the two sister dales of Low Dale and High Dale—both similar in character to Whisperdales. From High Dales farm, the 'road' also serves as the watercourse for the beck: quite a formid-able watersplash for a car! There is an alternative footway for walkers.

HACKNESS

Hackness, which stands at the lower end of these dales, is really the easiest approach to them. There is an adequate road from Hackness as far as Low Dale, after which it is better to continue on foot. Hackness might be described as the tiny capital of this corner of Yorkshire. All roads to and from Scarborough and the surrounding district converge at this charming village, and Hackness Hall, the ancestral home of Lord Derwent, with its beautiful park and gardens and lake, sets the seal on it. I like it best in summer when all the cottage gardens are ablaze with flowers, and the woods—real old English woods—are heavy with foliage. This is the English scene at its best: the hall, the church and the village set in a fair valley against a background of woods and hills, with the moors beyond. It has changed little since I was a boy, and I hope the Forestry Commission will not spoil it now.

LANGDALE END

There is a good choice of roads out of Hackness. One can go up the steep hill to the breezy heights of Silpho and Broxa, or take the famous drive through Forge Valley to Ayton and Scarborough (or westward to Thornton Dale and Pickering). I like to go to the delightful little village of Langdale End, with its tiny Moorcock inn, which hasn't changed a jot for fifty years, and where the pictures of Field-Marshal Lord Roberts and various other Boer War celebrities still grace the crowded parlour! I doubt if old Ada Martindale recognizes any later wars yet, God bless her! Generals apart, the scenery around this village is enchanting. 'Sugar Loaf' Hill, just beyond the inn, is a comical, conical-shaped, green hill which is irresistible; but the high spot of the district is the steep, wooded ravine of Langdale Ridge through which the young River Derwent runs.

All this is essentially walking country, and to appreciate it one must be prepared to climb the steep ridges and follow the wild moorland streams into the heart of these intricate hills and dales.

CHAPTER THIRTY-ONE

Middlesbrough

THE great iron and steel city of Middlesbrough, with its satellites, dominates the north-eastern corner of the North Riding around Teesmouth, and I must confess that I am in a quandary about it. My own instinct when I approach Middlesbrough is, I fear, to by-pass it altogether when I see the smokestacks and blast-furnaces in the distance: for this is the only part of the North Riding which bears any resemblance to the industrial West Riding, and as this book is intended primarily for the tourist and general reader, I feel bound to point this out. Fascinating as the story of Middlesbrough is, from its obscure beginnings on the mudflats of the Tees in the early nineteenth century to its present importance as a great industrial city, I do not suppose that the average tourist will wish to spend much time there—unless he is very steel-minded or iron-souled.

On the other hand, nobody can understand the strength and character of the people who have made this part of Cleveland famous throughout the world unless they pay it a visit. By night, when the steel furnaces are ablaze and the myriad dock and harbour lights are twinkling, Tees-side has a dynamic beauty of its own. I like to approach it along the Whitby-Guisborough road on a clear night when, from certain vantage points, one can pick out not only the fiery glow of Middlesbrough but also the dancing green and yellow lights of Teesmouth, until gradually the whole panorama of the great steel country around Middlesbrough is revealed—a thrilling sight.

But to get a more realistic view of the great steel city and its satellites, one should approach it from Redcar and Dormanstown through South Bank; or from Thornaby-on-Tees; or again from Wilton, where vast new ICI works are springing up.

By day, let us admit that it has its share of ugliness, as well as its power and glory; and let us be thankful that the industrial part of Cleveland has been confined to a relatively small corner of this vast Riding—Tees-side and the strip of country between Guisborough, Loftus and Skinningrove.

But make no mistake about it, the story of the rise of Middlesbrough from an obscure village in 1805 to one of the greatest iron and steel cities of the world is as thrilling as any romance. Until the early part of the nineteenth century, sleepy-looking Yarm was the chief port and shipbuilding centre on the Tees, with nearby Stockton taking second place. The mudflats nearer Teesmouth frustrated all attempts to contruct shipyards and docks at Middlesbrough.

But from 1805 onwards, a determined attempt was made by some far-sighted men to develop Middlesbrough (which was so much nearer the sea) as the great port for the Tees. The Tees Navigation Company was formed, land was acquired, and, later, the 'O.M.E.' (the Owners of the Middlesbrough Estate) set to work. The 'New Cut' was completed in 1810, and between 1830 and 1840 the first big dock was constructed. From that time, modern Middlesbrough developed with astonishing rapidity.

In addition to the opening of the river to shipping, other factors played an important part in this expansion: the extension of the new (Darlington-Stockton) railway to Middlesbrough; the development of ironstone mining in the surrounding Cleveland district; and the erection of the first smelting plant at Middlesbrough. While all this was going on, the great South Gare breakwater was completed, and Middlesbrough went from strength to strength.

By 1860, the tonnage of ocean-going shipping on the Tees was about four hundred thousand tons; by 1913, it had grown to over four million tons. Simultaneously, the iron and steel business had developed on the same gigantic scale.

This all sounds easy and inevitable to us today; it is the familiar pattern of the Industrial Revolution that transformed the whole of the North of England. But Middlesbrough might still have been a name on the mudflats if the right men had not appeared at the right time. Many of them became national figures, such as, for example, Edward Pease (the 'Father of Railways'), and his famous son, Joseph Pease, M.P. (who perhaps did more than anyone else to make modern Middlesbrough), and their descendants. Others were Henry Bolckow, John Vaughan, Sir Lowthian Bell, Sir Arthur Dorman—and many more.

Today, Middlesbrough steel and the name of Dorman Long are famous all over the world, and the Middlesbrough blast furnaces and rolling mills are never still. Many of the great bridges of the world, such as the Sydney Harbour Bridge, Lambeth Bridge, the Storstrom Bridge in Denmark—the longest in Europe—the Menai Bridge, Tyne Bridge, and other fine bridges, including Middlesbrough's own famous Transporter Bridge and Tees Bridge, were built in this city.

Everything in steel, from needles to girders is made at Middlesbrough—and much else besides. For Middlesbrough, is today a city of many industries. Apart from the actual processing and manufacture of iron and steel, the manufacture of machinery and the erection and construction of great buildings and bridges, Middlesbrough is actively engaged in ship-building and repairing, while at the docks ships come and go to and from all parts of the world. In addition, there is a great chemical industry, as well as brick and chimney construction (Middlesbrough firms have built some of the highest chimneys in England), and a host of other trades.

The crowded town bears the marks of this feverish activity and expansion, but it has some fine parks and buildings, including a Catholic cathedral and several other notable churches, museums and schools.

All this from the mudflats—and a first-class football team into the bargain—is surely a remarkable achievement.

CHAPTER THIRTY-TWO

The Yorkshire Coast

THE only way to see the Yorkshire coast properly is to walk along the cliffs or by the seashore. The so-called coast road deviates too far inland and misses many of the spectacular features of this rugged coastline, whereas the tortuous—and more or less continuous—footpath along the cliffs and down into the creeks and coves reveals many a splendid panorama that the motorist never sees. It is, however, a test of physical endurance which not everyone can pass. And it takes time. Fortunately there are offshoots from the coast road to the principal harbours and to some of the smaller ones, while the main road itself does follow the coast now and again.

REDCAR

The popular part of the coast begins at Redcar, which lies just south of Teesmouth, very near the industrial belt, and is yet surprisingly fresh and clean. It is the natural playground for Tees-side, a kind of Yorkshire Blackpool, though it is too flat and monotonously of a pattern to fire the imagination. The best features of it are the fine long promenade and magnificent stretch of sands, with the charming green embankment. Redcar racecourse is an added attraction.

All the way down the Yorkshire coastline you find these superb golden sands, ideal for children, such as I have never found elsewhere in England in the same profusion. Redcar has miles of sands, and so have neighbouring Saltburn and most of the other resorts; so that one can usually have a private corner of beach to oneself.

Marske-'by-the-Sea', between Redcar and Saltburn, lies rather away from the sea, but has its own superb beach and sands. It used to be a small village but has grown into a sizable and very pleasing little residential town, and is now part of Saltburn. Marske Hall, a seventeenth-century mansion, was for many years the home of the Dowager Marchioness of Zetland.

SALTBURN

Saltburn-by-the-Sea, a little to the south, occupies a striking position on a terrace above the sea, with a five-mile stretch of glorious sands. The four-decker houses and hotels along the front have a grave dignity and Victorian charm which always pleases me. With their now somewhat dingy glazed frontages, they begin to look like a period piece whose like we shall probably never see again. Even the names of some of the hotels and crescents, the Zetland, the Alexandra, the Queen and Britannia, are in keeping with the period. Do not imagine, however, that Saltburn is a back number. The hotels are modernized, and the town is very much alive and beautifully kept. The Cleveland Hills beyond make a fine backcloth to this dignified resort.

SKINNINGROVE

The twisting, hair-raising coast road between Saltburn and Skinningrove, despite the intervening iron- and steel-works, is worth any motorist's consideration, if only as a test of driving. Even by day, ugly as much of this part of the coast is, it is surprising how much natural beauty remains just outside the steel belt. One passes through an extraordinary mixture of fair woodlands, spectacular ravines, and pit-heads all jumbled together. Grim places like Brotton, Carlin How and Skinningrove, have farms and pleasant rural scenery between, and a fine stretch of coast just beyond. Skinningrove both repels and fascinates me: the little houses seem so needlessly ugly and poverty-stricken, but the enormous complex of buildings, aerial railways and shafts make a striking picture, while the little harbour below is as attractive as all harbours are.

For those who wish to cling closer to the coast and do not mind a narrow secondary road, I can recommend the road that goes down to Skinningrove harbour and then hugs the coast road through Upton and Street Houses. It has the advantage of going within easy walking distance of Boulby cliff— reputed to be the highest cliff on the English or Scottish coasts (666 feet)— and reveals wonderful sea views before descending the steep Boulby bank to the Staithes road. But I must confess that the real coastal scenery does not begin for me until I approach Staithes.

STAITHES

For those who wish to avoid the industrial belt altogether, therefore, I would suggest making a start at Staithes. My own favourite approach to

Staithes (after the footpath way) is from the famous Whitby-Guisborough moor road mentioned above. There are several offshoots from this road, leading to Staithes, Saltburn, and other places on the coast, and each of them passes through remarkable scenery, starting from the bare moors and plunging through deep, wooded defiles, with vistas of blue sea far beyond. One goes by way of Grinkle Park, past the old mansion of that name, which has been converted into a modern luxury hotel in beautiful grounds.

Another road runs through the villages of Roxby and Dalehouse, but the one I like best is the parallel road that starts from the village of Scaling, on this bleak moorland road, and goes along Ridge Lane to the sea. This little country ridge road straddles two ravines, with the twin becks of Easington and Roxby on either side, and then sweeps down to Dalehouse and the sea. Although recent tree-felling has stripped these glades of some of their glory, this is still a lovely stretch of English scenery, culminating in a fine view of the sea.

The approach to Staithes by road is, at first sight, disappointing. The usual rash of new red-brick houses on the outskirts of the village is followed by some ugly boarding houses, but the old village lies far below in a narrow coomb between the cliffs, and, as one descends the steep road, the true character of the place is soon apparent. Only a sea-loving race could have built a village like Staithes, with every conceivable obstacle in the way. The houses are built at all angles and some of them seem in imminent danger of falling over, but they have stood there for centuries.

Staithes (pronounced 'Steers' or 'Steease') means literally a quay, wharf or landing-stage, or a sea-wall with a ledge or platform. And that is precisely what Staithes is. It is also the Scandinavian word for harbour.

There is nothing of the pretty-pretty about Staithes. It is one of those places you like or dislike at sight. It is a grim, grey, workaday, uncompromising sort of place, with a cobbled stone main street and a general air of sturdy aloofness and independence. Seen on a dark, stormy day it is very grim indeed! Even the Lion inn is a Black Lion, and the old Cod and Lobster on the quayside is tarred black too. Staithes is not going to unbend to please a mere tourist. There is no mistaking the Yorkshireness of Staithes: it is written all over its face. I love that steep main street plunging down to the sea, and the stone houses huddled together on either side—and above and below too! The little shops at the lower end seem infinitely more exciting to me than the large city stores. As you wander about there, you are sure to see some of the old women walking to and fro in their picturesque Staithes bonnets which they have worn time out of mind. They give almost a Breton touch to the place and are the only concession to woman's natural vanity. They wear them with such an air, too, as if they realize how becoming they are. I always look for a pretty young face beneath one of them, but they all seem to be old and weatherbeaten at Staithes, and yet with that comely beauty that age can bestow. The fishermen, too, wear blue jerseys with a special cablestitch, one of which I have long coveted.

At the very bottom of the hill, the impossible road swings behind the Cod and Lobster and you find yourself on the open sea front—the *staithes* —at last. And what an incomparable sea front it is, with the harbour wall and the great cliffs all round! Truly a wonderful setting. There are sure to be one or two old fishermen leaning over the rail in front of the Cod and Lobster brooding darkly on the wide sea.

I talked to old Tom Verrill, 't'owdest sailor now living in Staithes'. I found him sitting outside his pleasant 'Anchorage' at the bottom of the hill and smoking his pipe in the sun. Nearly ninety he was then; and he could look back to the days when Staithes was what he called 'a proper place', when the fishing fleet had 'great "yaels" eighty to ninety feet in't keel'. He didn't think much of the present generation. 'Nothing at all,' he told me candidly. His father and grandfather were fishermen before him, and in that 'awful race' with the men of Blythe—an historic race between two rival crews, from Staithes to Whitby—his father was the coxswain of the winning Staithes boat. He said to me: 'The King of England sent for mi feyther two or three times to talk to him about t' biggest race that ever was rowed in the North, but he wouldn't go: him was too busy fishing!'

He told me also that he had seen 'raws and raws of houses at Steease weshed into t'sea'. 'You'll niver sit in Captain Cook's cottage ageean,' he went on gloomily, 'because it's nut theear any longer.' (Rival claimants to the title, please note!) 'It's weshed away long sin. And Steease isn't like what it was at all.'

Like a lot of the old breed of fishermen, the 'Captain' takes a poor view of the 'new' harbour and sea-wall built in 1924. 'It isn't a job at all,' he said. 'They should have asked two or three of the old fishermen to tell them where to put it and how to do t'job reight.' Then, his mind wandering into other channels, he suddenly said, 'Talk about Franchmen! There never wor a good Franchman. They do you right and left,' he added darkly.

His near namesake, Mr Frank Verrall—a retired master mariner, 'and a square-rigged Master too'—was a mere seventy-seven and looked younger. He went to sea at sixteen in a square-rigged, three-master sailing ship, the *Champion*, from Liverpool to Montevideo, and was away on one voyage for three years and four months. He remembers the days when Staithes had sixteen yawls, each manned by ten men, and from forty to fifty cobles. Staithes cobles were the finest ever built, he said; and he, too, agreed that Staithes is now only a shadow of what it used to be. 'All the young men go to the iron mines now,' he said, 'they won't have the sea.'

Mr James, the Chairman of the Harbour Commission, gave me rather a different version of the harbour controversy. He said one old sailor had prophesied that when the new harbour was built 'there weeant be a fisherman left by Staithes Fair'; they would all be drowned. But they all died natural deaths. Some of the old fishermen believed that the harbour wall had been wrongly sited owing to the currents and shallow water, but actually it was correct. The fact was that they resented any interference with their old methods. It was not the harbour wall but the development of the iron mines—and the growth of Whitby—that was responsible for the decline of Staithes as a fishing port. The trade had gone farther south and north—and Staithes, which used to be the principal fishing port on the coast, with a couple of hundred fishermen and seventy skippers, is now almost purely a mining village.

Sometimes—if you are patient—you can hear some of the older men exchanging reminiscences in the bars of the Cod and Lobster or the Lion, but the Staithes men are slow to speak of their own achievements and slow to unbend. The Cod and Lobster itself could tell many stories if walls could speak. It could tell of fierce gales when the sea poured into the cellars and the barrels were all afloat. Three times, they say, it has become a total wreck and been half washed away; but there it is, rebuilt and shipshape again, brooding like the fishermen themselves over the restless sea.

PORT MULGRAVE

Just before entering Hinderwell from the direction of Staithes, a by-road turns towards Port Mulgrave. This little, deserted harbour of Port Mulgrave is well worth a visit. The road swings past the village on a ledge slightly reminiscent of the Grande Corniche, with superb sea views, and, far below, is the tiny harbour. The road stops short at the last houses, but a cliff path continues down to the harbour. The view from this vantage point is as fine as anything on the coast, and the 'toy' harbour makes an ideal bathing pool.

Port Mulgrave dates from the time when iron ore was mined at Grinkle mine, near Dalehouse. It was transported through a two-mile tunnel to this specially constructed harbour, and there loaded on to boats and shipped to Jarrow.

Today, Port Mulgrave is deserted. The stone cottages that bear witness to its former activity, and a few boys swimming in the harbour, were the only signs of life I saw. But the general setting is entrancing and those in search of a quiet bay might find it the place of heart's desire.

RUNSWICK BAY

At Hinderwell, the road forks to Runswick Bay. As at Staithes, the approach is spoilt by the inevitable new housing estates, but when one reaches the last hotel overlooking the lovely bay, the breathtaking view more than compensates for all this, especially if one has the good fortune to see it on a bright summer day. Runswick is the perfect picnic bay—a great arc of blue sea far below, with cliffs to north and south culminating in the bold headland of Kettleness. Many people, daunted by the steep, twisting road down to the bay, content themselves with the view from above; but they miss the rich beauty of this unique resort. Runswick is a dream-village which can hold its own with any on the Cornish Riviera. It is a prettier place than Staithes or Robin Hood's Bay, and the bay itself and the lovely sands are more suitable for children. The little red-roofed cottages with their almost tropical gardens look too good to be true. In early summer, when the gardens are at their best, they are an artist's paradise.

Though Runswick has been largely transformed from an old fishing hamlet into a holiday resort with a special appeal to children, it does not make it less attractive to me. Runswick used to live entirely by the sea. Names like Patton and Clark and Taylor go back for generations. Inshore fishing was the main industry then. Fifty years ago more than a dozen cobles used to put out to sea regularly. Now it is down to 'two and a booat'. 'T'young 'uns weeant have it,' one old sailor said. 'I doubt there weeant even be yan booat next winter.' 'Today there's nowt but yan chap crabbin' and another salmoning.'

It seems a pity, but there it is. . . . In the beautifully kept chapel in the heart of the village the organ is dedicated to 'Coxswain Robert Patton, V.C.

of the sea, who gave his life to save another in February, 1934'. The family of this hero are still living in the village, and the gallant Runswick lifeboat, with Tom Patton (now retired) as coxswain, has a proud record of service.

TOWARDS KETTLENESS

If you can tear yourself away from Runswick you will find that the coast road makes a wide sweep past the charming village of Ellerby to Lythe; but a mile before reaching Lythe, another by-lane turns towards the coast again in the direction of Goldsborough and Kettleness. Goldsborough is a tiny village consisting of a few farms and the Fox inn; but on a hill in the fields of Green Pastures farm is to be found the site of a Roman encampment. This stretch of the coast is noted for its ancient British and Roman associations, and it is believed that the Romans had a landing place between Goldsborough and Dunsley.

Kettleness, just beyond Goldsborough, is another isolated village, with high cliffs and a coastguard station. From the headland, there is a delightful view of Runswick, and at low tide one can walk to it across the sands. The headland, with its twisted and forlorn appearance, shows the remains of the old alum workings of over a century ago. In a landslide at this point the old village fell into the sea in December, 1829.

This is a fascinating part of the coast, and ideal for exploring and walking. The cliff path past the coastguard station towards Sandsend points the way.

LYTHE AND MULGRAVE CASTLE

Lythe village, at the top of the famous Lythe Bank, is notable for its fine church of St Oswald on the hill top, and for the nearby seat of the Marquis of Normanby—Mulgrave Castle—which is on the right of the road as one descends to Sandsend. The eighteenth-century castle, which has been much altered and improved, stands near the ruins of the original castle, and is surrounded by an extensive park and woodlands. The woods may be visited for a slight charge against a ticket. Dickens was a frequent visitor to Mulgrave. The country around Mulgrave, and the villages of Dunsley, Hutton Mulgrave, Newholm and East and West Barnby provide a delightful little tour.

SANDSEND

The main road from Lythe descends by leaps and bounds to sea level again at Sandsend, as if impatient to reach Whitby which can be seen in all its glory from the top of Lythe Bank.

Sandsend is a small, select holiday resort—an appanage of Whitby—built around the old village. It has an old-world charm, with modern comforts —a useful combination. Its little bridges and twisting main road effectively control the passing traffic, and its riding stables and bathing beach are well known to holidaymakers. The ravine leading to Mulgrave woods makes a perfect background. It is a pity, however, that the railway company built such a hideous viaduct at the entrance to the village and placed such an ugly barricade alongside the line in the direction of Whitby. If one approaches Sandsend from the north, this particular eyesore is not so noticeable; the golfers who play on the adjoining Whitby course probably do not notice it at all if they follow the rules and keep their eye on the ball.

And so over the new stretch of road to Whitby.

WHITBY

If you enter Whitby from the West Cliff, you come at once into the modern part of the town, high above the sea. With one or two exceptions, the new hotels and boarding houses are attractive, and the older Crescent has charm and distinction. The promenade, with its lawns and flowerbeds merging into the green top of the cliffs, is a delight. At the farther end— beyond the sunken Spa which is a remarkable building feat—stands the fine statue of Captain Cook gazing over old Whitby, and the sea.

It is right that Whitby should claim him, for though he was born at Marton-in-Cleveland, it was at Whitby that he learned the trade of the sea; it was from there that he first sailed; and it was in Whitby that were built his famous ships that were to take him round the world. In Grape Lane, over the one iron bridge that still links the new town with the old, you will find the house where he lived between his voyages. What a pity it is that this has not been acquired by the town and made into a Cook museum. As it is, you will find some of Cook's relics and trophies housed in the Pannet Park museum, which is one of the most interesting and well-kept small museums in the country.

As you turn round the corner of the oddly named Khyber Pass, you get the best view of the old town and the harbour—a cluster of red pantile-roofed houses huddled together against the background of the East Cliff, with the estuary of the River Esk between. It is a pity, in a way, that the old and new towns could not have been kept quite apart, but that was impossible. If you live in Whitby for any length of time, you soon get used to this juxtaposition of old and new, and you accept it. It is not correct to say that all the old town lies across the river mouth: quite a bit of it straggles over the west side by the fishing harbour, as you will find if you wander through narrow Haggersgate, or climb up the steep and cobbled Flowergate; or walk through Baxtergate, one of the shopping streets.

There is in fact a third Whitby—the Georgian Whitby—which reveals itself in many a lovely terrace (like St Hilda's) and in streets like Bagdale. This was the Whitby built when the old shipowners, bankers and sea captains were piling up their fortunes and spreading their wings.

But as you cross the iron bridge and walk down Grape Lane, or up Bridge Street into Church Street, you are conscious of a distinct change. It is like walking into another age. The old houses and streets are very shabby now, and there are gaps here and there where some have been pulled down; but how astonishing they are, with their ghauts and wynds climbing tier on tier, and with rambling yards and dark passage-ways between.

One of the things that astonishes me about Whitby—and some of the smaller coastal villages—is the amazing skill of the old builders in building these houses and streets in such 'impossible' positions. We seem to make such heavy weather today about putting up a few houses on perfectly level sites, with the advantage of modern machinery and methods, that it passes my comprehension how these old builders managed to construct houses in such situations, in such a relatively short time.

If you climb up one of those Church Street stairways, up several flights and past a large chapel poised half-way up the cliff, you will find a workshop occupied by the two Varley brothers,[1] both approaching eighty years of age, and one son. The first thing one notices is the magnificent view of the harbour from the windows, then the beautiful smell of processed woods, Spanish mahogany, cedar wood, walnut and beautiful veneers. Next one sees some exquisite piece, a bureau, a cabinet, or a chair on which one of the Varleys is at work. The Varleys are famous for their craftsmanship. They are in the true line of Chippendale and Hepplewhite, and their work is known and treasured far and wide. In other quiet corners, one may see some of the old jetworkers at their benches cutting those beautiful brooches and cameos which seem to be coming back into fashion again, for Whitby has been famous for its jet for centuries.

The old Whitby townspeople thought nothing of climbing the 199 steps to the abbey; they were so accustomed to climbing the 99 steps to their own houses that another 100 was neither here nor there! Nowadays,

[1] Mr Ernest Varley, the gifted head of the firm, has since died, but his son and brother are carrying on this famous business.

what a fuss we make of it. What panting and scrambling, stopping and starting again, and aching and creaking goes on when we make our way to the old abbey on the cliff.

The abbey *is* Whitby: certainly it makes Whitby what it is, for, wherever one turns, the ruined abbey, which has inspired so many pictures, dominates the scene. And what an incomparable setting it has, perched on the east cliff, 250 feet above sea level, and looking like a beacon, a mute and glorious witness to the Age of Faith.

One cannot look at the abbey without thinking of the remarkable St Hilda, the first abbess, who ruled over the first abbey in the seventh century. And when one thinks of Hilda, one thinks of Caedmon, the poor, tongue-tied cowherd who used to slip away from the feasts (where everyone was expected to sing) because he was ashamed of his illiteracy. One day, Caedmon had a vision and was told to 'sing the beginning of created things'. Next day he told his story to St Hilda, and from that time he began to write the first true English verse. If for nothing else than this, Whitby Abbey would be a place of pilgrimage and a shrine; but Caedmon was only an incident in its exciting story. Its history cannot be told in detail here. Amongst other things, the date of our Easter was settled at Whitby at the great Synod of 764. After many vicissitudes, a new and mightier abbey was built between the eleventh and twelfth centuries, the influence of which extended far beyond the confines of Whitby, over the wild moorlands around. It is the ruins of this Benedictine abbey church that one sees today, and they tell their own sad story.

The rugged parish church of St Mary, which stands just below the abbey on the cliff top, is a wind-buffeted legacy from the twelfth to fourteenth centuries. One has only to look at the weatherbeaten tombstones to realize what fierce storms this old mariners' church has withstood. It makes a fitting companion to the old abbey beyond.

The first thing to strike the eye on entering the church is the astonishing amount of timber that fills it—the enormous pews, galleries and pulpit. I have heard it said that some of the larger pews, with their wide doors, were designed for the comfort and convenience of ladies in crinolines; some of them are big enough to hold a family party.

In 1612, the old high-pitch roof was taken down, and the present flat roof is believed to have been erected by Whitby ships' carpenters, who must also have been responsible for the cabin-like windows put in at a later period. At any rate, no church could look more like the interior of a ship than this old, much altered and much battered parish church of St

Whitby Abbey stands high on the cliffs overlooking the North Sea, a mute and glorious witness to the Age of Faith.

The North Bay at Scarborough. An unusual view of this famous resort, taken from the walls of the castle on the Headland.

Mary on the hill, which has withstood so many fierce nor'-easters. And yet, somehow, despite the excessive amount of timber that greets the enquiring eye, despite the massive Cholmley pew (1700) that obscures the fine Norman chancel arch, despite the enormous three-decker pulpit (with the large ear trumpets, specially made for a deaf minister's wife) and despite the hidden altar, I like the old church very much and never miss an opportunity of exploring it. It has seating accommodation for 2,000 people, and is full of fascinating pieces, including a chair commemorating the Rev. Wm. Scoresby, the famous explorer.

The best way to find old Whitby is to wander about the streets and yards near the market place and town hall, and along the harbour side where one meets the fishermen. Whitby is full of old customs,[1] and of old inns. Many of the inns are sadly decayed or modernized, but the old Smugglers in Baxtergate (now a café) is interesting. The White Horse and Griffin in Church Street is said to have been the place where Cook planned his voyages, and where Dickens sometimes stayed. Lewis Carroll, too, spent several long holidays at Whitby during his Oxford days and stayed at No. 5, East Terrace. His first writings were published in the *Whitby Gazette* in 1854.

If you look beyond the picturesque old streets and houses and enquire into Whitby's history, you will find yourself involved in a story that goes back to the earliest times. Whitby is perhaps the most ancient seaport on this northern coast. It witnessed the coming of the Romans, the Vikings, the Danes, the Normans, and many other invaders. But it is its seafaring traditions which are still most fresh in the memory of Whitby men, for Whitby ships were famous throughout the seven seas and were once reputed to be the best and stoutest bottoms afloat. Many of them were engaged in the whaling industry, and others in general trade. Whitby enjoyed its most prosperous period in the early nineteenth century, and the yards were full of ships; but with the decline of sailing ships and the coming of steam power and heavier ironclads, the trade moved farther north and Whitby's great days were over. No writer has portrayed this aspect of Whitby's history better than Storm Jameson—a native of the town.

Today, small ships are being built again in the yards, and the local fishing fleet carries on the old tradition in its 'keel boats' and the harbour is full of life again when the Scottish herring fleet arrives in the late summer. But the main industry now is in catering for visitors. It remains to be seen what effect the new potash discoveries will have on Whitby in future years.

[1] See the late Mr Shaw Jeffrey's *Whitby Lore and Legend* for a detailed account of these.

N

The real charm of Whitby today is its friendliness. It is one of those small towns that have retained their individuality and old-world character in spite of modern developments. It is still a closely-knit community of friendly people with the fisherfolk at the heart of it and the bankers, butchers, bakers, barbers, innkeepers, printers, solicitors, fruiterers, stationers, booksellers, wine merchants, all huddled together, cheek by jowl, in a few narrow streets. All of them seem to belong to one large family, and they all read the *Whitby Gazette*. Everybody knows everybody else, and most of them belong to the Yacht Club, the Conservative Club, the 'Lit & Phil' or the 'Amateurs', and they are always meeting along Baxtergate or Flowergate or Skinner Street, or at one of the numerous bars, and exchanging the latest gossip.

Whitby has not yet (fortunately, as I think) become too popular and prosperous like some of the larger seaside resorts. Of recent years—in common with most other seaside resorts—it has suffered from an influx of motor coaches from the big industrial cities, and its quaint streets are sometimes full of strange people wearing weird hats and behaving in a very un-Whitby-like manner! But this only occurs during the brief holiday season. For the rest of the year, Whitby preserves her dignity and charm.

To see the town at its best, one should go there out of season—say between October and April—when its streets and sea front are deserted save for its own people—and one should see the 'prospect of Whitby' from the sea. Then, when the sun is shining on the rust-red roofs across the harbour, the old town looks like a dream.

ROBIN HOOD'S BAY

The road out of Whitby turns away from Saltwick Bay and swings towards Hawsker on its way to Robin Hood's Bay, quite a long way from the sea. One must persevere through a maze of new houses before one comes at last to the Victoria hotel, when the sea comes into view again and the steep road plunges down to the old village below. The last twisting street is so steep that the village is hidden until one is really on top of it; but it is worth the struggle. Many people like it better than any of its rivals; others are disappointed, partly, I suspect, because they never discover the real 'Bay' (as it is known locally). It is an elusive place, but it improves vastly on closer acquaintance.

I like to turn aside (to the left) just below the first few houses at the top of the steep main street, where narrow little passage-ways lead into the interior of this old fishing hamlet. This, to me, is the most fascinating part of Robin Hood's Bay. There are tiny little squares and miniature streets and alleys with delightful stone cottages tucked away in unexpected corners. It is like a toy town. This medley of cottages, shops, inns and cafés is the heart of the village, as many artists have discovered. Eventually the street leads past the Dolphin hotel to the Bay hotel on the edge of the sea. Robin Hood's Bay has always been a favourite spot for painters; it contains a number of studios, and a flourishing Fylingdales group of artists holds exhititions there.

Although 'Bay' resembles Staithes and Runswick in its steep setting, it is different in character from either of these places. It is more compact and rather shut in, and it is more rugged than Runswick Bay. It is much bigger than it appears at first sight. Every nook and cranny on the cliff has been used to build on. Occasionally a cottage falls in the sea, but nobody seems to mind. Others cling to perilous ledges and look as though they might topple over at any minute.

The bay itself is strewn with slabs of granite and is full of deep pools and sea-anemones. There are no sands, save under the cliffs in the direction of Ravenscar. 'Bay' is essentially a fishing hamlet with a long history of in-shore fishing, which Leo Walmsley—a native of Robin Hood's Bay—has so vividly described in his *Three Fevers* and other 'Bramblewick' stories. Now, alas, its great fishing days are over, but there are plenty of retired master mariners lurking in those solid-looking houses and they can tell you some fine yarns of the old days.

For the rest, 'Bay' is a hive of activity in summer when its narrow streets are swarming with visitors. I, for one, never grow tired of it—in season and out of the season.

THE 'FLASK' AND 'FALCON'

Between Robin Hood's Bay and Scarborough, the road takes a sweep inland, and clings to the edge of Fylingdales moor. The Falcon and the Flask inns are the twin attractions on this isolated moorland road. The Flask is the first inn one passes after leaving Robin Hood's Bay, and, as it is on the main road, it is a favourite calling place. More than once after crossing Fylingdales moor in a storm I have found refuge in its cosy bar.

The Falcon, a few miles nearer Scarborough, used also to be on the main road, but it has now been by-passed by a short new section of road. It is well worth the slight detour involved.

RAVENSCAR

Three twisting miles down this branch road bring one to Ravenscar, a scattered village in grey stone on top of the cliffs. Here one has
a fine view of the coast, with the great sweep of Robin Hood's Bay
below. On a clear day, the view is entrancing, but sometimes a sea-fret
intervenes. Personally, I enjoy a partial sea-fret: it gives character to the
scene.

To get the best possible view, one should continue along the road to the
Raven Hall hotel which stands on the top of the cliffs and commands one
of the best sea views I have ever seen. Raven Hall was once an old manor
house, and was, I believe, built by an ancestor of Mr Christopher Fry, Mr
W. H. Hammond, who also created the famous terrace gardens and
financed the Scarborough-Whitby railway, besides building and maintain-
ing the little Ravenscar church.

I imagine that this benefactor would be considerably surprised to see the
luxurious modern hotel that has been created from the old hall. It is the
complete self-contained holiday resort, with its own bathing pool, golf
course, putting green and tennis courts, and beautiful gardens—all on top
of the cliffs.

But the real wonder of Ravenscar is the great Scar itself, and to appreciate
it one should go down the twisting footpath towards the beach and see it
from below. This is rugged coastal scenery on the grand scale. There are
great bluffs of rock and grassland, and one tremendous, awe-inspiring cliff
soars sheer out of the bed of the sea to a dizzy height of 600 feet. High
above, on a ledge of rock, the turreted bastion of the terrace garden of
Raven Hall can be seen looking like the outer walls of Elsinore. This is a
sight worth seeing, but when the northern sea-fret is creeping over the
Scar, there is something deeply moving—and perhaps a little fearsome—
about it all.

A secondary road from Ravenscar follows the coastline and goes through
the secluded village of Staintondale, with its picturesque cottages and cosy
Shepherd's Arms. Staintondale has its own sporting pack of hounds. This is
a beautiful bit of coastal scenery, with the green fields running down to the
cliff edge, and revealing a vista of the distant white cliffs of Flamborough
Head.

Hayburn Wyke nestles in a densely wooded glade below, and has its
own popular hotel and woods well known to thousands of tourists, as is
the famous walk down to the little creek below.

SCARBOROUGH

Many people make the mistake of following the main road into Scarborough Town, and thus get involved in the built-up area, instead of following the coast road—which, in this case, really does lead to the coast.

By taking the left fork at Burniston, one enters Scarborough by the North Bay foreshore, near the bathing pool. The route is then along the famous Marine Drive by the edge of the sea, with the great cliff of Scarborough Castle and Headland on the right. At the further end of the Drive, the road passes the docks and fishing harbour, and the somewhat incongruous amalgam of medieval England ('Here dwelt King Richard III'), modern cockshys, and a crowded south shore. This is a part of Scarborough I hurry past, but at the end of this popular beach Scarborough comes into its own again, with the splendid Spa and the Grand Hotel recalling bygone glories.

Still following the main road, one turns towards the Valley Gardens and then sharp left to the Crescent and the Esplanade. This is the really elegant part of Scarborough. Seen on the right sort of sunny day, I doubt if there is any other resort in England to compare with it. Passing many fine hotels, one comes to the lovely Esplanade leading to the gardens. From almost any corner along this stretch of promenade, the view looking towards the sea, with the old castle on the cliff and the great sweep of the bay, is beyond words, but I think the most striking view is from the further edge of the fine bowling green at the Clarence gardens where the whole magnificent stretch of the bay, the gardens and Castle Hill are revealed in all their glory.

The enchanting gardens—both on the north and south cliff—are one of Scarborough's glories; the whole of the undercliff beneath the Esplanade has been converted into a series of ornamental terraced gardens which in summer are a pure delight. Everything in Scarborough is on the grand scale, from the hotels to the bathing pools and golden sands.

There is grace and dignity on the famous Esplanade, and along the nearby Crescent. It is true, alas, that many of the famous houses have been converted into hotels or galleries. Wood End, the home of the Sitwell family (a detached house at the end of the Crescent), is now the Natural Science Museum, but this enables the public to explore the house that Sir Osbert Sitwell has made famous in his reminiscences. (Some of his original manuscripts may be seen there.) Lord Londesborough's old house nearby is now the Turkish baths, and another beautiful mansion has been turned into an art gallery. All this may be lamented, but outwardly this corner of Scarborough has not greatly changed and the public are free to enjoy it. Scarborough may not be the exclusive resort it once was, but it is still elegant and beautiful—like a gracious lady who has lost her fortune but remains charming and irresistible.

Everything I have said about the remarkable building and engineering feats at Whitby and elsewhere along this rugged coast applies also to Scarborough, where every kind of natural obstacle has been overcome to develop this fashionable resort. High bridges span the ravines, twisting roads and paths climb from the sea to terraces above.

One of the best viewpoints from which to get a picture of Scarborough is from the castle itself, which occupies a commanding position between the two bays. From the castle ramparts one can see all Scarborough at one's feet—and half the North Sea. Another fine vantage point is Oliver's Mount.

There is not much left of the castle beyond the shell of the massive keep, the outer walls, and a truly astonishing well. But the position it occupies is magnificent, even though the actual site chosen on the Headland was not quite impregnable. Built in Stephen's reign (1135–64) the castle played a part in much turbulent history. Several times it was besieged and starved into submission. Civil wars apart, it has been attacked at different times by French, Dutch and German forces. The walk round the Headland is one of the most bracing and exciting on the coast.

Coming out of the barbican into the road again, Scarborough's fine old parish church is immediately to the left. On the outside wall of the churchyard, a tablet indicates the position of the grave of Anne Brontë—the meekest of the three sisters—who came to Scarborough in a forlorn fight for life and died here within a few days.

There is, of course, much else to see in Scarborough. There is Oliver's Mount and the Mere, and the famous cricket ground where one can watch the *élite* of the cricket world during the Scarborough Festival in September, and where I have seen Bradman bat and Lindwall bowl. There is the wonderful Open Air Theatre which attracts thousands during the season, and there are the famous shops and hotels in and around Westborough and St Nicholas Street which are so popular with the ladies. But above all this, there is an air about this northern resort which lifts it high above the rest.

Not for nothing is it called the Queen of Watering Places.

FILEY

South of Scarborough, the coast road passes Cayton Bay—a superb holiday bay—overshadowed, alas, by unsightly caravan settlements above. Shortly afterwards, the lovely sweep of Filey Bay—a perfect arc—comes into view, with the famous Brig at one corner and Flamborough Head at the other.

Filey marks the division of the North and East Ridings; but what do Ridings matter when one comes to Filey with its incomparable sands, seven miles long, its bathing and riding, and its exquisite setting? Once the most exclusive of the smaller resorts on this coast, Filey is still an elegant younger sister to Scarborough, with excellent hotels of its own. And even though Filey, too, has been somewhat hemmed in by modern camps and caravanserais, it is one of my first loves and I will not hear a word against it.

The white cliffs between Filey, Reighton Gap, Speeton, Bempton and Flamborough Head are the most spectacular on this coast and should not be missed.

Envoi

So much—or so little—about this fair Riding. There is much else that I should like to have said about its people, its customs and its beauties; but my space is exhausted while the country itself is inexhaustible.

But perhaps I have said enough to send some reader off on his own pilgrimage of discovery—and that is the only way really to appreciate this rich and fair North Riding.

Of one thing, at least, I am quite certain: in no other corner of England is a kindlier welcome to be met. North Riding people are the most friendly and hospitable one could wish to meet anywhere. They like others to enjoy their beautiful countryside—their moors, dales and parklands—provided, of course, that visitors observe the customary courtesies of the countryside.

Long before the new National Park was contemplated, North Riding farmers and landlords threw open their gates to strangers and friends alike; and I have no doubt that they will continue to do so, so long as their confidence is not abused.

Make friends with the farmers and villagers, and you will be welcomed everywhere with the old traditional North Riding salutation:

'Coom thi ways in, an' sit ye doon!'

Good luck—and God-speed!

Index

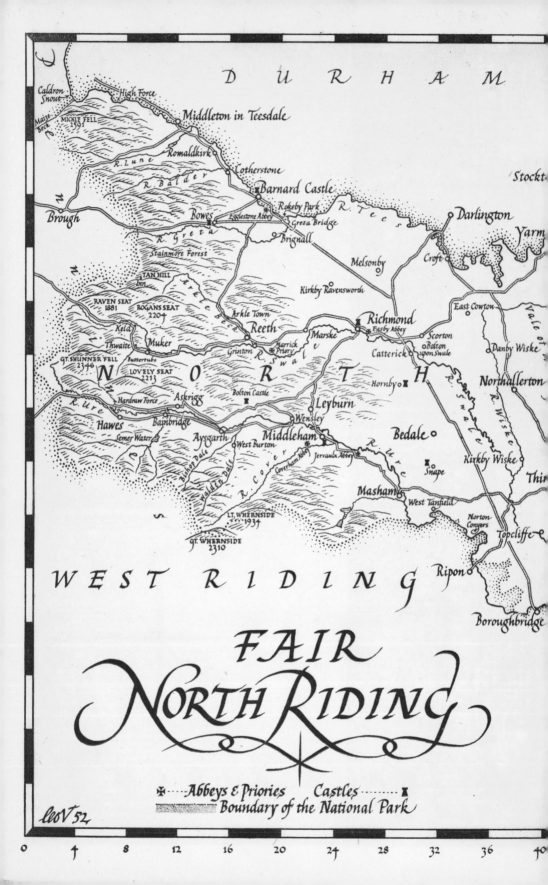

FAIR
NORTH RIDING

Abbeys & Priories ⊕·········· Castles ········ ⚔
▬▬▬▬▬ Boundary of the National Park

leoV 52

0   4   8   12   16   20   24   28   32   36   40